WORKPLACE
BULLYING

CLINICAL AND ORGANIZATIONAL PERSPECTIVES

—— **JUDITH GENEVA BALCERZAK** ——

NASW PRESS

National Association of Social Workers
Washington, DC

Darrell P. Wheeler, PhD, MPH, ACSW, *President*
Angelo McClain, PhD, LICSW, *Chief Executive Officer*

Cheryl Y. Bradley, *Publisher*
Stella Donovan, *Acquisitions Editor*
Sharon Fletcher, *Marketing Manager*
Julie Gutin, *Project Manager*
Don McKeon, *Copyeditor*
Juanita Ruffin Doswell, *Proofreader*
Lori J. Holtzinger, Zinger Indexing, *Indexer*

Cover by Britt Engen
Interior design and composition by Xcel Graphic Services
Printed and bound by P. A. Hutchison

First impression: November 2015

© 2015 by the NASW Press

Library of Congress Cataloging-in-Publication Data

Balcerzak, Judith Geneva.
  Workplace bullying : clinical and organizational perspectives / by Judith Geneva Balcerzak.
    pages cm
  Includes bibliographical references and index.
  ISBN 978-0-87101-490-0 (pbk.)—ISBN 978-0-87101-491-7 (e-book) 1. Bullying in the workplace. 2. Bullying—Prevention. I. Title.
  HF5549.5.E43B356 2015
  658.3'82—dc23
                    2015030333

Printed in the United States of America

Table of Contents

Foreword

As attorneys with a combined experience of over 50 years in the field of employment law, we have seen dramatic changes in the protection the law affords to workers. Most of us have a sense of the dismal working conditions endemic at the beginning of the 20th century. Although worker-manned machinery facilitated mass production, tort law failed to protect the worker against serious bodily injury or death, and no compensation was afforded for injured and disabled employees. In response to deadly mine explosions and machinery accidents, workers' compensation laws were enacted to protect against the hazards of an unsafe workplace. Not until the 1970s, with the passage of the Occupational Safety and Health Act, were employees entitled to environmental protections, including those against deadly chemical exposure, unsafe machinery, excessive temperatures, and workplace pollution.

Whereas safety issues were improving, America's legal system essentially failed to address the lack of equitable opportunities for all. A major step forward occurred with the passage of the Civil Rights Act in 1964. It outlawed discrimination in nearly every aspect of American life. Enactment the following year of Title VII specifically targeted discrimination in the workplace. This legislation explicitly prohibits employment discrimination based on race, color, religion, sex, and national origin and created an enforcement agency, the Equal Employment Opportunity Commission. Next came the Age Discrimination in Employment Act of 1967, which forbids employment discrimination against workers age 40 and older. Enforcement provisions were added to Title VII in 1972. In 1990 the Americans with Disabilities Act expanded Title VII's protections to citizens with physical and mental disabilities. The Civil Rights Act of 1991 brought further changes to Title VII litigation. Its greatest change was authorizing plaintiffs to recover punitive damages.

Notwithstanding the passage of the aforementioned laws for workplace protection over the past century, the tragic truth is that no law has been passed in the United States to protect workers against the pervasive existence of mobbing and bullying. Like an oasis in a legal desert, Judith Geneva Balcerzak's work deals with this untamed issue. Until now, no body of work has approached this matter so effectively and thoroughly. Balcerzak addresses the sociological, economic, psychological, and physiological implications of the bullying threat with depth and clarity. Her analysis of the plight of victims of emotional abuse in the workplace is well documented and consistent with our observations and professional experience. Balcerzak has taken on this profound challenge and captured the heretofore elusive solutions.

Only a writer as astute as Balcerzak could present her readers with such an incisive, academic perspective on a workplace plague that has been tolerated far too long, infecting countless workers at all levels of the employment spectrum. Readers will find this definitive work indispensable to understanding the economic, social, and psychological impact of mobbing; its prevalence throughout the United States and globally; and the measures needed to eradicate the abuses and injuries resulting from such conduct. This book is a breakthrough in social work literature. May it provide the inspiration and impetus to craft state and federal legislation that will withstand political influence, corporate self-interest, and legal inequities that have impeded essential progress toward equal justice under the law.

Georgianna Regnier and Richard Regnier

About the Author

Judith Geneva Balcerzak, PhD, MSW, LCSW, has worked as a clinical social worker for over 35 years. Licensed in California since 1981, she has spent decades working in health care in the public and private sectors. Balcerzak teaches in the Marriage and Family Therapy Master's Degree Program at California Lutheran University in Thousand Oaks, California. She also teaches in the Psychology and Sociology Departments at Ventura College, where she developed the Human Services Degree and Certificate Programs. After completing her MSW at Wayne State University (Detroit) in 1977, Balcerzak has been a resident of California since the early 1980s. In her private clinical and consulting practice, Judith has encountered many clients, students, and organizations with workplace bullying problems. Balcerzak's recent doctorates in social work and organizational psychology are examples of her passion for lifelong learning. An avid sailor and scuba diver, Balcerzak and her husband, Daniel Jordan, PhD, ABPP, divide their time between Ventura County, California, and the island country of Dominica in the eastern Caribbean. Their commitment to human rights and social justice is central to their values and practice.

Acknowledgments and Dedication

As a clinical social worker, university professor, and former health-care administrator, I had always been interested in organizational functioning and its impacts on individual well-being. After retiring from a meaningful career as a senior administrator of health services in a large public agency, I returned to one of my lifetime passions: teaching at the graduate and undergraduate university levels and in our local community college system.

In 2005 one of my students gave me a book and said, "Dr. Judi, I don't know why, but I think you would enjoy this book and get a lot out of it." The book was *Mobbing: Emotional Abuse in the American Workplace* by Davenport, Schwartz, and Elliott (2002). I was surprised to discover that a name existed for what had happened in my own professional life while working in the public sector. I also discovered that my own story was not unique. Without pointing fingers or identifying any person by name, I will simply state that the system that was designed to protect me had failed me. Those events were life changing. Fortunately, I had the resilience and resourcefulness to land on my feet and reinvent myself in midlife. Today my passion for understanding the dynamics of workplace bullying remains fierce.

Since leaving my public-sector position in 2001 and after learning about the signs, symptoms, causes, and effects of workplace emotional abuse, I have amassed an extensive library—more than 300 research articles and texts—related to bullying in the workplace. This compilation of literature answers some questions that I had and that emerge when I lecture on this topic. My hopes in sharing my findings are fourfold:

1. To provide a clear understanding of the nature of workplace bullying and examine studies both in the United States and globally.
2. To help social workers and other clinicians provide support and treatment to people who have been harmed by bullying in their organizations.
3. To provide a blueprint for organizational leaders who want to prevent abuses in their work environments or correct them if they are occurring.

4. For public policies to be developed to protect and prevent these types of workplace injury. Included in these policies would be the Healthy Workplace Bill (HWB), legislation that as of May 2015 has not yet passed in any of the 26 states or two territories in which it has been introduced.

The time is now for social work and other health-care professions to address this cause in advocacy, education, and petition. Having the endorsement of the National Association of Social Workers (NASW) for this book will give these efforts new voice. Thank you to Stella Donovan, acquisitions editor for NASW Press. You have been patient and encouraging.

Thank you to David Yamada and to Gary and Ruth Namie for your pioneering efforts in identifying workplace bullying, crafting language for the HWB, and spearheading grassroots efforts across the United States for its passage. Thank you also for granting permission to reference many of your works. A special thanks to my colleague, dear friend, and mentor/adviser for my original research for this project, Stephen Daniel. Steve, your eye for detail, excellent conceptual skills, and tireless editing helped tremendously. Thank you to Benjamin Weisman, to whom I first presented my ideas for study in this domain. Thank you to Richard and Georgianna Regnier for your reading of this work and providing its foreword. A special thanks to attorney Jane Oatman, who championed my cause as I "fought Goliath" 14 years ago! Ms. Oatman continues to represent the interests of emotionally injured workers in the public and private sectors. I thank my former adviser and major professor, Ted Goldberg, retired chair of the Group Work Division at Wayne State University's School of Social Work. Ted remained a lifelong friend after I completed my MSW in 1977. Ted, from you I learned to teach with compassion without sacrificing academic rigor.

Thank you and "I love you" to my husband, Daniel David Jordan. Dan, your excellent copyediting, your challenges to clarify my thinking, and your very helpful commentary continue to be valuable, along with your love, support, and encouragement.

I dedicate this work to my parents, Hazel and Stanley Balcerzak. My mother, Hazel Marie Mathis Balcerzak (1923–2008) was a pioneer in her generation and was deeply committed to human rights and social justice. My father, Stanley Marvin Balcerzak (1916–1994), the son of Polish immigrants, grew up during very hard times in U.S. history. He would be proud of my efforts to create better work environments for all.

To clinicians, organizational leaders, and lawmakers: Bullying is real, and its effects can be brutal. Our track record in the United States compared to the rest of the developed world is abysmal. We need the knowledge, skill, policy, and legislation to address this plague.

Finally, to any worker who has been bullied in the workplace: Do not give up hope. Trust yourself. Get information. Get help. You are not alone. Know that you have a right to survive, to thrive, and to engage in meaningful life work—with dignity.

Preface

In my initial quest for reliable and valid information about bullying, I wanted to examine and perhaps challenge some of the popular opinions about the phenomenon. I was particularly curious about the validity of anecdotal information about victims, perpetrators, and risk environments. Are victims really innocent? Is it true that targets are generally high-functioning, well-adjusted workers who contribute positively to the workplace, or are they workers with performance problems? Are perpetrators always mean and "evil," or are their actions misunderstood and misinterpreted? Do bullies scan the horizon looking for opportunities to be hurtful to others, or are bullying behaviors merely opportunistic responses to workplace dynamics? Are risk-prone environments highly dysfunctional systems? Are they usually typified by low morale, emotional tyranny, and lack of emotional safety? Can organizational problems be resolved with policy and training, or are there additional dynamics that need attention if the workplace is to remain bully-free? What about legal protections for workers? Are any protections readily available? What laws address the needs of bullied workers, and what else is needed?

This book examines the definition, causes, effects, and prevalence of workplace bullying and mobbing and identifies solutions from a variety of theoretical perspectives. It includes an exploration of the history of the definition and conceptualization of mobbing, its role in high-risk professions, and the personality traits of people who are mobbed and their persecutors. This work also identifies organizational practices related to the risks of mobbing, strategies for prevention, social work's role, and the role of other clinical disciplines in treating physical and psychological symptoms resulting from mobbing.

I have addressed the need for an integrated framework identifying organizational vulnerabilities and leadership strategies; provided suggestions for victim survival, clinical assessment, and treatment for targets of abuse; and highlighted organizational prevention and best practices for remediation. The laws and public policies currently in place and those in development are examined. Finally, I have explored larger public policy issues and human rights concerns.

To establish the breadth and scope of the problem from a global perspective, citations include research from countries and cultures where literature sources originated. The conclusions of this work provide a basis for social work scholars and practitioners to include this growing social problem as a domain in which to intervene and call for social change.

1

Introduction to Mobbing in the Workplace and an Overview of Adult Bullying

In the early 1980s, German industrial psychologist Heinz Leymann began work in Sweden, conducting studies of workers who had experienced violence on the job. Leymann's research originally consisted of longitudinal studies of subway drivers who had accidentally run over people with their trains and of banking employees who had been robbed on the job. In the course of his research, Leymann discovered a surprising syndrome in a group that had the most severe symptoms of acute stress disorder (ASD), workers whose colleagues had ganged up on them in the workplace (Gravois, 2006). Investigating this further, Leymann studied workers in one of the major Swedish iron and steel plants. From this early work, Leymann used the term "mobbing" to refer to emotional abuse at work by one or more others. Earlier theorists such as Austrian ethnologist Konrad Lorenz and Swedish physician Peter-Paul Heinemann used the term before Leymann, but Leymann received the most recognition for it. Lorenz used "mobbing" to describe animal group behavior, such as attacks by a group of smaller animals on a single larger animal (Lorenz, 1991, in Zapf & Leymann, 1996). Heinemann borrowed this term and used it to describe the destructive behavior of children, often in a group, against a single child.

This text uses the terms "mobbing" and "bullying" interchangeably; however, mobbing more often refers to bullying by more than one person and can be more subtle. Bullying more often focuses on the actions of a single person. Although differences are subtle, sometimes, but not always, mobbing can refer to an institutional or systemic process in which many of those in administrative authority are involved in trying to force an employee out of the workplace via over-direction and overdocumentation. In such instances, administration even supports the original perpetrator because that support serves a function for the organization. Leymann's definition described *mobbing* as "hostile and unethical communication directed in a systematic way, by one or more people toward another person or group, occurring often (almost daily) over a long period of time, generally at least six months" (Leymann, 1990, p. 120). This early description of the syndrome suggested that mobbing behavior involves ganging up on a targeted employee and subjecting that person to severe, emotionally damaging harassment. Leymann's definition specifically *excluded* temporary or transient conflicts and focuses on the area in which a psychosocial situation begins to result in a psychiatric or psychosomatic illness. Bullying behaviors may include insulting comments about a person's private life or background, humiliating or intimating behaviors, rumors or false allegations, and exclusion from customary workplace socialization (Salin, 2003b).

Building upon his body of data, Leymann wrote in the late 1980s and early 1990s that a significant problem of emotional abuse of workers by coworkers had been documented in Sweden and in other countries. These abusive attacks, according to Leymann, could have severe occupational and psychological consequences for the injured worker (Leymann, 1990). Although mobbing is not a new phenomenon, much research has been conducted in the past two decades to provide understanding of the causes and effects. By the time of this writing in 2015, mobbing and bullying have been identified and studied in most developed countries around the globe and in many emerging countries as well.

This volume explores the history of the understanding of the symptoms of mobbing, the personality traits of people who are mobbed and those of their persecutors, organizational practices related to mobbing and its prevention, social work's role in treating symptoms resulting from mobbing and in addressing this workplace malady, and, finally, larger public policy issues and human rights concerns. To establish the breadth and scope of the problem from a global perspective, citations include research from countries or cultures where a literature source originated. In addition, to separate academic literature from mainstream conversations, general Internet sources, or "blogging," references will be made to the academic institutions from which they originate where appropriate.

HISTORY AND CONCEPTUALIZATION OF MOBBING IN THE WORKPLACE

Bullying in schools has been examined in research and social psychology literature for decades. Data suggest that school bullying is a universal occurrence in developed countries (Rayner & Cooper, 1997). Beyond the relatively rare case of school shootings, bullying at school can result in many negative mental health consequences for the victim and target, including anxiety and depression (Chapell et al., 2006).

Until Leymann's work, bullying in the adult work world had received no attention, but recent studies have suggested that the same patterns identified when children bully other children can carry over into the adult workplace. Unfortunately, mobbing victims are often portrayed as being at fault for the treatment they receive from others (Davenport et al., 2002). Theorists today are challenged with producing evidence and analysis of the long-term effects of the victim's experience.

Mobbing includes hostile and unethical communication directed in a systematic way by one or a number of people, usually toward one targeted individual. These behaviors occur often, even daily, and persist over a long period of time (Leymann, 1990). Prior to Leymann's work, bullying of adults had been discussed only from the perspective of social structure and the ways in which victims risk expulsion from the workplace. Since Leymann's findings, however, attention has been given to victims' symptoms and resulting disabilities (Leymann, 1990, in Davenport et al., 2002).

A distinguishing feature of mobbing or bullying is that it is a *process*, rather than an *event or act*. Bullying is *not* normal conflict and is not the same as more general workplace incivility. Bullying involves repeated and persistent negative acts toward another in which a perceived power imbalance exists, creating a hostile work environment. Not all acts are necessarily perceived as bullying in each situation: The *severity*, *duration*, and *intent* of the threats are important in defining and identifying specific behaviors such as mobbing or bullying (Salin, 2003a). Individual acts may seem inconsequential when viewed in isolation but may have negative consequences when used in a systematic way over a period of time and can result in dire outcomes. Critical events in the process from bullying to mobbing to expulsion from work go through four critical-incident phases (Leymann, 1990).

The first critical-incident phase occurs when a triggering situation or enabling environment is perceived as a conflict (usually over work). This usually lasts a fairly short time. Analyses of organizational practices and policies have shed light on the notion of an *enabling environment*. These will be examined in depth in chapter 7. The original critical-incident phase ends when the targeted person's coworkers and management begin what become stigmatizing actions.

The second critical-incident phase is the actual process of bullying and stigmatizing. While many of the actions might occur in normal, everyday work life, when they occur within the frame of harassment they produce injury. The actions have in common the objective to "get the person," or to inflict punishment. This second critical-incident phase includes behaviors such as rumormongering and ridiculing the victim, withholding communication from the victim, isolating the victim, assigning meaningless or humiliating tasks to the victim, and violence or threatening violence (Leymann, 1990).

The third critical-incident phase involves intervention by management, usually via human resources (HR). By this point, the victim has become a "case" for HR, and ironically those around the target often assume that the victim is the problem. Because the victim is typically under extreme duress and work performance may have become impaired, he or she may be receiving disciplinary action, warnings, write-ups, and constant scrutiny.

Finally, the fourth critical-incident phase is commonly known as *expulsion*. Expulsion can take on many forms, ranging from the victim's illness and long-term medical leave to relocation, degrading work tasks, and psychiatric treatment. In some instances, the person may be fired or resigns, with or without another career plan in place.

As with sexual harassment and stress, a consensus on the resulting effects of mobbing has not been reached. Like other forms of aggression and abuse, outcomes data about the impact of workplace bullying are sparse. Because definitions of workplace mobbing or bullying are mixed, theorists have borrowed from various sources in attempts to quantify the rates and severity of mobbing at work. Three sources exist in this effort: (1) definitions that deal with people who have severe clinical (psychiatric or other medical) outcomes from being bullied at work, (2) definitions that explore the concept within the general population of workers or employees, and (3) incidence studies that ask whether a person has ever been bullied (Rayner, Sheehan, & Barker, 1999).

An important feature of bullying is that it involves an injury, not an illness. Symptoms of this injurious syndrome do not develop in isolation but evolve as a result of behavior inflicted on a person by others over time. Symptoms may range from mild to extreme, but they are almost always significantly disruptive to the victim's life inside and outside of the workplace. The symptoms often lead at least to voluntary resignation or involuntary dismissal. Leymann (1990) also estimated that 10 to 15 percent of suicides committed annually in Sweden have bullying as a background or precipitating factor.

Mobbing behaviors themselves are many and varied. Einarsen (1999) delineated five major categories that constitute workplace bullying strategies:

1. Changing the work tasks of a worker in some negative way or making the tasks difficult to perform
2. Social isolation by noncommunication or exclusion
3. Personal attacks or ridiculing or insulting remarks
4. Verbal threats through criticism or public humiliation
5. Spreading rumors

Bullying acts can be divided into seven groups: calling out, scapegoating, harassment by someone in greater power, unreasonable relocation of workspace, unreasonable increases in workload, isolating or ignoring the target, and physical abuse (Harvey, Heames, Richey, & Leonard, 2006).

These acts may be committed voluntarily or unconsciously, but all cause humiliation, offense, and distress. They all interfere with work performance and cause unpleasant work environments (Harvey et al., 2006).

Other theorists identified the 10 most common forms of workplace aggression as gossip, interrupting others while they talk or work, flaunting status or authority, belittling another's opinions, failing to return phone calls or memos, giving another the "silent treatment," yelling insults or shouting, using verbal forms of sexual harassment, staring or giving dirty looks, and intentionally "damning with faint praise" (Koonin & Green, 2004).

Any of these behaviors can be perpetrated by one person or by several people against a single target. The direction of emotional abuse can be lateral (peer to peer), downward (superior to subordinate), or upward (subordinate to supervisor or manager). While downward abuse is perhaps the most common, lateral and upward abuses also occur with some frequency.

Leymann's original typology included 45 mobbing behaviors (Davenport et al., 2002). These are organized into five categories of varying degrees:

1. **Self-Expression and Communication.** This includes behaviors that affect self-expression and the way communication happens, including restricting opportunities for employees to speak, constantly interrupting the person when he or she is speaking, restricting opportunities for self-expression, yelling at or scolding the victim in the presence of others, constantly criticizing the victim's work performance, making threats, and denying the target contact with others.
2. **Social Relationships.** This comprises attacks that include not speaking to the victim, prohibiting the victim from speaking to others, locating the victim's workspace to somewhere far isolated from others, forbidding colleagues from talking to the victim, and acting like the victim is invisible.
3. **Attacks on Reputation.** These offenses include unfounded rumors, ridicule, treating the victim as mentally ill, forcing the victim to undergo psychiatric examinations, mockingly imitating the gestures and voice of the victim, ridiculing the victim's private life or nationality, forcing the victim to do a job that affects the person's self-esteem, constantly questioning the person's decisions, calling the victim demeaning names, and sexual innuendoes.
4. **Attacks on Quality of Work Life.** These attacks include failure to assign any specific job duties, taking away the person's work assignments, giving the person meaningless jobs, giving the person tasks well below his or her qualifications, overloading the person with new tasks far above the individual's qualification (thus inviting failure), and causing damage that creates financial costs for the person.
5. **Attacks on Health.** Finally, mobbing behaviors may include direct attacks on the person's health with harmful practices, such as forcing the target to do strenuous work beyond his or her physical capacity, threatening violence, using light violence as a threat of greater violence to follow, and physical abuse.

Leymann's structural definition of bullying addresses the scope, severity, variety, and degree of emotional assaults in a comprehensive manner. It seems to be the most inclusive and best suited to describe the problems addressed in this text. Leymann's scheme includes conceptualizing mobbing as a process, not just an event, and describes the environmental conditions experienced by the victim during the injuring process.

In most European countries, workplace bullying has been made illegal. In the United States, however, organizations and legislators are only recently becoming aware of the types of workplace incivilities that can be considered mobbing. Considering the harm that bullying can cause to the targets, one could easily label these acts as unethical and unwelcome in organizations, workplaces, and academia.

However, these behaviors do exist and can create serious, lasting damage to individual workers, workplace morale, productivity, and organizational goals (Bandow & Hunter, 2007). Consensus from general clinical experience among professionals working in occupational health settings is that immediate and grave psychosomatic effects are observed in other victims.

Among the social consequences, expulsion rates are high among targets. Prior to leaving a bullying workplace, targets can have many periods of illness with high use of sick leave. They may be forced to undergo psychiatric examinations and diagnoses (Leymann, 1990). Regardless of whether the person leaves the abusive workplace, the effects are often long lasting. In addition to clinical outcomes, the person is affected socially by being isolated and stigmatized and may elect voluntary unemployment rather than continuing to endure ongoing daily injury. Subjective experiences can include feelings of desperation, hopelessness, anxiety, and great rage about the lack of legal options. Psychological symptoms may include depression, acute stress, anxiety, psychosomatic illness, and suicide. Suspicions also hint that the experiences can produce a compromised immune system, so targets may be vulnerable to diseases (Leymann, 1990). These concerns will be addressed more fully in chapters 5 and 6.

PREVIOUS EFFORTS AT EXPLAINING WORKPLACE BULLYING

Previous authors, such as Geffner, Braverman, Galasso, and Marsh (2004), addressed workplace emotional abuse from an organizational behavior perspective. Others identified workplace stressors and precipitating events by pointing to organizational structure and practices as primary conditions for workplace bullying. Some authors, such as Namie and Namie (2003) and Davenport et al. (2002), focused on supporting victims from a self-help perspective. Some theorists demonized perpetrators for their cruelty, while others pointed to the target person's pathology as the cause of their vulnerability. Still others suggest that workplace mobbing is a multifaceted, multidimensional problem requiring multidisciplinary solutions (Rayner, Hoel, & Cooper, 2002).

A systemic, multifaceted, multidimensional explanation and a multidisciplinary approach to the topic seem to be the most rational and inclusive strategy. It would allow for broad interpretations and offer the most options for prevention and redress. Rayner et al. (1999), for example, stressed the need to avoid fragmentation into discipline-specific definitions and solutions. The process of mobbing or bullying might be metaphorically described as a game or a battle. Participant narratives compiled via focus groups by Tracy, Lutgen-Sandvik, and Alberts (2006) identified phrases such as "strategic attacks," "playing the game," and "I had no rights" as common themes. The narratives were saturated with metaphors of beating, physical abuse, and death. Respondents cited feeling "abused," "ripped," "broken," "scarred," and "eviscerated." Another used the term "nightmare" to describe her experience. One respondent said she felt as if she was "going crazy" or "being tortured." Mobbing can have social, emotional, physical, and psychological effects on targets. Almost all of the effects are painful. Some effects can cause short-term or even long-term disability.

Options for targets of emotional abuse can seem limited. Victims must understand that what they are experiencing is workplace bullying and that it is not normal or acceptable. After this first step of naming the condition, targets have choices. Victims who seek assistance are advised by employee-assistance professionals (EAPs) to explore all options and to take control of their situations. This may be difficult for any number of reasons. A worker may have very real barriers that prevent leaving. Alternative employment may be difficult to secure. They might lose accrued benefits. Job markets remain tight for mid- and late-career professionals. An injured worker may be too anxious, depressed, or debilitated to make changes or may not believe that change is possible (Davenport et al., 2002).

Targets of bullying often need professional therapeutic intervention. With help, victims may identify a recourse they might not yet have tried or considered. Victims can explore all other options, including short-term, intermediate, and long-term planning, but often first need to feel safe before they can take any action or do any planning.

The most extreme type of workplace bullying is actual physical violence. Physical violence may be either a one-off event or the final result of an escalating pattern of bullying. According to the National Institute of Occupational Safety and Health (NIOSH), workplace violence is a leading cause of occupational injury and death. NIOSH includes threatening behavior, verbal or written threats, harassment, verbal abuse, physical attacks, and bullying as examples of workplace violence (NIOSH, 1996).

The U.S. Department of Labor's Occupational Safety and Health Administration (OSHA) has estimated that nearly 2 million American workers report having been victims of workplace violence each year. Unfortunately, many more cases go unreported (U.S. Department of Labor, 2002). While determining the extent to which any of these incidents are related to bullying is impossible, logic would suggest that there is a relationship.

Organizations often invest time and resources into workplace communications training, but estimates are that less than 5 percent of training courses for the workplace deal with verbal abuse (Brennan, 2003). However, verbal abuse can make up to 90 percent of all reports of violence at work! Brennan proposed categorizing verbally abusive statements at work into five groups: (1) inappropriate language, (2) general statements criticizing the organization but not the person, (3) communications that are patronizing, (4) threatening or offensive statements, and (5) statements about a person that are not true.

Australian researchers Hartig and Frosch (2006) described mobbing as a "silent and unseen" occupational hazard. They posited that, since bullying is more frequent, it is a more serious safety and health issue than any other workplace risk but cite a lack of clear state and federal legislation as a serious deficit.

A number of factors can be associated with the likelihood of the onset and continuation of mobbing. Some of these can include workplace politics and corporate culture, unclear management expectations, dishonesty, withholding information from employees, discouraging responses, high tolerance for poor performance, and employees feeling taken for granted. These environmental symptoms can increase the likelihood of workplace emotional abuse of employees and will be discussed later in this book.

"Power distance" is a term used to describe the way people with different degrees of organizational power relate to each other at work (Breckler, Olson, & Wiggins, 2005). The term refers to relationships between people with unequal status. Data suggest that the greater the power distance, the more likely an organization's hierarchy will accept workplace inequalities and authoritarian values. Organizations with larger power differences are more autocratic, a relevant factor because workers in the United States tend to be somewhat more tolerant of autocratic bosses than workers in other developed countries (Vega & Comer, 2005). Differences in the data on workplace may reflect these somewhat different value systems, because bullying in the United States is most often perpetuated more by managers or supervisors toward subordinates, while emotional abuse in places such as Scandinavia tends to occur more between peers. That is, less downward bullying occurs in Scandinavia, perhaps because Scandinavian countries tend to be typified by work environments with less power differential and more egalitarian status between workers and their supervisors. This is also a statement about supervisory relationships in the American workplace!

LEGAL DILEMMAS AND EMERGING POLICY

Debate continues about whether discharge resulting from a supervisor's environmental harassment is a tangible employment action. Although legal options are discussed more fully in chapter 6, it should be noted here that for any legal action to be levied, one of the first questions to consider is whether the complainant is able to establish specific "intent" by the perpetrator (Gray, 2004). A second question in determining the relevance of legal action is whether the employer can be found liable for workplace harassment. In both cases, the burden of proof is on the *employee* to establish both intent and employer liability. Circuit courts in the United States have not been consistent in rulings with regard to this type of litigation (Gray, 2004).

Since the 1960s, most citizens of the United States have come to rely as employees on some protection of the country's civil rights laws. The specific intent of these laws is not always clear or consistent. With Title VII of the Civil Rights Act of 1964, it became unlawful for an employer to discharge an employee or otherwise discriminate against an individual with respect to his or her compensation, terms, conditions, or privileges of employment based on the individual's race, color, religion, gender, or national origin (Davenport et al., 2002). Later legislation included the Age Discrimination in Employment Act of 1973 and the Americans with Disabilities Act of 1990. These acts protected workers around issues regarding age, pregnancy, and disability. Legislation has only recently begun to address sexual orientation, although many states do provide protection in their employment discrimination statutes. The Civil Rights Act of 1991 implemented major changes that expanded existing federal antidiscrimination laws and overruled previous court decisions that had limited employees' rights to legal recourse (Davenport et al., 2002). A specific mobbing complaint may or may not fall under one of these categories because of a person's protected status. The Supreme Court of the United States has found that Title VII is *not* limited to economic or tangible discrimination but is also intended to protect people from a hostile or abusive environment at work. The court has ruled that Title VII is violated when a workplace is typified by ridicule, intimidation, threats, and insults that can alter the conditions of a person's employment. The claim of "hostile environment" has been used in cases of sexual harassment and other Title VII cases, but in bullying cases a hostile employment environment is generally based on general behavior—that is, nonracial and nonsexual types of harassment. In cases decided at the Supreme Court level, the court has identified factors such as frequency and severity of conduct, the actual threat or humiliation, and whether the offensive behaviors interfered with a worker's ability to perform job duties (Davenport et al., 2002).

While federal and state laws address what may look like bullying, bullying itself is often not illegal. In some instances the laws do not apply, or the legal options make cases too difficult to build. Harassment, if unrelated to gender, race, age, or any of the other Title VII–protected class categories, may be invisible (Namie & Namie, 2003). The presence of a law simply gives an individual or a group of individuals the right to sue but does not guarantee a favorable outcome for a plaintiff. Even when a settlement or award is paid, the award seldom justifies or rectifies the agony experienced during the mobbing process and after (Namie & Namie, 2003). Although injured workers have the right to seek redress through the legal system, those who file civil suits may undergo additional financial and emotional expense attempting to recover damages, and the results can be disappointing. These issues will be discussed again in chapter 5.

Unlike a generation ago, legal precedents today clearly provide protection for workers against sexual harassment. As Associate Justice Sandra Day O'Connor ruled in *Harris v. Forklift Systems* (1993),

> whether an environment is "hostile" or "abusive" can be determined only by looking at all the circumstances. These may include the frequencies of the discriminatory conduct; its severity; whether it is physically threatening or humiliating, or a mere offensive utterance; and whether it unreasonably interferes with an employee's work performance. (Vega & Comer, 2005, p. 105)

The Supreme Court in the *Harris* case determined that psychological harm was not necessary to prove that a workplace is hostile. Instead, a plaintiff need only provide evidence that a *reasonable* person would find the behavior offensive if that person were in the victim's position (Vega & Comer, 2005). In two similar cases, *Burlington Industries v. Ellerth* and *Faragher v. City of Boca Raton*, the Supreme Court ruled that employers are responsible for taking preventative action and remedying sexual harassment (Vega & Comer, 2005).

Most citizens of the United States do not yet enjoy safeguards protecting them from emotional harassment at work that are similar to the legal protections, now more clearly defined, prohibiting sexual harassment. In fact, workplace bullying itself is not yet illegal in many states (Vega & Comer, 2005). Unfortunately, the United States has lagged far behind other industrialized countries in creating an awareness of workplace bullying. By some estimates, the United States is at least 20 years behind its Scandinavian and Western European counterparts (Namie & Namie, 2003), based on the recentness of legislation, the paucity of precedent-setting cases that have been tried in courts, and the reluctance of states to pass legislation prohibiting workplace bullying. For example, the National Board of Occupational Safety and Health (NBOSH) in Stockholm, Sweden, has been publishing and distributing Leymann's educational materials since 1989. The first measures against victimization at work came into law in Sweden in early 1994. Australia passed its Public Sector Ethics Act in 1994, identifying respect for persons as one of the five ethical obligations required in the workplace. In Germany, the KLIMA Association was founded in 1998 to help victims of mobbing in business, in the government, and in society. In the United Kingdom, public service unions began to survey their work-forces as early as 1996 (Namie & Namie, 2003). Vega and Comer (2005) suggested that the lack of attention, until recently, to the concept of dignity in the workplace organizations in the United States has supported, and perhaps even encouraged, both mild and more serious types of emotional harassment that American workplace laws do not fully cover. Others surmise that because workers in the United States are marginally more comfortable with more autocratic management styles than workers in other countries, they may have been historically more willing to accept management's more arbitrary directives and actions (Vega & Comer, 2005).

Social conditions become social problems when interest groups raise public awareness about the existence of the conditions. The term *claims-making* describes the activities of interest groups (claims-makers) whose grievances about a social condition are brought to public awareness (Hewitt, 2007). When a claims-maker's cause becomes widely recognized by a society, the social condition becomes known as a *social problem*. The process from initial claims-making to widespread social recognition of the concern as a social problem takes time—often years or decades. The social problem of abusive work environments has undergone such a claims-making process. It began Western Europe and Scandinavia, migrated to the United Kingdom and Australia, and is finally gaining recognition in the United States. The relatively slow claims-making process for identifying and defining social problems may account for the marked lag in data collection and analysis in the United States as compared to other developed nations in the West.

PREVALENCE OF MOBBING IN THE AMERICAN WORKPLACE

No single social institution or group has been able to measure accurately the degree to which individuals are emotionally harmed at work by colleagues, superiors, or subordinates. The diversity of approaches has resulted in a knowledge base that is fractured at best, and data are conflicting. Because most clinical disciplines, including social work, clinical psychology, psychiatry, and family counseling, have been somewhat delayed in addressing workplace mobbing, more data have been collected by scholars in HR, business administration, risk management, and organizational psychology. Scholars within individual professional disciplines such as medicine, nursing, and higher education have also contributed to the existing knowledge base of mobbing by studying workplace abuse within their own fields.

Data capturing the incidence and prevalence of emotional abuse at work are difficult to gather for a number of reasons. Self-reports by victims tend to under-represent emotional abuse and violence at work because victims are often reluctant to report such activity (LaVan & Martin, 2008). Studies examining specific work environments can be helpful by allowing for inferential estimates of the prevalence of mobbing in the United States and providing an idea of the frequency of emotional violence, but they do not address qualitative differences in mobbing experiences, nor can they identify precipitating events or outcomes.

Some of the best estimates of the prevalence of mobbing in the American workplace originally came from the Wayne State University researcher Loraleigh Keashly (Namie & Namie, 2003). Keashly presented the evidence, based on a 2000 survey of 1,335 Michigan residents, to what was then the Campaign Against Workplace Bullying (it is now known as the Workplace Bullying Institute [WBI]). Data were collected through voluntary, anonymous online surveys. Women constituted 50 percent of the bullies. Bullying was more prevalent than actual illegal discrimination; in 77 percent of instances neither the bully nor the target was identified as a member of a protected status group (that is, a group protected by civil rights legislation). Nearly all the bullies were bosses (81 percent) with the power to terminate targets at will (Namie & Namie, 2003). Results reported at the Workplace Bullying 2000 Conference in the United States provided convincing evidence of workplace mistreatment in 17 percent of its Michigan respondents via a self-selected, online sample. If that figure is extrapolated to the nation, one in six Americans may be bullied each year. Other estimates are that American workers have a 25 to 30 percent lifetime risk of being bullied at work, and at any one moment in time 10 percent of the U.S. workforce is experiencing some degree of bullying (Tracy et al., 2006).

Sexual harassment and general workplace harassment among 1,500 university employees were compared by University of Chicago researchers Rospenda, Richman, Ehmke, and Zlatoper (2005). They found similar characteristics between the two phenomena. Findings suggest that traditional measures of both job stress and workplace harassment are related to physical health symptoms and injuries, including workplace accidents. These findings also suggest that negative outcomes associated with workplace harassment tend to persist over time. Many injured workers have physical and psychological symptoms that persist long after the bullying situation is no longer part of their lives. The authors also found that some effects are lifelong.

Bullying at work can be more crippling and devastating than all other work-related stress put together. Einarsen (1999, in Harvey et al., 2006) asserted that bullying activities in the American workplace are escalating and have increasingly negative impacts on workers. According to the 2006 study, women tend to bully other women, men tend to bully other men, and the bully is usually the target's supervisor. Targets of bullying have stress-related health symptoms and generally feel unsupported. Rarely are bullies punished or held accountable. Targets often lose their jobs due to voluntary or involuntary termination. Finally, feelings of safety in the workplace have dropped dramatically since 1990 (Harvey et al., 2006).

Up to 90 percent of American workers will experience workplace abuse at some time in their lives, according to P. R. Johnson and Indvik (2006), suggesting that verbal abuse is the great secret of the American workplace and that it is more pervasive than most realize. Projections are that between 70 and 90 percent of abusive communication is perpetrated by superiors upon subordinates (P. R. Johnson & Indvik, 2006). An opinion survey of 1,300 workers conducted by the Opinion Research Corporation found that 42 percent of respondents experienced being the targets of yelling and verbal abuse, and 20 percent admitted to yelling at coworkers. Overwork, stress, and lack of job security were all cited as precipitating stressors. Two out of every three people who tried to defend themselves against demeaning behavior found that rather than helping them toward problem resolution, their defense triggered retaliation (P. R. Johnson & Indvik, 2006).

A sample of 4,832 university employees participated in a 2004 cross-sectional survey studied by Rospenda and Richman. Using an instrument called the Generalized Workplace Harassment Questionnaire (GWHQ), 2,416 men and 2,416 women responded to questions about having experienced bullying in the work setting. The GWHQ is a 29-question instrument asking respondents to indicate on a three-point scale (1 = never, 2 = once, 3 = more than once) if they have experienced any of the listed bullying behaviors at work. Researchers sorted workplace aggression into three types: subtle and covert, overt, and severe. Findings showed that subtle, covert forms of workplace aggression are more frequent than overt types. Subtle, covert forms of aggression included verbal hostility and manipulative behaviors (Rospenda & Richman, 2004). Overt forms of aggression, including humiliation, negative comments, yelling, gesturing, and talking down to someone, are also more frequent than more severe forms of aggression. Severe forms include behaviors such as threatening, hitting, pushing/shoving, throwing something, or making jokes about the person (Rospenda & Richman, 2004).

Data from an American study indicated that 14 percent of university students employed in entry-level positions in a variety of professions had experienced several types of abusive behaviors. The most common abuses were intellectual degradation, being publicly demeaned, being addressed sarcastically, being targets of temper tantrums, and being subjected to unreasonable work demands. Most respondents chose to deal with negative behaviors indirectly, by avoiding or ignoring the harasser. However, some 13 percent chose to leave their work prematurely (Keashly, Trott, & MacLean, 1994).

Unfortunately, some recent trends in the American workplace focusing on excellence and quality have increased pressure on employees, lead workers, supervisors, and managers, creating environments at high risk for bullying. Institutionalized bullying can result when an organization values high performance and high efficiency over human identity. When production demands threaten employment security, bullying is reinforced (Koonin & Green, 2004). OSHA identifies environmental conditions and triggers that correlate with increases in workplace assaults of all types as of 2004. Although policies and procedures have fallen within the purview of individual states and individual employers, organizations need to inventory the emotional climates of their work environments and take actions to prevent abuse before it occurs (Koonin & Green, 2004). Chapter 7 will include training guidelines from OSHA for preventing workplace violence. Where appropriate, these guidelines can be specifically applied to preventing and remediating bullying at work.

Social work research has relied on international data collected for estimates of the incidence, prevalence, and severity of workplace mobbing. Despite the prevalence of workplace emotional abuse in the United States and the implications for clients who are targets, limited information exists addressing how social workers and other clinicians can address this growing concern. Chapters 6, 7, and 8 will address clinical interventions and the role of social work. If clinicians in the United States are to be equipped to address the psychological damage created by workplace emotional abuse, they need comprehensive information about the nature, causes, and effects of the condition to identify treatment goals and measure effectiveness. If HR professionals and attorneys are to raise their awareness of the risks, liabilities, and responsibilities for prevention and remediation, the role of employers needs to be clarified through legislation and regulation.

2014 DATA FROM THE WORKPLACE BULLYING INSTITUTE

As with family violence and sexual assault, good data about workplace bullying remain difficult to collect because of underreporting by victims and misunderstanding by the general public. The most reliable data to date have been collected by the WBI, founded by Gary and Ruth Namie. For over a decade, the WBI has conducted annual data-collection efforts via self-report surveys. The following data are cited from the 2014 Workplace Bullying Institute U.S. Workplace Bullying Survey. In January 2014, 1,000 American adults responded to this online survey administered by Zogby Analytics, commissioned by the WBI (Namie, Christensen, & Phillips, 2014). Extrapolating to the American population, highlights of the results are summarized as follows: 27 percent of Americans have suffered abusive conduct at work, another 21 percent have witnessed it, and 72 percent are aware that workplace bullying happens, while only 28 percent are unaware of any workplace bullying. These estimates of bullying in the American workforce are alarming. Based on current workforce population data, more than 36 million American workers have been bullied in the past year or at some point in their work histories. More than 28 million workers have witnessed another being bullied. Only 75,000 perpetrators of workers would have admitted to histories of bullying others, and more than 26 million have not witnessed bullying directly but believe that it does occur.

A number of studies have indicated that up to 60 percent of victims are women and up to 69 percent of perpetrators are men. However, when women are the bullies, they are most likely to bully other women. Data also suggest that 77 percent of bullying cases are same-gender incidents, making sexual discrimination cases difficult to substantiate. Slight differences in gender and job loss data suggest that although

82 percent of targets lose their jobs, only 18 percent of perpetrators lose theirs. Female targets are the more likely candidates for job loss. Discrimination exists in how organizations respond to female perpetrators. In 30 percent of the instances, a female who bullies a male will lose her job, as compared to only 11 percent of females who bully other women. It appears that it is more acceptable for a woman to bully another woman than it is for a woman to bully a man (Namie et al., 2014).

Regarding race and bullying, 2014 data suggest that nonwhite groups are much more vulnerable to bullying, with Hispanics as targets 33 percent of the time and African Americans targeted 32 percent of the time, followed by Asians as targets 19 percent of the time. By definition, bullying complicates, increases, and aggravates any mistreatment created by racial or sexual discrimination. Because employers are obliged to comply with federal and state laws prohibiting discrimination, nonwhite workers represent a legally protected status group, but actual discrimination is sometimes difficult to prove.

Perpetrators apparently act alone in 77 percent of cases, with mobbing—abuse by multiple perpetrators—occurring 23 percent of the time. Data about the rank of perpetrators in relation to those bullied continue to reflect a tendency for bullying to be top-down, or inflicted by someone of higher rank than the target. More than 56 percent of bullies are the bosses of the victim, 33 percent are coworkers, and 11 percent are subordinates. According to the 2014 data, bullying is created by a combination of bosses, peers, and subordinates 14 percent of the time. Unfortunately, even as recently as 2014, employers tend not to be sympathetic or responsive to worker complaints of bullying. WBI data from 2014 indicate that 72 percent of the reactions of employers condone or sustain bullying.

With an absence of state or federal laws to prohibit bullying and promote civility in the workplace, employers have little risk exposure for bullying incidents or outcomes. Although a wise and proactive employer would take precautions to prevent or redress bullying when it occurs, 2014 WBI data suggested that in 66 percent of the instances, employer reactions were to deny, discount, defend, or rationalize bullying behavior, leaving the bully or bullies unchecked. In only 28 percent of instances did employers acknowledge and show concern, take steps to remediate, or exercise a zero-tolerance policy for bullying. This leaves American workers and workplace environments at very high risk for abuses.

What about observers? WBI data from 2014 showed that others did nothing 38 percent of the time or participated in isolating the victim or siding with the perpetrator (11 percent). Only 29 percent of observers or witnesses openly provided assistance to targets or made an attempt to intervene.

Outcomes for victims are grim. In 61 percent of cases, targets left the workplace voluntarily, were forced to quit because conditions worsened, or were terminated by the employer. Perpetrators, on the other hand, were punished, terminated, or left voluntarily only 21 percent of the time. These data sadly suggest that the victim, not the bully, is asked to make sacrifices or accommodations when targeted, because six times out of 10 the former lose their jobs when they bring the issue to light.

Regarding ownership of responsibility, the 2014 survey data suggested that most respondents were unlikely to blame the victim for the situation. Only 20 percent of respondents attributed the target's skill deficiency or personality flaw as the reason for the abuse. Skill deficiencies or personality problems of bullies were deemed responsible by 41 percent of respondents. Twenty-eight percent of respondents blamed the employer for failure to address or prevent abuses, and 10 percent cited a society that supports abuse and aggression as the cause. Contrary to some popular myths, victims tended to be viewed by respondents as compassionate, kind, cooperative, and agreeable. Targets were viewed as aggressive or abusive by only 21 percent of respondents (Namie et al., 2014).

Although no state has yet passed the HWB (discussed later), the data from Namie et al. (2014) suggest that 93 percent of the American public are aware of bullying and want laws to address it. The question asked in the survey: "Do you support or oppose enactment of a new law that would protect all workers from repeated abusive mistreatment in addition to protections against illegal discrimination and harassment?" Almost two-thirds (63 percent) of respondents answered that they strongly supported such legislation, and another 30 percent said they would somewhat support such laws.

In summary, respondents believe that bullying exists, generally see it as more top-down, state that women and nonwhite workers are more likely targets, view the loss of employment as much more likely for victims than for perpetrators, and find targets to be generally pleasant colleagues with adequate work skills but bullies to be less pleasant and with greater skill deficits. Most admit that organizations do little to prevent or remediate bullying and would welcome legislation to prevent or redress workplace emotional abuse.

PREVALENCE OF MOBBING IN THE INTERNATIONAL COMMUNITY

Most industrialized countries, including much of Europe (including Scandinavia and the United Kingdom) and Australia, have regarded bullying at work as a social problem far longer than has the United States. Studies have been conducted for decades, and more data exist in industrialized nations *other* than the United States. Swedish psychologist Heinz Leymann's groundbreaking work in 1990 marked the beginning of what would become an explosion of international interest and data collection on the mobbing syndrome (Leymann, 1990). Coining the term "mobbing," Leymann emphasized that these hurtful behaviors occur daily or almost daily and persist for a long period of time. Because of the severity and frequency, the actions result in psychological and social misery, as well as physical symptoms. Early estimates based on observations by industrial health physicians indicate that grave psychosomatic effects of mobbing could be observed in targets of abuse and that 10 to 15 percent of the suicides in Sweden each year could be attributed to mobbing (Leymann, 1990).

In the United Kingdom, labor unions have taken the lead in studying mobbing and in educating the public about it through national awareness campaigns. Researchers have worked in collaboration with unions to design and analyze surveys of workers and work environments (Namie & Namie, 2003). One such study was conducted in 1996 by UNISON, a union for public service organizations. It found that 66 percent of all respondents had experienced or witnessed mobbing. Of those who admitted having been bullied themselves, 74 percent said that management knew about the bullying and did nothing. Eighty-three percent of bullies were managers, and 94 percent of respondents said that they thought bullies would not receive any consequences. More than 75 percent of those who said they had been bullied reported some negative effects on their physical or emotional health, including stress, depression, and reduced self-confidence (Namie & Namie, 2003).

In another study in 2000, 1,100 workers in the National Health Service of southeastern England were surveyed about their mobbing experiences. Of those who responded, 38 percent reported having been emotionally bullied in the past year, and 42 percent reported having witnessed another being bullied. Staff who had been bullied reported lower levels of job satisfaction and higher levels of job-induced stress, depression, and anxiety. Affected workers were also more likely to leave their jobs (Cusack, 2000).

Workplace bullying in the National Health Service is such an important issue that it has been examined by other researchers as well. One theory has been that the nature of health-care organizations themselves may actually foster or sustain organizational bullying. Factors such as high stress levels, inadequate training, rapid organizational change, pressure from management, and unrealistic performance goals may all contribute to workplace bullying by creating a climate of tension and uncertainty (Randle, Stevenson, Grayling, & Walker, 2007).

In the United Kingdom, researchers identified a sample of 4,500 employees, about 800 of whom were clerical/secretarial support staff. A combination of surveys to identify those who had been bullied in the previous two years was administered and then followed by semistructured interviews with a sample of respondents who had reported having been bullied. All interviewees felt that being bullied had harmed their health in some way. All reported having lost confidence and self-esteem during the bullying experience; 8 out of ten complained of stress. One interviewee mentioned an increase in the use of analgesics and alcohol. One complained about being in a constant state of anxiety. Most complained of more frequent illnesses, such as headaches, colds, and flu. All said that the experience had affected their work performance (M. Thomas, 2005). Other researchers estimated the social costs of mobbing in the United Kingdom to exceed £680 million in 2007 and reported that there are increases in the number of cases reported annually (Whittaker, 2009).

A national survey of the workforce in Ireland surveyed 4,425 workers by mail about their experiences with mobbing. Results concluded that of those who responded (1,057, or 23 percent), 6 percent admitted having been bullied frequently in the preceding 12 months, and 17 percent admitted having been bullied occasionally in the previous year. Of those who had been bullied, 67 percent described the leadership style of their organizations as laissez-faire, and only 18 percent described it as democratic. Of those bullied, over 70 percent cited poor management styles as a significant factor contributing to their bullying experiences. Limited prospects for promotion, lack of recognition for accomplishments, and lack of control over work or workload were the most frequent areas of job dissatisfaction for bullied employees (O'Moore & Lynch, 2007).

English health-care employees experienced what they considered to be harassment, according to Quine (1999). In a sample of 1,580 individuals who admitted to having been bullied and harassed, most had high stress levels and a strong desire to leave their jobs. Most felt less job satisfaction than their peers. The study concluded that workplace harassment results in severe psychological distress for victims.

The Second European Survey on Working Conditions, based on face-to-face interviews with 16,000 workers throughout the European Union, identified 8 percent of all European workers as being bullied each year. An expanded projection indicated a 5 to 10 percent annual rate of emotional abuse at work. These estimates exceeded those of people reporting workplace sexual harassment, which was identified as 2 percent (Steensma & van Dijke, 2006).

Australian theorist Kelly blamed the increase in workplace bullying on the increase of competitive pressures, the diminished commitment to fairness or social justice, and a predominance of business values over human values (Kelly, 2007). Australia has made some institutional commitments to identify, penalize, and reduce the incidence of bullying, through occupational health and safety legislation in some states. Unfortunately Australia's Workplace Relations Amendment (Work Choice) Act of 2005 has the capacity to counter or weaken such measures. This law has made it more difficult for workers to file suit and less likely to receive judgments in their favor. An opinion by the Supreme Court of New South Wales stated that only 10 percent of instances of workplace bullying are actually reported. Differences in estimates seem to be in the ways that survey questions are asked. If a person is simply asked, "Have you ever been bullied?" respondents tend to report affirmatively only 8 or 9 percent of the time, but if respondents are provided a list of 23 predefined negative acts and then asked which they have experienced, 24 percent or more report having been victimized in some way (Kelly, 2007).

A 2004 Australian study examined 800 workers in tertiary education, health care, and long-distance hauling (Mayhew et al., 2004). Its authors concluded that emotional abuse at work is increasing and that covert forms of occupational violence over time, such as bullying, can be equal in traumatic impact to the harm caused from actually physical assault. Citing Leymann and Gustafson (1996), who addressed psychological disability by measuring the health effects of bullying at work, the researchers found extremely degraded health profiles for the 62 patients/victims of mobbing selected for their study. Citing Einarsen and Mikkelsen (2003), Mayhew et al. (2004) examined health status of 64 victims of mobbing and found high incidence of generalized anxiety disorder and posttraumatic stress disorder (PTSD).

Spanish public university system employees served as the subjects for studies of three campuses in 2006 where administrative and services personnel, along with educational and investigative personnel, were queried about the problem of psychological harassment within the university system. A total of 7,432 people responded anonymously via a mail-in survey. Although 54 percent of respondents claimed they had never experienced or witnessed emotional abuse at work, the remaining 46 percent said they had experienced or witnessed abuse at some time in their lives. Of these, 23 percent said they had witnessed or experienced workplace bullying in the year prior to the survey. The most frequent types of psychological harassment cited by respondents were lack of information to do their jobs well, excessive criticism, public undervaluation, and restricted promotional opportunities (Lopez Cabarcos & Vasquez Rodriguez, 2006).

Turkish white-collar workers were studied in 2006 via a 20-item inventory of bullying. A good response rate of 79 percent (944) of 1,200 people surveyed indicated that 55 percent had been bullied at work in the past year. The most frequently reported types of bullying reported were overwork (70 percent), destabilization (55 percent), threats to professional status (42 percent), and threats to personal standing (32 percent). The destabilization category included acts such as persistent attempts to demoralize the person, removing areas of responsibility without consulting the person, undervaluing the worker's efforts, and shifting goals without informing the worker (Bilgel, Aytac, & Bayram, 2006).

An Australian study of 500 nurses in the metropolitan area health services of New South Wales (Hutchinson, Wilkes, Vickers, & Jackson, 2008) queried professionals employed mostly in clinical nursing positions and management. An exploratory factor analysis identified the most prevalent abusive behaviors nurses had experienced in the previous six months. Following the initial definition of bullying, respondents were asked to answer 23 seven-point scale items measuring their experiences (ranging from "never" to "constantly") of bullying acts in the 12 months preceding the survey. Results suggested that in the professional context, an attack upon a person's reputation might be used as a strategy to render a person more deserving of more overt forms of bullying to follow. Slanderous gossip, then, may make one more vulnerable to other forms of abuse.

Industrializing parts of the world, such as India, have identified and examined workplace emotional abuse. A cross-sectional survey was conducted among 174 physicians in a government medical college in the state of Tamil Nadu. Of the respondents, 115 were postgraduates, and 59 were junior doctors. Although bullying was common in junior medical doctors (nearly half reported having been bullied), survey results suggest that 90 percent of bullying incidents go unreported (Bairy et al., 2007).

China has studied bullying as well. A study of 142 high school teachers there measured the impact of bullying on affective (or emotional) commitment to the job. Perhaps not surprisingly, findings suggested that workplace bullying had a significant negative correlation with affective commitment to work, while satisfaction with coworkers and supervisors had a significant positive correlation with affective commitment to work (McCormack, Casimir, Djurkovic, & Yang, 2006).

Workplace mobbing seems to be universal, although rates vary across types of settings. The literature sources surveyed in this section are by no means exhaustive but share many features in common. Bullying causes misery when it occurs. Victims are likely to terminate employment early to escape. Up to 20 percent of a workforce may be bullied at any one time. Mobbing tends to go unreported or underreported.

Other writers have suggested that rather than gather quantitative data about incidence, prevalence, severity, and duration, researchers should focus attention on the subjective experiences of targets of bullying to measure the breadth and scope of this malady (Liefooghe & Davey, 2002). Problems may exist with definitions and lack of consensus about what constitutes abuse. Poor management practices seem to be at least one source of the malady. Later sections of this book will explore practices and policies that may place organizations at risk. These are relevant to a discussion of mobbing because many high-risk organizational factors might be identified and remedied by analysis and intervention.

ECONOMIC CONSEQUENCES OF WORKPLACE EMOTIONAL ABUSE

Significant economic consequences for unchecked emotional abuses at work include wasted wages for paying a worker who does not have an actual job description or tasks to perform after the worker's duties have been stripped away as part of a mobbing process, extensive use of sick leave by targets of abuse, significant drops in production rates in organizations where mobbing is prevalent, costs of interventions by human resource officers, and costs associated with personnel and external consulting fees. Estimates of economic impact can be staggering. Studies suggest that individual cases of mobbing can last as long as 10 years (Leymann, 1990).

Long-term financial consequences for abused workers and their families can be dire, according to data from the nursing industry in the United Kingdom. Victims may be coerced to resign, or they may accept early retirement due to ill health. Those who leave their jobs because of bullying often develop alcohol-related problems, eating disorders, panic attacks, and nightmares, all of which can prohibit successful future employability. In addition to effects on victims, their families and friends can be affected as well (Randle et al., 2007).

Loss of productivity suggests that emotional abuse at work creates a financial burden for the health-care system in the United States. At one hospital alone, costs for losses of productivity due to incivility at work may have exceeded $1.2 million annually (Hutton & Gates, 2008). These researchers identified the financial costs of workplace violence at millions of dollars each year. They posited that early diagnosis of a hostile work environment and interventions to change the milieu can be cost-saving measures.

Direct costs such as disability and workers' compensation claims, medical costs, and legal expenses for wrongful dismissal lawsuits contribute to the high price employers pay for unchecked emotional abuse of workers in the United States (Tracy et al., 2006). Indirect costs are difficult to calculate but may include low-quality work, high absenteeism, reduced productivity, and damage to public image. Davenport et al. (2002) cited increased employee turnover, increased use of sick leave, increases in unemployment claims, increases in workers' compensation claims, and high litigation costs as the real and potential costs employers incur for failure to address abusive conditions in the workplace.

Workplace bullying can damage an organization's productivity and public image, all of which will eventually affect that organization's bottom line. Ultimately the costs for these problems are passed along to the consumer, who is generally forced to absorb the expense increases in costs for goods and services (Ambrosino,

Heffernan, Shuttlesworth, & Ambrosino, 2005). The potential for public-sector financial risk and liability increases as workers become unable to return to meaningful employment. Long-term unemployment or permanent disability can force a previous wage earner onto public-assistance rosters for health care and financial support. At a macro level, lack of individual employment can ultimately affect the business sector as well when a displaced worker has a reduced capacity for participating in the marketplace for the purchasing of goods and services. All of these effects point to the need for further analysis of the causes of bullying, the maintenance factors in the bullying syndrome, any preventative measures for organizations, and the most effective treatments for employees when injury has occurred. If work environments are to be lower in risk for emotional abuse, the conditions at all levels are relevant to the discussion.

Additional costs to workplaces where emotional abuse is pervasive can include expenses for overtime wages, reduced morale, low productivity, increased error rates, higher health-care costs (medical and psychiatric), administrative costs for investigating complaints, and damage to public image and trust (Koonin & Green, 2004). Vega and Comer (2005) proposed that organizational costs can have a domino effect, creating additional negative impact on organizations. Nontargets can be drawn into the abuse and suffer personal distress that affects their productivity as well. Perhaps the greatest cost to organizations is the loss of qualified professionals, a loss triggering lengthy and expensive recruitment, hiring, and training in a high-turnover organization (Vega & Comer, 2005).

Often the brightest, most talented, and most dedicated employees are at risk for leaving because of bullying (Namie & Namie, 2011). Good people generally will not remain in an abusive environment. They may also be targets precisely because they excel in their roles. Turnover rates are always costly, and costs for exposure to litigation vary, but in a few well known cases, such as the 2001 *Doescher v. Raess* case, plaintiffs were awarded large sums. The judgment in another case, a 2005 lawsuit filed against the City University of New York by former employees Salerno and Aleandri, awarded the plaintiffs a combined settlement of $1.4 million (Namie & Namie, 2011). Additional costs cited by Namie and Namie include those for disability claims, absenteeism, and worker apathy. Court decisions in 2000 awarded damages of $740,000 for a case involving workplace bullying, and another case awarded $325,000 to a bullied plaintiff (Pfaffenback, 2000, in Fox & Stallworth, 2009). Direct costs to employers include time, labor, overhead, litigation settlements, costs for replacing employees, workers' compensation claims, health care, and costs for security. Indirect costs cited include defects in the quality of products and services, loss of productivity, lost revenue, increases in workers' compensation insurance premiums, and excess capacity (Cascio, 2000, in Fox & Stallworth, 2009).

Abuse is costly to organizations. It destroys networks of communication and increases the likelihood of early departure of both targets and nontargets (Tracy et al., 2006). Victimized workers have frequent absenteeism and may develop permanent disabilities with corresponding decreased earning capacity. Workplaces where abuse occurs incur costs for legal expenses, consulting fees, recruitment and retention expenses, and high use of medical benefits. Problems with recruitment and retention, employee health effects, reduced productivity, and legal counter-measures by employees are all potential hidden costs of workplace emotional abuse (Glendinning, 2001).

The impacts of bullying and emotional abuse on an organization can be significant. Intangible costs include reduced productivity, loss of creativity and low innovation (Vega & Comer, 2005). Efficiency declines when work environments become toxic. Although direct financial costs to organizations can be devastating for such expenses as legal defense, workers' compensation claims, consultants, and reduced output, the greatest losses are those of qualified personnel, requiring extensive hiring and training. The importance of people as resources cannot be overstated.

WORKPLACE ENVIRONMENT AND WORKPLACE HEALTH CONSEQUENCES OF BULLYING

Catastrophic drops in production rates, frequent personnel consultations, more union involvement in case-dispute resolution, and a general lowering of job commitment have been found to be common in emotionally abusive work environments. Leymann's original work cited a cost between $30,000 and $100,000 per year for an employee exposed to mobbing (Leymann, 1990; Sheehan & Barker, 1999, in Vega & Comer, 2005).

Estimates are that mental illness in the United States causes lost productivity of about $17 billion each year. A Massachusetts Institute of Technology (MIT) study in 1995 found that untreated depression, a common but serious mental illness, costs $23.8 billion annually in lost productivity and absenteeism, with direct treatment and rehabilitation costing some $12.4 billion annually. In addition, lost earnings because of depression-related suicides cost over $7.5 billion each year (Ambrosino et al., 2005). Each year some 85 percent of industrial accidents and 32 percent of worker-related accidents and heart attacks are attributed to employee stress. According to most leading theorists, mobbing is among the most severe forms of workplace stress.

Rospenda et al. (2005) suggested that some lack of control over job tasks may be inherent in certain types of work, especially if that work is dangerous. Wide variability exists in the extent to which workers lack control over their jobs and the extent to which this lack of control results in stress. Nonetheless, conclusions suggest that interpersonal relationships at work that are characterized by abuse or harassment are unnecessarily very stressful to victims. Conclusions also highlight that the stress created by workplace harassment is more serious than mere task-related or role-related workplace stress. In addition, workplace emotional abuse results in more symptoms of mental illness than any other type of work-related stress.

A study in the early 2000s by the University of Manchester Institute for Science and Technology in the United Kingdom found a modest but notable correlation between absenteeism and four groups of people who differed in their experience of bullying. More than 5,300 participants from 70 organizations responded to a four-part Likert-type scale about the effects of bullying on targets. From 27 to 33 percent of respondents felt that bullying had negatively affected their places of work. Respondents were divided into four groups: those who had not been bullied or witnessed bullying, those who had witnessed bullying, those who had been bullied within the previous five years, and those who were currently being bullied (Rayner et al., 2002). Respondents who were currently bullied used the highest number of sick days, followed by those who had been bullied in the past and those who had only witnessed bullying. Respondents who had not been bullied and who had not witnessed bullying took the fewest days off. On average, respondents who were currently bullied had taken off three and a half days more in the past six months than those who were neither bullied nor had witnessed bullying (Rayner et al., 2002).

A 2006 study by Hartig and Frosch suggested loss of productivity in the workplace as a consequence of unchecked bullying. A survey conducted by the South Australian Working Women's Centre in 1997 (New South Wales Department of Commerce, cited in Hartig & Frosch, 2006) identified that 70 percent of the respondents reported taking time off as a result of being bullied at work. That survey also noted that 75 percent of workers used sick leave, while the remaining used workers' compensation.

A study of verbal abuse within the nursing profession suggests that the impact on the workplace decreases the quality of patient care, produces job insecurity, fosters low morale, and reduces job satisfaction. A meta-analysis of a previous study that had surveyed 500 nurses in a local county medical community confirmed that verbal abuse was the most frequent (64 percent) form of mistreatment of nurses by physicians. Although not as frequent, sexual abuse (35 percent), threats (23 percent), and physical abuse (10 percent) were also notable (Diaz & McMillan, cited in Keashly et al., 1994).

Other data also suggested that targets can spend great amounts of time (more than 50 percent of their time) at work defending themselves, preparing grievance reports, or building up support networks (Canada Safety Council, 2005, in Hartig & Frosch, 2006). In a report by the Victoria's State Services Authority from a survey of over 14,000 workers, more than one in five (over 20 percent) had been bullied or harassed by colleagues or managers. Another 40 percent had witnessed someone else being abused (Tomazin, 2006, in Hartig & Frosch, 2006).

Harvey et al. (2006) identified major negative impacts of bullying on organizational functioning. These include impairment of employees' task-specific abilities, creation of a climate in which high-achieving employees no longer exert extra effort to do well, and creation of "strategic myopia" in the organization, which lessens organizational flexibility and responsiveness to change. In these ways, bullying can act as a type of "organizational cancer," killing the organization.

Davenport et al. (2002) suggested that mobbing affects not only individual victims but also team functioning. The quality and quantity of work produced can suffer. Communications and teamwork can break down. Employees can become split or factionalized. An organization's reputation can suffer. Relationships can suffer, and energies begin to revolve around the bullying process, diverting attention from the organization's actual mission and goals.

Voss, Floderus, and Diderichsen (2001) studied 3,470 employees from the Sweden Post (Sweden's postal service). The focus of the study was the use of sick leave by employees and the physical, psychosocial, and organizational factors that contributed to its use. Questionnaires were sent to respondents who completed and returned them anonymously. Response rates were high at 76 percent, with mild differences between male and female respondents. Most respondents reported working when ill, but, among other findings, 16 percent of the female respondents reported being bullied at work. This was linked to a doubled risk of the development of illness and the use of sick leave in women. For men, concerns about reorganization were correlated the most highly with self-reports of anxiety (Voss et al., 2001). The large sample size and the high rate of return lent strength to the study in spite of the limitations of self-report survey methods.

Studies of work environments using the GWHQ survey indicate a reduction in employee morale and a reduction in job satisfaction in work environments where emotional abuse is prevalent (Rospenda & Richman, 2004). When bullying occurs, it may trigger involvement by HR, EAPs, and unions. A work environment can develop a heightened emotional state, drawing energy and attention away from work tasks (Tracy et al., 2006).

Additional findings from using the GWHQ include high levels of workplace anxiety (Voss et al., 2001). Workers other than targets can experience emotional stress reactions, low self-confidence, and poor goal clarity about work tasks (Vartia, 2001). Absenteeism, decreased organizational commitment, decreased productivity, general lack of civility among workers, and poor communication are all byproducts of workplace mobbing (Hutton & Gates, 2008).

Mental and physical health needs were surveyed in a study by Hoel, Cooper, and Faragher (2001, in Rayner et al., 2002). Respondents were asked about bullying and health status. For physical health concerns, 82 percent of those previously bullied and currently bullied complained of physical health concerns, and 34 percent of those who had witnessed bullying complained of health problems. Regarding mental health, 9 percent of those currently bullied and previously bullied reported mental health concerns, compared to only 3 percent of those who had only witnessed bullying. Although these findings implied a correlation between illness and bullying, it is not known if the health of participants with exposure to bullying would have been similarly compromised had they not experienced or witnessed bullying.

Finally, interpersonal reactions in the workplace are job stressors linked to increased risk of illness and injury. Rospenda et al. (2005) examined the cross-sectional and lagged effects of both sexual harassment (SH) and generalized workplace harassment (GWH). The sample in their study included faculty, graduate student workers, clerical/secretarial staff, and service/maintenance workers at a large Midwestern university who responded to a survey. This sequential type of study involved surveying respondents at four points in time from 1996 to 2002. The findings, reported earlier in this chapter, suggested that GWH was positively correlated with an increase in illness and injury.

Researchers caution against underestimating the effects of workplace emotional abuse on work team members who observe abuse, citing anxiety, dismay, powerlessness, and revenge as common occurrences in the witnesses of abuse. A particular admonition is that for workplaces where bullying has become operational or "normalized," it can be difficult for victims or advocates to challenge it and effect any real change (Randle et al., 2007).

To the degree that workers are emotionally injured at work, one can expect increases in rates of expulsion, psychiatric illness, physical illness, suicide, and death. The economic consequences for organizations and society are also apparent:

> We must assume that the economic consequences—like the psychosocial— are considerable. A person can be paid without having any real work to do for years. Long periods of sick leave, a catastrophic drop in production by the whole group, the necessity for frequent intervention by personnel officers, personnel consultants, managers of various grades, occupational health staff, external consultants, the company's health centers, and so on. All this extra effort, combined with the loss of productive work can be costly. (Leymann, 1990)

PERSONAL CONSEQUENCES OF WORKPLACE MOBBING

The experiences of targets will be examined in chapter 5. However, a few examples of personal consequences are included here. Performance-based destruction is described in recent work by Harvey et al. (2006). Grouping this destruction into four areas, the authors posited: (1) Bullying can affect daily task-specific abilities of employees, such as employee motivation, task learning, and team interdependence. (2) Employees who tend to be ambitious and who will go the extra mile for the organization may have their prosocial behavior discouraged. This second area of destruction can be found, then, in a decrease in *organizational citizenship*, or helping others and civic virtue at work. (3) Bullying creates myopia in the firm by controlling change agents and increasing levels of general control. (4) Tolerance for bullying can become so toxic that the organization suffers from cancerlike malignancies, creating a reputation that the organization is a bad place to work (Harvey et al., 2006). A bad reputation can have major implications for hiring but also for risk assessment, liability issues, public opinion, and financial viability.

While the relationship between bullying and health problems may seem obvious, it is not always straightforward. Longitudinal data collection has been very limited and difficult to obtain. Targets have reported such symptoms as anxiety, depression, sleep problems, appetite disturbance, and sadness. The most severe symptoms for some are cognitive effects, such as poor concentration, insecurity, lack of initiative, and irritability (Bjorkqvist et al., 1994, in Rayner et al., 2002). Work performance almost always suffers for targets, along with a reduced commitment to remain in the job, loss of efficiency, diminished motivation, and serious compromises in job satisfaction (Rayner et al., 2002).

Workplace bullying can have severe outcomes for targets. Two hundred subjects responded to a Web survey in 2003 (Namie & Namie, 2003). Respondents included 154 targets and 46 witnesses of workplace emotional harassment. Of those who identified themselves as targets, 79 percent reported feeling stressed, 64 percent felt depressed, 64 percent reported chronic fatigue, 59 percent said they lacked confidence in themselves, 59 percent said they felt humiliated and guilty, 58 percent had obsessive thoughts and nightmares, 56 percent reported poor concentration, and 53 percent admitted difficulties with sleep. Targets were more likely than observers or witnesses to experience general stress and mental pressure, but both targets and witnesses reported greater stress than people who were not exposed to workplace abuse. Davenport et al. (2002) suggested that mobbing and bullying are mentioned in the same list as homicide, rape, and robbery as workplace crimes.

Tracy et al. (2006) used metaphors to describe the experience of being bullied, including feeling as though in a battle, undergoing water torture, torn apart, or in a nightmare. All authors concluded that being the target of bullying puts an employee at risk for injury, illness, and accidents. For a few, it can result in assault toward the perpetrator or others. In some isolated cases, an injured worker retaliates with violence, including murder and suicide, referred to in American popular culture as "going postal." Clearly, the costs for unchecked workplace emotional abuse are significant and substantial enough to warrant preventative strategies.

Damage to health from emotional abuse at work is real. A host of stress-related conditions can be attributed or exacerbated by a hostile work environment, such as compromised immunity, gastrointestinal disorders, hypertension, increased sensitivity to allergens, and headaches, to name only a few. In addition, targets experience very real psychosocial effects, such as damage to social relationships, economic damage, and loss of professional identify.

Although some unhappiness on the individual, organizational, and macro levels of work may be an inevitable part of life, many types of individual suffering, workplace devastation, and workplace economic costs could be avoided by recognizing and preventing emotional abuse at work. A later chapter will address organizational prevention and remediation. Chapter 2 will address theoretical explanations for the causes of mobbing and potential solutions for prevention and remediation.

SUMMARY

Although social work practice within the workplace has been a recognized domain for many decades, little has appeared in social work literature to address the identification, prevention, treatment, and remediation of actual workplace emotional abuse that is created and sustained by bullying in work organizations. Social work's ethical traditions advocate for understanding and intervening in the environment where problems occur (Woods & Hollis, 2000), but most non-social-work-oriented organizations do not have the benefit of social workers to address problems occurring within the workplace. Some might argue that "personality and environmental systems are inevitably intertwined" and that it is not often easy to differentiate between the two. The remaining chapters focus on answers to a number of questions about victims, perpetrators, risk environments, social work practice, and public policy.

This book provides for an integrated framework identifying organizational vulnerabilities, leadership strategies, survival tactics for victims, clinical assessment and treatment for targets of abuse, organizational prevention approaches, best practices for remediation, and the laws and public policies currently in place and in development. This work makes an argument for including this social problem as one of the domains where social work scholars and practitioners should direct their attention and intervene to improve the lives of people in American society.

2

Multiple Theoretical Explanations for Mobbing

This chapter surveys various theories that can help to explain emotional abuse in the workplace. It provides an understanding of the many theories for the phenomenon of emotional abuse at work and the need for a multidimensional model of addressing, treating, and preventing individual bullying and group mobbing in the workplace.

THEORIES OF AGGRESSION AND SOCIAL INFLUENCE

Like those of other psychological and sociological phenomena, theories of mobbing, aggression, and bullying are many and varied. Each definition depends on the perspective taken by each author or the theoretical perspective. For any given event or process of bullying or mobbing at work, the entire social context in which the behavior occurred must be considered (Lawrence, 2001). Gravois drew a parallel between workplace bullying and behaviors occurring spontaneously in nature, stating that

> when songbirds perceive some sign of danger—a roosting owl, a hawk, a neighborhood cat—a group of them will often do something bizarre: fly toward the threat. When they reach the enemy, they will swoop down on it again and again, jeering and making a racket, which draws still more birds to the assault. The birds seldom actually touch their target (though reports from the field have it that some species can defecate or vomit on the predator

with "amazing accuracy"). The barrage simply continues until the intruder sulks away. Scientists call this behavior "mobbing." (Gravois, 2006, p. 1)

Workplace mobbing was seen as a "silent and unseen epidemic" by Australian researchers Hartig and Frosch (2006). Acknowledging that mobbing behaviors, when viewed in isolation from each other, may seem trivial within the holistic context of a work environment, they emphasized the importance of understanding the cumulative process of loss of control experienced by mobbing victims. Within this framework, workplace aggression or bullying can be better understood.

Social psychology has long addressed the phenomenon of aggression in human relationships, as outlined by Baron, Byrne, and Branscombe (2006). Drive theories of aggression propose that aggression stems from external conditions that create or arouse an individual or collective motive to inflict injury or harm on others. One of the earliest and most prevalent drive theories is the *frustration-aggression hypothesis,* a view that suggests that individual frustration is a powerful determinant of aggressive behavior. In spite of its popularity and frequency of reference, the frustration-aggression hypothesis has not been well substantiated.

Another social psychological theory, the *social learning model,* suggests that people learn to act in aggressive ways by observing others displaying aggressive behavior. Baron et al. (2006) described a number of these models. In the social learning model, when individuals are exposed to high levels of aggression—for example, in television, films, or video games—the repeated exposure strengthens knowledge structures related to aggression, such as beliefs, attitudes, and internal working models. Other social psychology theorists suggest that the strongest push toward aggression is direct provocation, especially provocation that is arrogant, harsh, or condescending. Another theory proposes that the emotional state of heightened arousal, produced through fear, terror, anxiety, or panic, can increase a tendency to behave aggressively. Still another theory purports that hostile expectations or biases (that is, assumptions) that others will behave aggressively can heighten an individual's tendency to be aggressive.

In cultures of honor in which there are strong norms approving aggression as an appropriate response to insults to one's honor, aggression is often triggered by the word or actions of another (Baron et al., 2006). Other theories imply that the roots of aggression lie within the perpetrator, who may be a type A personality, prone to interpret or project evil intent from others, narcissism, or sensation seeking (Baron et al., 2006). Some social psychologists interpret bullying as a need for power or a need for belonging, suggesting that bullies have lower self-esteem than nonbullies and that bullies attack others to build their own self-images (Baron et al., 2006).

A distinction in how different types of aggression might be categorized is found in the difference between hostile aggression and instrumental aggression. Hostile aggression is often impulsive rather than planned, and the goal is to hurt the target in some way. By contrast, instrumental aggression is motivated by goals *other* than directly hurting the target, such as getting something of value (Breckler et al., 2005). Within these definitions, injury to a victim in a robbery would be an example of instrumental aggression.

Relational aggression, or behavior that is designed to damage the relationships of others, can be viewed as instrumental aggression. The goals of relational aggression include such outcomes as trying to get another person to dislike a peer, verbally threatening to exclude a peer, and not inviting a peer to a social event (Breckler et al., 2005). Adolescent girls are at risk for relational aggression. For people in the lesbian, gay, bisexual, and transgender communities, it might include threats to "out" someone (that is, reveal that person's sexual orientation). Under this definition, workplace emotional abuse is a form of instrumental aggression of the relational aggression variety. Social psychology recommends reducing relational aggression at work by reducing aversion within the workplace. Aversion reduction could then serve as a deterrent to workplace emotional abuse and will be examined in chapter 7.

Aggressive behavior is complex, and a stronger theoretical framework is needed to understand it from an organizational behavior perspective. Stewart's work (2007) suggested that individuals differ considerably in their tendencies to behave aggressively toward others or to attack in response to environmental stimuli. Considerable evidence also concludes that people who are inclined by individual or personal temperament to be aggressive are more likely to engage in antisocial behavior, including engaging in direct harm toward others. Such factors as a desire for revenge, variability in locus of control, and negative emotional states might be examples of individual temperaments prone to aggression. Situational factors influencing aggression at work can include role conflict and ambiguity, perception of organizational injustice, and a perception of psychological contract violation (someone breaking informal rules of conduct).

The perception of organizational injustice as a predictor of aggression was examined by Kennedy, Homant, and Homant (2004). The research was exploratory, directed at determining whether subjects' perceptions of injustice would predict their support for aggressive behavior. The goal was to provide a foundation for the future development of theory, and the intention was to examine any possible relationships between variables in attitude. The authors administered a questionnaire to a convenience sample of 139 subjects recruited through seven classes in psychology, human services, and criminal justice at two Midwestern universities. The outcomes reflected a high correlation between workplace aggression and perpetrators' perceptions that they are or were being treated unfairly. Individual differences in the perceptions of injustice did not appear to be related to the differences in organizational support for aggression within each of four scenarios in which participants judged the degree to which they thought aggression in a social situation was justified. Although the researchers made no claims to generalizability of the findings because of the self-report design and the sampling strategies, support or approval for workplace aggression was identified as more of a personality variable than any pattern of response to various themes or situations.

Social influence can be examined from a number of perspectives. Defined as efforts by one or more individuals to influence the attitudes, beliefs, perceptions, or behaviors of one or more others, social influence is a common feature of everyday life (Baron et al., 2006). *Conformity, compliance,* and *obedience* are three types of social influence all relevant to the discussion of emotional bullying at work. Conformity is social pressure to behave in ways that others in a group find desirable. The wish to conform with others' expectations can be difficult to resist. Studies have suggested some aspects of group behavior that can be somewhat predictive. The higher the cohesiveness of a group, the greater will be the conformity within the group. It is interesting to note that group size can affect conformity, but only up to a point. Up to five people in a group increases conformity, but as additional numbers are added to group size, conformity levels off and can even decline (Breckler et al., 2005).

People's desire to conform can affect the likelihood of workplace mobbing. The desire to be liked and accepted is a powerful human motivator. A desire to be seen as "right" can also increase conformity. When people are unsure of what is considered appropriate behavior in a situation, they are more likely to react or behave like those around themselves (Baron et al., 2006). So, in a work situation where someone is being mobbed, even those who may have no personal motive for bullying the target may be encouraged or enticed to go along with others because of social influences, including conformity. By contrast, people are less likely to conform when (1) they have a strong desire for individuation; (2) they have a strong need for personal control; or, in some cases, (3) when they lack the ability to conform because of disability, gender, or another reason (Baron et al., 2006).

Compliance is the willingness to respond to the direct request of another. Compliance can be based on friendship or liking. It may be influenced by a hope or promise of reciprocity, or it may occur after an easier request has already granted (Baron et al., 2006). For decades, Madison Avenue (that is, advertising) has used principles of compliance and conformity to sell people products they may not need or even know they wanted before being exposed to the manipulation of marketing. Conformity and compliance may also underlie workplace emotional abuse. Some workers, then, may go along with bullying to feel accepted, to avoid feeling excluded, in hopes of avoiding abuse themselves, or for the promise of personal gain.

Finally, principles of obedience to authority may be operating in mobbing. Obedience to authority has been studied during laboratory experiments and in real-life situations such as combat (Baron et al., 2006). A few factors that influence obedience include whether a person will or will not be held personally responsible for his or her actions and the presence of outward signs of authority, such as uniforms, badges, insignia, or special titles, all reminding others to obey those in charge. Another factor influencing obedience is a gradual escalation of an authority figure's orders. As discovered in many experimental situations (Milgram, 1963; Zimbardo, 1973), destructive levels of obedience can emerge very quickly. Noninvolved observers of mobbing may be persuaded to participate in the process by group pressure, environmental enticements, and failure of the organization to intervene, especially if key perpetrators seem to be those high in authority or popularity. Techniques to resist this type of social influence might include questioning the motives of the authority figure and understanding the power that authority figures represent in one's life.

Accountability in the workplace can have an effect on the bullying behavior of some workers toward others (Harvey, Treadway, Heames, & Duke, 2009). Accountability is the perception of justifying or defending one's conduct to others when either rewards or approvals are inherent in the conduct (or consequences for failures of conduct). Accountability theory states that there is a significant role for interpersonal expectations that may be emphasized in the consequences of actions, such as emotional abuse. Accountability theory suggests that if bullying is "tolerated" at work, it can become an ethical norm. An implicit endorsement of dysfunctional behavior affects entire organizations and will ultimately affect productivity. Mobbing then may persist when no one is held accountable for bullying acts or their consequences.

In addition to personal factors that can influence abusive behavior at work, stress is highly correlated with aggression in organizations. Situational stressors can include any condition or circumstance at work that produces a negative emotional reaction, such as fear, anxiety, anger, or frustration (Stewart, 2007). Some common job stressors include workloads that prevent one from pursuing other goals, conflicting roles in organizations, and ambiguous job descriptions. More will be examined in a later section to address how stressful work environments can be fertile ground for emotional abuse.

Neuman and Baron (1998) addressed social determinants of workplace aggression. Their findings suggest that social factors that seem relevant to aggression in workplaces include

- the perception of being treated unfairly;
- events in the workplace that produce frustration;
- an increase in the diversity of the workforce, with exposure to groups of whom one has no or little understanding; and
- norms that allow for aggressive behavior.

Neuman and Baron also identified situational determinants of aggression. These may include abandonment of social contracts between employers and workers and layoffs, or downsizing. Data also seem to suggest that observers as well as victims can be harmed by these events (Neuman & Baron, 1998).

Concepts from social psychology concerning influencing others can help to explain how and why people treat others in abusive ways at work. While these explanations are not complete when examined alone, they begin to make sense when one considers personality, environment, and larger macro systems as significant influences in the mobbing syndrome. Even though early views of aggression have focused on reactions within an individual, context remains an important consideration in the understanding of human aggression. In examining the issue of workplace bullying, context or social backdrop matters (Lawrence, 2001). Behavior does not occur in a vacuum. The purpose of this work is to identify and analyze the myriad social and behavioral influences underlying a workplace problem.

THEORIES OF THE INDIVIDUAL

A variety of theories focus on the individual and his or her development. They focus on many aspects of personal and social development and include attitude formation, social comparison, attribution, conflict, symbolic interactionism, social identify, social perception, anomie, and muted group theory. These are outlined here, with a focus on their relationship to bullying in the workplace.

Attitude Formation

Social psychologists use the term *attitude* to refer to people's evaluations of their social world (Baron et al., 2006). Attitudes are formed via a number of processes in human experience. The process of learning through observing others, or social learning, is one significant way in which people acquire new information and develop new behaviors. Another way of learning is by association or classical conditioning, in which a previously neutral stimulus acquires the capacity to evoke a strong positive or negative reaction through repeated pairing with a more benign stimulus. The process of classical conditioning has major implications for attitude formation. A person learns that when one stimulus or event occurs, a second will follow soon (Baron et al., 2006). People may form attitudes based on the association one person or event has with another. An important feature of classical conditioning is that it can occur when one is not even aware of its occurrence. An example might be: If Employee A observes Supervisor X frowning and showing signs of displeasure each time that Supervisor X encounters Employee B, Employee A will learn from Supervisor X or other managers to respond to Employee B (a previously neutral cue) with frowning and displeasure. Classical conditioning, then, can occur when Employee A learns to react negatively to Employee B without having any actual reason for doing so.

Another form of behavioral conditioning is instrumental conditioning, which simply increases or decreases the likelihood of repeated behavior by a rewarding or punishing consequence. Quite simply, with regard to attitude formation, responses that lead to positive outcomes or those that help to avoid negative outcomes are likely to be stronger or more frequently used. Any of these forms of learned behavior can impact workers and their participation in or tolerance for bullying others. People can learn behaviors by what sorts of consequences they or others receive for those behaviors. If bullies were consistently apprehended and punished with reprimands, warnings, threats of demotion, or actual job loss, bullying would be unlikely to persist in any workplace for long.

What happens, however, is that bullies often have their negative behavior ignored or even rewarded, so there may actually be positive consequences for their actions. For example, Employees A, B, C, and D may be involved in mobbing Employee T. If management sees Employee T as the cause of the problem rather than Employee A, B, C, or D, and if Employee T is disciplined while Employees A, B, C, and D receive either no consequence or some form of reward for their actions, offenders like Employees A, B, C, and D are very likely to repeat the bullying behaviors in the future. Those who observe the reward are more likely to follow.

Social Comparison

Social comparison is the process by which people compare themselves to others in order to judge the validity of their social reality. To be similar to others whom one likes often involves adopting attitudes that those others hold (Baron et al., 2006). Attitudes function in a variety of ways for humans. They may permit expression of central beliefs and values, or they may enhance self-esteem. To some degree they may help a person to manage others' views of him or her via a mechanism called *impression management,* or self-presentation. These principles may be operating in bullying situations. Otherwise uninvolved individuals or groups may tolerate or even participate in mobbing or bullying because of a desire to be similar to those they like and for a need to enhance their own self-esteem.

Explicit attitudes are those that one can identify and report consciously, while *implicit attitudes* are those about which one is not aware (Breckler et al., 2005). Situational factors may determine the extent to which attitudes influence behavior. The ease with which attitudes come to mind, or *attitude accessibility,* is one influence on behavior. Another influence might be the *extremity of attitudes,* or the extent to which individuals feel strongly about an issue. Finally, personal experience with objects and people can affect how one behaves toward those objects and people. In short, attitudes do affect behavior. It stands to reason, then, that if a person is unpopular, envied, or evokes resentment in others, then that person may be at higher risk for being targeted for emotional abuse. Inconsistencies between implicit and explicit attitudes are not uncommon. One can consciously support an issue or policy but may have other feelings about the issue or policy at a preconscious or subconscious level. Or someone may express admiration for a person he or she subconsciously envies. Because implicit attitudes are automatic and below conscious awareness, people may not realize that their implicit and explicit attitudes toward a victim might vary. While bullying behaviors are overt and intentional, the underlying reasons for them may not be within one's immediate awareness.

In addition to situational influences on attitudes, irrational behavior may seem to become more rational by the process of *dissonance reduction.* Dissonance reduction is the social process by which one becomes able to view his or her actions as more rational, deserved, appropriate, or right, by means of rationalization (Breckler et al., 2005). Dissonance reduction may operate in mobbing situations because perpetrators and observers may cognitively disown the irrationality of workplace bullying and justify it as a rationale consequence for the target or victim.

Attitudes and behavior are relevant to the discussion of mobbing because understanding how attitudes are formed and how they persist can help to explain how otherwise well-intentioned people can purposely inflict harm on someone else. Perpetrators may develop or learn their attitudes via social learning, classical conditioning, instrumental conditioning, and social comparison. The element of social comparison may be involved if mobbing is motivated by jealousy or resentment. The accessibility of attitudes and personal experience with the object of an attitude can determine the role of those attitudes in the bullying process. Finally, bullying behavior may be influenced by both explicit and implicit attitudes.

Attribution

Attribution theory posits that humans seek to identify the causes of others' actions by attaching meaning or interpretation to those actions. People do this to understand others' behaviors and to gain knowledge of their dispositions and traits (Baron et al., 2006). Quite simply, attributions are one's attempt at making sense of the social world. *Causal attributions* are the human attempts to know why others behaved as they have or why events turned out the way they did. To some extent, attributions are what are termed *projections* in personality theory. They are judgments about why an event or a behavior occurred.

Social psychology predicts that it is human nature for people to be more or less self-serving in their attributions. It is normal for people to attribute positive behaviors in themselves to their own internal qualities and negative behaviors in themselves to external conditions. When the actions of others are judged, Yagil (2005) suggested that the reverse is generally true—that is, people tend to view the positive actions of others as environmentally caused and the negative actions of others as internal, even character-dependent traits. This may be a significant aspect of difficulty between employees and supervisors. An employee may attribute a supervisor's negative behavior toward that employee as the supervisor's internal problem, unrelated to the employee's own actions. This may contribute to the perception of oneself as a victim and not responsible for events that occur. Supervisors may likewise attribute the perception of a subordinate's positive behaviors as influenced by environmental conditions and negative behaviors, including performance problems, as purely the result of the employee's internal makeup. Suggestions are that such dichotomous thinking is not conducive to good relationships between supervisors and subordinates or between workers and peers.

According to the concept of causal attribution, in one's attempts to answer the question *why* in others or outcomes, one can focus on three major types of information: *consensus, consistency,* and *distinctiveness.* Consensus is the extent to which some people react to some event in the same manner as others do. Consistency is the extent to which a person responds to the same situation or event the same way on different occasions. Distinctiveness is the extent to which an individual responds in the same manner to different events or situations (Baron et al., 2006). According to social psychology and other social science disciplines, human perceptions are subject to a variety of distortions, including the following:

- One can be unaware of subtle external factors that may influence behavior.
- One can underestimate the power of external influences on behavior.
- One may not have the cognitive resources or abilities to take situational factors into account when explaining the behavior of others.

Finally, Western culture, as an individualistic one, emphasizes the importance of personal, internal causes of behavior rather than contextual—that is, external causes (Breckler et al., 2005).

A common attribution that may represent a distortion of reality is referred to as the *just world belief* or *hypothesis.* Just world belief suggests that humans need to believe that the world is fair and just, that people usually deserve what they get, that hard work and honesty bring rewards, and that laziness and dishonesty do not pay. If people did not believe that the world is just, then hard work and investing could be in vain (Breckler et al., 2005). The possibility that the world is *not just* is so threatening and anxiety provoking that people tend to blame or derogate victims who are suffering in negative circumstances, such as unemployment, HIV/AIDS infection, intimate-partner violence, financial destitution, and homelessness. In principle, just world belief denies the contextual aspects of individual human suffering. Just world thinking blames victims or targets for the suffering experienced from bullying rather than attributing blame to perpetrators, workplace conditions, or principles of social functioning as causes.

The idea of a "just world" helps one to understand the conclusions by Steensma and van Dijke (2005–2006) concerning attribution styles and practices. The extent to which just world belief can be measured and correlated with both self-esteem and victimization in an abusive workplace was examined. Outcomes suggested that targets of bullying seem to attach a higher importance to negative situations than do nontargets. "Importance" may be necessary but not sufficient to cause feelings of hopelessness, depression, and helplessness. Data also suggested a relationship between negative events and the perception of injustice. The more negative events one experiences, the more one is inclined to see injustice (or unfairness) in outcomes. Because bullying at work often continues unchecked for a long time, one can be tempted to view victimization as a personality or behavioral problem of the *victim* (just world belief) rather than viewing bullying as *injury* inflicted by another or as the result of workplace practices or workplace culture. It may also be true that victims of bullying might attach or attribute higher importance to negative situations than do nonvictims. It could be that once a person is a victim, he or she knows more about the pain caused by negative events and is sensitized to that pain. When this is true, interventions or treatment recommendations might include "reattribution" training for victims, so they can learn to place less importance on negative situations and to be less inclined to interpret events as unfair.

In some studies, employees attributed the abusive behavior of supervisors as external factors affecting work safety and well-being (Yagil, 2005). Evidence also suggests that viewing a supervisor's behavior as negative may even result in an employee perceiving himself or herself primarily as a victim and not at all responsible for any aspect of an event. A covariation model of attribution proposes that one makes causal judgments by determining whether a behavior correlates with a person or situation (Breckler et al., 2005). It might be, then, that perceptions and even aggression at work result from common errors such as information-processing errors that include inappropriately attributing cause to correlative features of people and situations.

Conflict

Evidence from a number of sources indicates that conflict is very often a condition of the onset of a mobbing process. Ayoko (2007) suggested that the greater the degree of conflict in a work group, the less goodwill and mutual understanding will exist and that conflict hampers task completion. In a study that specifically addressed the issue of task conflict contributing to features of distrust and resentment in work groups, some evidence hinted that a greater potential for conflict occurs in more culturally diverse work groups, a factor perhaps related to social psychology's concepts of *in-groups* and *out-groups* (Ayoko, 2007). In-group and out-group refer simply to those others whom one deems to be more or less like oneself.

Demographic makeup of groups can influence communication, because people are more inclined to communicate with others most similar to them. When group members experience others as being like themselves, they tend to be more open. When group members perceive others as being dissimilar to themselves, they will tend to be less self-disclosing and more closed. In-group/out-group differences in the workplace can make task coordination, communication, and efficiency more difficult and conflict more likely.

Mixed evidence may suggest that workplace bullying is also more likely when a workplace involves a high degree of task conflict. People may react to conflict with either competition or cooperation. While some degree of competition is not necessarily negative, high levels of competition at work are more strongly correlated with bullying behaviors (Ayoko, 2007). Some interpersonal difficulties and disagreements are a normal part of human interaction. Only a thin line exists between interpersonal conflict and aggressive behaviors that can be labeled as bullying. Data from Ayoko's study suggest that reactions to task conflict may result in an increase in either competition or cooperation. Lower levels of conflict and competition might be related to improvements in cooperation, but it may be that if competition due to conflict is high, then a greater likelihood exists that mobbing incidents will occur. Ayoko concluded that low levels of brief, intense conflict could be linked with increased productivity but that conflict of a longer duration can damage the workplace. In addition, communication is always an important element in the outcomes of conflict. There is some suggestion that lower levels of communication openness are linked to higher levels of destructive reactions to conflict. When levels of productive or constructive reactions to conflict exist, levels of workplace bullying tend to increase (Ayoko, 2007). The lower the level of communication openness, the greater the level of destructive reactions, possibly even bullying.

An earlier study of workplace conflict and bullying examined differences between *task-related conflict* and *relationship-induced conflict*. Task-related conflict involves not agreeing on the work to be done or how to do the work. Relationship-induced conflict involves interpersonal frustration and personal clashes (Ayoko, Callan, & Hartel, 2003). Semistructured interviews in 1997 examined types of conflict, frequency and duration of conflict, intensity of conflict, and emotional responses in groups where conflict existed. These findings suggested that high levels of bullying behaviors are linked to increases in counterproductive behavior and prolonged conflict. Some evidence also points to the seriousness of conflict increasing with the numbers of people involved (Ayoko et al., 2003). According to Einarsen (1999), escalated levels and frequency of conflict are related to increases in bullying.

Symbolic Interactionism

Symbolic interactionism is a general sociological model not limited to the field of social psychology. Symbolic interactionism, a pragmatic approach, proposes that people attempt to meet the demand of their environments in practical ways and to make practical adjustments to their surroundings (Hewitt, 2007). Briefly, symbolic interactionism posits the following. Humans use signs and symbols to help them make meaning out of their surroundings. Symbols are signs that give meaning to experience. Language is one such symbol, as is overt behavior. In nature, signs or symbols stand for the presence of important conditions, things, and events. One learns natural signs through experience. Signs may be public or private and are learned through each individual person or animal. Finally, the meaning of a sign or symbol is embedded in the ways that an individual has learned to respond to that condition, thing, or event (Hewitt, 2007). Quite simply, symbolic interactionism serves an evolutionary function: It aids in survival. Symbols transform the nature of the environment in which people live into identifiable and understandable patterns. Symbols make it possible for the behaviors and attitudes of one person or group to be reproduced by another person or group and for an individual to be part of the environment in which he or she is responding (Hewitt, 2007). This can help to provide another aspect of a theoretical understanding of the mobbing phenomenon, because mobbing or bullying behaviors include interpreting events and acting on those interpretations. Mobbing thus can be learned and reproduced by one or more people as a means of survival, but mobbing incidents will have different meanings for—and different effects on—different people, depending on their own histories and experiences. Conduct is interpreted through one's own subjective frame of reference.

Social Identity

Contrasts exist between *personal identity* and *social identity*. One's personal identity can be unique to the person who owns it, while social identity is generally understood as the self as a member of a group. An important component of an individual's identity comes from group membership. Human nature includes a desire to maintain a positive identity, including a positive social identity (Baron et al., 2006). Rather than being opposite, these two distinctions exist on a continuum. A number of judgments or processes contribute to social identity. *Intragroup comparisons* refer to a tendency to judge oneself compared to other members of one's same group. *Intergroup comparisons* refer to the tendency to judge one's own group from another group. Judgments may depend on *justice ethics*, such as universal rules regardless of social relationships, or *care ethics*, involving concern for the welfare of others (Baron et al., 2006). Emotional abuse of others and the response to such abuse may be influenced by one's personal identify, one's social identity, one's intragroup comparisons, one's intergroup comparisons, and the degree to which one's sense of right and wrong are driven by justice ethics as opposed to care ethics. These may be difficult to identify or measure in cases of workplace bullying, but the possibility that they can influence the propensity for emotionally abusing others at work can certainly be considered. Social psychology continues to focus its attentions on identifying and measuring identity, social comparisons, and quality of ethical orientation in individuals and groups.

Anomie

Anomie is a term used to define the breakdown of social bonds between an individual and the community. The term, credited to French sociologist Émile Durkheim in the late 1800s, results from a "disconnect" between one's social identity and a social norms. Anomie is most likely to exist when there is a mismatch between personal or group standards and wider social standards. It also results from a lack of a social ethics. Conversely, when there is sensitivity to mutual needs in the division of labor, anomie cannot exist. Durkheim's use of the term as it relates to industrialization refers to a condition in which rules within organizations cannot adjust to changes because of organizational inertia. Psychological ownership can be seen as the feeling of being psychologically tied to an object (Pierce et al., cited in Aleassa & Megdadi, 2014). Organizational inertia leads to a lack of workplace norms, making individual psychological ownership of one's work almost impossible. When such anomie is prevalent and psychological ownership is missing, both unethical behavior and bullying are more likely to exist and are very related to each other.

Social Perception

In human interactions, social perception can be complex. Almost everyone observes the outward appearances of others, but perceiving the meaning behind behaviors is not always easy or accurate. Nonverbal communication, perhaps one of the earliest forms of human symbolic behavior, does not involve the content of spoken language but rather relies on more subtle cues of facial expression, eye contact, and body language (Baron et al., 2006). From an evolutionary perspective, the ability to read nonverbal messages seems related to basic survival instincts. Even though nonverbal communication is not universal, it can provide useful information in human interactions. Data suggest that women are somewhat better at reading the nonverbal cues of others than are men, yet this can create both advantages and disadvantages (Baron et al., 2006). From an evolutionary perspective, sensitivity to nonverbal cues has probably helped with survival. In human interactions, however, attention to nonverbal cues may create conditions in which one overinterprets or overattributes the actions and intentions of others. Misattribution can lead to conflicts and ill will and may contribute to workplace emotional abuse. Nonverbal communication and the social perception of meaning are both relevant to a discussion of emotional bullying of adults toward other adults in the workplace. Since social perception is subjective and nonverbal communication does not have universal meaning, social cues can be ignored, misread, and misinterpreted, possibly contributing to the initiation of a conflict event or other origins of mobbing.

In summary, concepts of self and others, how behaviors are interpreted, how one's ethical framework operates, how messages are sent and received between people and groups, how group affiliation affects self-identity, how judgments about human behavior are made, how people behave in the presence of others, how conflicts are negotiated, and the meaning each person brings to each experience are all relevant aspects of social problems in general and workplace mobbing specifically.

Muted Group Theory

Another theory worth considering for understanding why mobbing behaviors develop and persist can be found in the concept of *muted group theory*. Borrowing from the field of linguistics, muted group theory includes a number of basic assumptions (Lutgen-Sandvik, 2003). First, because many of the differences experienced by men and women are rooted in traditional gender-role-defined division of labor, women and men comprehend the world differently. Second, because men have historically dominated most work environments, a predominantly male worldview prevents the views of women or other nondominant groups from being recognized or validated. Finally, to participate in society, women and others with less power have needed to reframe their experiences into the accepted dominant view.

Muted group theory posits that as women continue to consciously and verbally reject the dominant language and symbolic representation, common public expressions will change. An example of that change is that although the women's movement was well underway in the 1960s and 1970s, terms like "sexual harassment" and "sexism" in the workplace have only been highlighted as workplace concerns for the past 25 years. For clarification, a muted group is not a silent group. The concept of a muted group refers to the degree to which workers feel free to say what they want to say at work or feel the need to re-encode their thinking to make it better understood in the work environment (Ardener, cited in Lutgen-Sandvik, 2003).

Muted group theory might be relevant to an understanding of workplace bullying because people organize their experiences into stories by using language, the symbolic representation of events. In a work environment, organizational language is dominated by those with power in the organization. The dominant language reflects organizational goals and might not reflect the workplace experiences of organizational subordinates. Lutgen-Sandvik (2003) argued that, to some degree, a workplace mutes all employees. Workers enter an organization in a muted state and rely on implicit or explicit directives from more powerful people in the organization about norms of behavior, actions, and communication. Because muting of subordinates by superiors is inherent in most supervisor–employee relationships, the most egregious level of silencing is experienced when an employee is targeted for abuse. When agreement about a situation by an employee and that person's superior is in question, muted group theory assumes that resolution will always be in favor of the superior's point of view (Lutgen-Sandvik, 2003). A construct like this can help to explain environmental conditions that may affect the development of workplace bullying. Bullied targets are often those with less formal and informal power in an organization. The relative lack of power may be triggered or exacerbated by the target's membership in a muted group, such as being female, being a member of a minority racial or ethnic group, being of other than heterosexual gender identity, being part of a minority religion, or having a disabling special-needs condition.

THEORIES OF INDIVIDUAL PATHOLOGY

Individual Pathologies as Predictors of Aggression

Although some correlates of workplace bullying can be understood in terms of social functioning and context, certainly other theories suggest that bullying behaviors originate with the personality of the perpetrator. Fitness (2000) theorized that perpetrators learn angry scripts in their families of origin and that these scripts are relied upon in situations involving struggles of power and control. This theoretical perspective also suggests that anger is associated with tense, energized feelings and a predisposition to attack others. In intimate relationships, there may be an opportunity to confront, verbally and nonverbally, the anger target. In marriage and other intimate-partner conflicts, an anger-prone person at least has an opportunity to communicate feelings and engage partners in communication that may lead to conflict resolution. At work, however, the anger target may be in a position of greater power, so confrontation and communication might not be possible. Employees tend to assume a more submissive response toward those who control their future employment. Workers angered by subordinates may have the freedom to confront subordinates, but lower-power workers generally do not have this same option with their superiors.

Concepts of power and powerlessness are not static or constant in human relationships. Instead, they are relative and often defined by subtle and even assumed rights and relationships (Roscigno, Lopez, & Hodson, 2009). Studying how power unfolds within social interactions is one broad and significant topic of ongoing research in sociology. Any workplace is a potential arena for issues of power in relationships. Differences in social-class status and occupation can be important. Workers who are well paid may have some inherent occupational protections in the forms of higher education and greater knowledge but may also be more astute at utilizing remedial measures, such as grievance procedures and various forms of protection for employees.

Pathology of Bullies

A number of authors are cited in Vickers (2001) in a work on the pathology of bullies. These various authors discuss antisocial or sociopathic personality. Vickers created an argument for showing how bullies have sociopathic tendencies such as

- taking pleasure in the suffering of others,
- gross dishonesty,
- participation in illegal acts such as theft,
- aggressive physical and sexual behavior,
- substance abuse,
- low self-esteem and personal insecurities,
- professional obstruction, and
- need to control others through the use of aggression.

Such people might be diagnosed with antisocial personality disorder, a diagnosis from the American Psychiatric Association's (APA's) *Diagnostic and Statistical Manual of Mental Disorders* (5th ed.; DSM-5; 2013). Antisocial personality disorder is typified by acts that violate the rights of others, including, but not limited to, repeated acts that are illegal, deception, impulsive acts, aggression and assaults, high-risk behaviors, irresponsibility, and absence of guilt or remorse.

Vickers's (2001) work suggested that some people experience perverse joy at the suffering of others through a process of systematic degradation of them. Vickers concluded that real evil is in finding pleasure in acts that hurt others. Making a clear argument for the overlap between bullying and evil, two phenomena must be considered: (1) intention to harm others and (2) the degree to which a perpetrator derives pleasure in hurting others. This definition suggests a personality that is like that of a sociopath. The role of the sociopath as bully might be better understood by the degree to which a sociopathic perpetrator feels remorse for his or her acts.

These behaviors are designed to hurt, exhaust, and ultimately defeat the target(s) of anger while gaining control of them and enhancing the bully's personal self-esteem. The definition includes deliberate acts such as stereotyping, exclusion, obliterating significant identifying details (for example, correct spelling of a name), rudeness, and broken commitments. Vickers's explanation of the character of bullies specifically excludes acts of interpersonal aggression between individuals or groups of relatively equal strength. Thus, bullying or mobbing requires an imbalance of power (Vickers, 2001).

However, not all bullies are evil; some do feel remorse but may, for example, feel pressured to engage in bullying behaviors. Naive perpetrators may also engage in bullying behavior without knowing that what they do is harmful or wrong. Still other perpetrators may be stressed themselves because of budget constraints, downsizing, role overload, or managerial pressures to perform. Vickers would not consider either of these latter groups to be sociopathic or evil but would instead focus attention on those people who might be diagnosable with antisocial personality disorder.

Irish researchers Seigne, Coyne, Randall, and Parker (2007) suggested that bullies have authoritarian personality styles—that is, bullies are high in control behaviors, low in permissiveness, and low in interpersonal warmth. That work suggests that people who are conflict prone have characteristics of type A personalities. If the presence of a type A personality is a correct interpretation, then those people would tend to be hard driving, competitive, aggressive, and hostile and have a sense of time urgency. Type A personalities are also more likely to express aggressive and hostile tendencies at work against people whom they perceive to be likely targets (Randall, cited in Seigne et al., 2007). Some evidence suggests that bully traits are somewhat stable traits in a personality and that social situations may influence the expression of these traits. From this theoretical perspective, one could assume that children who are bullies will grow up to be adults who are bullies (Seigne et al., 2007). All the theories are relevant to a multidimensional approach and multidisciplinary solutions.

Novick and Novick (1996, in Kilburg, 2009) suggested that features of sadomasochism are involved in workplace bullying. These include conscious or unconscious fantasies of beatings, using externalization and projection as defenses, conscious or unconscious delusions of omnipotence, and difficulty managing the externalization of these underlying vulnerabilities. Kilburg (2009) also suggested that mobbing or bullying occurs within a set of dynamics, including the environment.

A relationship has been established between childhood bullying and adult workplace mobbing or bullying. Recent estimates are that from 7 to 15 percent of children have bullying characteristics in their personalities (Harvey et al., 2006). Although some limited evidence may exist for a biological predisposition to bullying others, no definitive genetic link or predisposition has been established. Nonetheless, some convincing studies have emerged from Denmark, the Netherlands, Great Britain, Australia, Japan, Canada, and the United States supporting the notion of a biological predisposition to aggression. Harvey et al. (2006) categorized the notion of biological underpinnings for human aggression from three primary theoretical perspectives. First, there may be brain-related issues involving the frontal lobes, influencing self-control, maturity, judgment, tactfulness, reasoning, and aggression. In frontal-lobe theories, the prefrontal cortex's uptake or use of glucose is significantly lower for people with antisocial tendencies. Hence, they behave more aggressively than others because their brains have insufficient fuel for operating in this area.

In a second category of theories, findings suggest a mutation of genes that code for an enzyme called monoamine oxidase A. This is the enzyme responsible for the brain's production and metabolism of the neurotransmitters serotonin, dopamine, and norepinephrine. If some malfunction occurs in this production-and-synthesis process, a lack of appropriate levels of these important neurotransmitters may be linked to aggression and antisocial behavior. In children, these neurotransmitters can moderate childhood responses to environmental stress. In adults, imbalances in neurotransmitters can be linked to depression and irritability and other symptoms of various disorders.

A third and final category of biological predisposition theories favors the existence of an overly developed immune system in those who are aggression prone (Harvey et al., 2006). Although some evidence may suggest a biological vulnerability or predisposition for bullying, more reliable explanations draw from a social learning perspective. Social learning theory assumes that workplace bullies were bullied themselves as children or watched others being bullied. Bullying may then be considered an imitation of experiences the person had with parents, siblings, or caregivers (Harvey et al., 2006). This assumption holds when one considers the vast resources devoted to understanding violence in families and in intimate-partner relationships.

In other studies, researchers suggest a relationship between anger and negative behaviors such as violence and other forms of hostility, a relationship between anger and antisocial behaviors such as theft, and a relationship between anger and retaliatory actions or actions designed to get even (Fitness, 2000). In spite of some convincing correlations, little is known about the antecedent and consequent conditions between workers' individual characteristics and the incidence of anger. Fitness (2000) posited that hate is a power-related emotion rated by most laypeople as a motive for malice. Some scholars have purported that hate is related to disgust rather than anger and that it is more likely typified by avoidance rather than other overt actions (Oatley & Jenkins, cited in Fitness, 2000). Fitness and Fletcher (cited in Fitness, 2000) suggested that hate-eliciting events are more likely triggered by humiliation and demeaning treatment and that hate appraisals are associated with lack of power or low control in various situations.

Fitness (2000) also distinguished between different types of workplace anger episodes, examining similarities and differences among the anger experiences of superiors, coworkers, and subordinates. In a study of data from structured interviews with 175 respondents, Fitness's goal was to identify the causes, features, and consequences of workplace anger situations. Her findings suggest that various features of anger episodes differ according to the status of the respondent, with managers and supervisors angered by incompetence and behaviors that are morally reprehensible, coworkers angered more by public humiliation and morally reprehensible acts of others, and subordinates angered most by unjust treatment at work. Those findings also indicate that humiliating offenses produced greater hate intensities than nonhumiliating offenses. Hate was also related to situational power and whether an angered person considered that a triggering situation had been resolved (Fitness, 2000).

Understanding the characteristics of, and differences between, perpetrators is important, but most descriptions of perpetrator behavior and characteristics have been reported by the targets of bullying (Matthiesen & Einarsen, 2007). This suggests that descriptions are anecdotal at best and fraught with subjectivity and bias. They also indicate that three main conditions are present in bullying situations. Some of these are internal to the bully, while others are situational. First, the bully has deficits in self-regulatory processes with regard to threats to self-esteem. Second, the bully seems to lack social competencies. Finally, the bullying results can be called micropolitical behavior, a type of internal rivalry or competition (Neuberger, cited in Matthiesen & Einarsen, 2007).

Low self-esteem and poor self-regulatory processes can cause a person to overreact with anger and aggression to even benign or neutral stimuli. Some have suggested that bullying results from self-esteem that is a form of unstable high self-worth (Matthiesen & Einarsen, 2007). Clinical literature would refer to this kind of high self-esteem as *grandiosity*, which suggests early deficits in caregiver mirroring and attentiveness. People with these traits may respond to minor or trivial threats to self-esteem with aggression and anger (Zapf & Einarsen, 2002). Social competencies are related to the capacity for empathy. Social and emotional intelligence (EI) requires an ability to relate to others by detecting, understanding, and appropriately responding to the feelings of others (Matthiesen & Einarsen, 2007).

Like sex offenders, workplace bullies may have limited skills in close relationships and a hostile and nonempathic style of relating to others. They may lack skills in dealing with anxiety or insecurity in social situations but may not be aware of that sense of anxiety and might not be aware of the consequences of their behavior (Leymann, 1990). Finally, bullying may be related to the antecedent conditions such as workplace rivalry and professional competition. These can be particularly likely to occur when high degrees of role ambiguity and role conflict exist (Salin, 2003a). Micropolitical behavior might be a way to protect one's self-interest at work (Zapf & Einarsen, 2002) and might also be used to maintain one's status (Keashly, 2001).

Aggression could be due to the perceptions of injustice on the part of the bully and not because of organizational dynamics or individual situations at work. In a study of 139 subjects who were presented with four scenarios representing different levels and types of workplace injustice, participants responded to an eight-item aggression scale (Kennedy et al., 2004). Using these aggression-scale scores as predictors of aggressive actions, the researchers then predicted how likely respondents were to treat others in an aggressive manner if they felt their actions were justified. Aggressive behavior and the likelihood of an aggressive response corresponded to both the amount and type of perceived injustice:

- Distributive justice is getting a fair share of rewards for effort contributed.
- Procedural justice is the perception of the fairness in allocating rewards.
- Interpersonal justice refers to the consideration and courtesy shown to individuals during this process of distributing rewards.

Procedural injustice was judged to be the most unjust and led to the greatest frequency of aggressive responses on the aggression scale. Findings concluded that although a perception of injustice coupled with a perception of organizational tolerance can contribute to workplace bullying, support for workplace aggression is more a personality trait or variable than a response to a particular situation. The researchers also concluded that the most likely explanation for a high degree of aggression lies in hostile attribution. Those employees with high hostile attribution scores are more likely to be supportive of workplace aggression (Kennedy et al., 2004).

Others theorists suggest that a bully is an archetypal destructive person and that bullying by supervisors and managers is a form of destructive leadership (Harvey et al., 2007). Destructive leadership can negatively affect the goals of an organization and may create or contribute to organizational dysfunction. A combination of destructive leadership traits combined with certain situational or environmental conditions can create conditions that increase the likelihood of destructive forms of leadership. Citing bullies as a specific form of destructive leader, Harvey et al. (2007) admitted that the destructive forms of behavior committed by archetypal bullies may appear harmless when viewed in isolation. Only when repeated constantly do they become what Leymann (1990) referred to as "pernicious." Considering the conditions where bullies could do the most damage, bullying can only take place when the bullies feel that they have the blessing, support, or some implicit permission to behave in this way (Einarsen, 1999, in Harvey et al., 2007). Whatever the permissive climate, perpetrators have specific traits that distinguish them, including a tendency to be envious of the target, destructive narcissism, a type of fear coupled with antisocial behavior, a tendency to engage in negative life themes (such as death of parents, financial impoverishment, and physical harm), and characteristics of malice or evil (Harvey et al., 2007).

Glendinning (2001) posited that bullies love power, that they love to display their power, and that they love to remind others that they are powerful. One way to display power is to behave in a bullying manner with an audience. This will mean that many people know, understand, and will disseminate the notion that the bully is powerful. This pattern, in turn, may then be a factor that leads to the people then going on to form a collective that engages in mobbing.

Another theory identifies two kinds of bullies: those who make an early exit from the work organization and those who make a contribution to the organization and therefore remain. This theory also suggests that managers bully in a changing work environment because they do not have the selective abilities or emotional skills to adapt to rapid organizational changes (Seigne et al., 2007). A skill-deficit explanation suggests that managers who bully perceive some sort of threat and have inadequate abilities to manage effectively in challenging situations.

Occupational choice and character style were paralleled by Kohut's (1971) model (cited in Czander, 1993) of how one imagines himself or herself to be:

- The mirror-hungry personality style seeks attention, admiration, and recognition to compensate for inner experiences of worthlessness.
- The ideal-hungry personality style constantly seeks a relationship with another person that contains beauty, power, prestige, or money.
- The alter-ego-hungry personality style constantly needs a relationship with another to confirm and sustain its sense of self.
- The merger-hungry personality style seeks attachment to another to be able to fuse identities with that other person due to a fear of separation.
- The contact-shunning personality style avoids contact with others out of fear of both rejection and engulfment.

While an in-depth study of self-psychology from which this theory draws is not the focus of this text, an understanding of how character traits can influence occupational choices and reactions to workplace slights is relevant. When an employee works in an organization, he or she makes an investment in the "self system." If that person is bully prone, he or she has an already fragmented sense of self. If, then, a new colleague is added to the organization, the bully's fragmented sense of self makes it impossible for the bully to assimilate the new colleague into the work milieu, and the bully feels overwhelmed (Czander, 1993). It is very possible that people who bully another at work may be suffering from this sense of fragmented self, resulting in difficulties with success, failure, and limitations. As a contrast to notions of skill deficits or limited abilities, a *Kohutian* approach, then, would identify deficits in the self-structure and character in the bully. Such self-structure could result in an exaggerated sense of self-importance and a tendency to devalue or deidealize a potential target of bullying.

Scholars have recently begun to focus on human emotions from a more integrated perspective, agreeing that emotions probably do have biological underpinnings and that they may serve an evolutionary function linked to survival. Emotions seem to play an important role in the human capacity to adapt (Fitness, 2000). Evolutionary adaptations aside, from birth throughout their lifespan people continually learn and relearn from their families, from their communities, and from their cultures how to think about, talk about, and regulate emotions. While agreement does not exist about the characteristics of perpetrators in mobbing situations, bullies may have some unique characteristics unrelated to workplace conditions or personalities of targets. Some of the alternative explanations are examined in later sections of this volume.

Theories of Individual Pathology as Predictors of Victimization

For many Americans, workplace violence is best represented by the caricature of a recently discharged, crazed ex-employee who appears at the former worksite and violently attacks coworkers and managers. In reality, these types of violence rarely occur. What does occur are daily insults, threats, slights, harassments, and innuendos that have come to be known as mobbing. Personality disorders, "evil" personalities, a perception of procedural injustice, power imbalances, and social learning processes have all been identified as correlates of bullying. However, creating a profile of a bully remains a challenge.

Creating a profile of a likely vulnerable target is equally challenging. A major drawback to a clear understanding of victim characteristics is the fact that without controlled experimental studies of bullying in the workplace, victims must self-report; in turn, self-reporting generally means underreporting. Self-report methods of data collection also rely on the judgments and insights of the responder. Nonetheless, the available research about victimization provides some insights about how it operates and its effects on victims, perpetrators, and organizations.

Australian researchers Djurkovic and McCormack (2006) studied the relationship between negative affect and bullying and neuroticism. *Negative affect* is temperamental sensitivity to negative stimuli resulting in feelings of fear, anxiety, depression, guilt, and self-dissatisfaction (Clark, Watson, & Mineka, 1994). Data from 127 Australian university students resulted in a psychosomatic model of bullying suggesting that some symptoms preexist in those who report having been bullied. These included anger, anxiety, guilt, and nervousness, all of which can leave a person vulnerable to stress-related illnesses. Evidence suggests that these symptoms correlate with, but do not actually cause, a person's victimization. These symptoms may even be the *result* rather than the *cause* of targeting.

Histories of trauma have been examined with people reentering the workforce after extended periods away from work and for those who never worked outside the home. For example, social work literature suggests that a relationship exists between barriers to employment and histories of childhood sexual abuse (Lee & Tolman, 2006). Childhood sexual abuse is also linked to mental health problems and physical health problems in adults. Children who have been abused are more prone to depression, eating disorders, aggression, sexual deviance, being perpetrators of molestation, and having relationships with people who may be molesters. This wide range of outcomes suggests that a connection between childhood abuse and being a victim of workplace bullying and mobbing is perhaps likely.

Several studies have examined the targets of bullying to identify risk factors for victimization. A Norwegian study of 85 targets of bullying examined psychiatric characteristics and personality traits using the Revised Minnesota Multiphasic Personality Inventory (MMPI-2). Data revealed that targets had clinically elevated psychosomatic complaints, depressive thoughts, compulsive behavior, and paranoid thinking (Matthiesen & Einarsen, 2007, in Balducci, Alfano, & Fraccaroli, 2009). This study could not draw conclusions about "prebullying" personality traits, as the MMPIs were administered after the bullied employees had presented for psychological treatment.

In the 2009 study by Balducci et al., researchers used the MMPI-2 to investigate the relationship between being targeted for mobbing and psychological symptoms and personality traits. Participants in the study were 107 Italian employees who had presented for mental health services after allegations of having been bullied. Scores showed elevated scales 1, 2, and 3, suggesting neurotic style and a tendency to experience psychic pain with physical health symptoms and depressive symptoms. Scores also showed elevated scores on scale 6, suggesting paranoia and a tendency to attribute difficulty to external rather than internal causes. Surprisingly, only about half of the respondents showed evidence of PTSD. Symptom severity was related to the frequency of exposure to bullying, with the most severe instances of depression and suicidal ideation correlated to the greatest mobbing exposure. What should be noted is that because tests were administered after the mobbing experiences, there can be no assurance that the results were a cause rather than an effect of having been victimized (Balducci et al., 2009).

Another study identified two types of bullying targets. One type could not be distinguished from those in a control group, but the other type had higher levels of anxiety and depression and lower levels of social skill (Zapf, 1999, in Matthiesen & Einarsen, 2007).

A 2009 Norwegian study using the Five-Factor Model (or the Big Five) (Lind, Glasø, Pallesen, & Einarsen, 2009) examined the personality profiles of 435 healthcare workers employed in seven nursing homes. The Big Five are traits or dimensions of personality categorized as extroversion, agreeableness, conscientiousness, neuroticism, and openness to new experiences. The Five-Factor Model is sometimes used in nonclinical studies of personality, proposing that almost any personality trait that could be named will be related to one of the five dimensions.

The study suggested that the targets of bullying tended to have common characteristics. Targeted employees were highly *conscientious* (organized, self-disciplined, hardworking, conventional, moralistic, and rule-bound) and were also low on *agreeableness* (indicating a tendency to be cynical, rude, suspicious, uncooperative, ruthless, irritable, and manipulative (Pervin et al., 2005, in Lind et al., 2009). No attempt was made to establish causation; rather, the temperament traits could have reflected difficulties that may have either preceded or resulted from bullying.

Another Scandinavian study using the Big Five key dimensions of temperament examined 79 mobbing victims. About 75 percent of the bullied (targeted) group did not differ from a nonbullied sample; however, 25 percent of the bullied group scored higher on neuroticism and lower on agreeableness (Matthiesen & Einarsen, 2007). A type of sensitivity to bullying in people who are bullied might not be present in nonbullied peers, while it has not been determined whether this trait is a cause, an effect, or a mere correlation linked to some other characteristic. Nonetheless, trait scores are topics for consideration.

An understanding of EI is relevant at this juncture. EI involves self-awareness, motivation, self-regulation, empathy, and a person's adeptness in relationships. EI has been suggested as providing a new understanding of the leadership and teamwork needed for high-functioning work environments (Clarke, 2006). To the degree that either high or low EI is a factor in being targeted for emotional abuse, high EI could be necessary for healthy survival in the workplace. It could also be possible to teach EI via workplace training.

Studies of victims of schoolyard bullying suggest that targets are cautious, sensitive, and quiet. Those same studies suggest that victims tend to have lower self-esteem than nontargets and that they generally have few friends as sources of emotional support. Finally, schoolyard bullies' victims have higher rates of anxiety and depression than do children who are not targets (Olweus, 2002). Data from these studies suggest that victims are more passive, more submissive, and may inadvertently signal to others that they are insecure and vulnerable. Olweus also identified a subgroup of schoolyard bullies' victims called the *provocative victim*, characterized by a combination of both aggressive and anxious behaviors. Provocative victims may bully weaker or younger children while concurrently being bullied by stronger or older ones.

In a study of adults in the workplace, respondents were asked to recall childhood experiences of bullying. An association was found between childhood victimization and being an adult target. Former school victims were more likely to be exposed to bullying in their adult work environments (Smith, Singer, Hoel, & Cooper, cited in Matthiesen & Einarsen, 2007). The authors attempted to measure the relationship between histories of provocative victims, childhood targets of bullying, role conflict/role ambiguity at work, and self-esteem. Data were collected from labor unions in the greater metropolitan area of the city of Bergen, Norway. Results suggested that provocative victims have lower self-esteem combined with high levels of aggressiveness and lower social competence. Victims also reported higher incidents of childhood targeting for bullying. Researchers concluded that exposure to childhood bullying and exposure to bullying in previous employment situations were both positively correlated with adult exposure to bullying in current adult job situations. They also concluded that all targets of bullying, but especially provocative victims, suffer from lower levels of self-esteem, but uncertainty remains about whether lower self-esteem is an antecedent or a consequent condition in targets. Finally, victims were overrepresented in the proportion of respondents who experienced role conflict or role ambiguity (Matthiesen & Einarsen, 2007).

Harvey et al. (2006) suggested that victims of bullying may be divided into groups based upon self-esteem levels. A working model suggests that self-esteem might be understood in five operational domains, indicated by the following questions:

- Can the person relate to others in the organization?
- Does the person seem to have emotional stability and maturity in comparison to his or her peers?
- What are the professional and personal accomplishments of the potential victim?
- What is the character of the target or victim—that is, is he or she respected and supported by peers and others in the organization?
- Does the potential target have physical characteristics that differentiate him or her from others?

Self-esteem was found to be a component of all five dimensions. Potential mobbing targets might not have high scores in these dimensions or might score high on only two or three of them. It is the unique, almost uncanny "sixth sense" of the perpetrator or bully to be able to zero in on a dimension in which the potential victim is vulnerable (Harvey et al., 2006).

Some other models suggest that victims may appear to be passive and not well connected in their organization. The lack of social status in an organization can be self-perpetuating, and victims can respond with learned helplessness—that is, they may come to expect to be bullied. People who attempt to improve organizational climate and functioning, and newly hired employees in particular, may become targets (Harvey et al., 2006). Other data suggest that exposure to bullying predicts the onset of depression in those exposed to long-term abuse. Obesity and cardiovascular disease are cited as patterns in victims, and these could be outcomes rather than causal factors (Kivimäki et al., 2003). In some instances, bullying targets are actually strong individuals who are real competition to the bullies, true rivals in the work setting. These people might compete with bullies for power. Managers who attempt to change organizational cultures could perhaps fall into this category (Harvey et al., 2006).

Roscigno et al. (2009) suggested that relational powerlessness is a correlate of victimization, as is any variation in race or ethnicity that might create visible markers of differential status or power from the dominant race or gender. Women and minorities, then, have less power than do dominant-race men. Gender influences the likelihood of being bullied. Differences in status, pay levels, education, and knowledge can also create vulnerability to bullying, as does job insecurity. Some speculation exists that at a macro level, the worldwide increase in bullying is related to an upswing in less-than-secure job markets as the economies of the world teeter in uncertainty (Roscigno et al., 2009). People are simply more likely to put up with bullying and related bad working conditions because of job insecurity and lack of job choices.

Although targets of mobbing can sometimes be troubled workers with histories of performance problems and supervisory interventions, most theorists agree that victims are more likely to be high-functioning and capable people. While no one type of vulnerable person exists, victims are often trusting in nature, loyal to the organization, and strongly identify with their work. They may be creative and challenging of others but lack the political savvy to survive a highly polarized workplace (Noring, 2000). Whistle-blowers may threaten established formal and informal rules for workplace functioning and can be targets for mobbing. Other authors have proposed that victims tend to have a strong work ethic and a strong commitment to getting along at work, but even experienced team players may become targets (Davenport et al., 2002).

Rospenda and Richman (2004) suggested using a survey to measure GWH experiences to measure bullying. They tested the GWHQ in a survey of more than 1,700 current and former university employees. Results suggested that harassing experiences at work that included verbal aggression, disrespect, isolation/exclusion, threats/bribes, and physical aggression all produced psychological distress. The study did not indicate whether any psychological distress or symptoms existed prior to the harassment (Rospenda & Richman, 2004).

Westhues, in his 1998 study of professionals in a university setting, suggested that those academics in his study who were mobbed tended to be trusting, naive, politically inept, and high-achieving. Like Socrates, they tended to be "principled individuals who are inner directed." The mobbed academics were often not the kind of person who simply goes with the flow. Westhues conceded that skin color, physical appearance, foreign accent, and different social-class background than workplace peers' are all attributes about which a person can do nothing. However, an individual's direct workplace performance and demeanor are within the person's control. Westhues suggested that targets might be responsible for all or part of what they experience in victimization.

By contrast, Davenport et al. (2002) interviewed people who reported having been mobbed and found that they were actually exceptional individuals. Their professional careers demonstrated positive qualities of intelligence, competence, creativity, and integrity, high levels of accomplishment, and high dedication to the organizations in which they worked. The study concluded that even if one could make a case that certain personality traits or behaviors might contribute to mobbing, these traits should not be accepted as an excuse for the bullying syndrome. This caution is important because unchecked bullying has negative organizational outcomes, which will be discussed in chapter 7.

While specific personality qualities may place one at risk for victimization, other arguments suggest that multiple-role demands and stress can greatly affect a person's perception of workplace difficulty (Home, 1997). Little evidence exists, however, linking personal stress or role overload with emotional victimization at work. Since most existing data are obtained via self-reports, and since victimization tends to go underreported, accurate estimates are very difficult to project. By the time a person self-identifies with victimization, he or she may have developed mild to severe symptoms of disorders, further confusing the picture and making any cause-and-effect relationship between personality and victimization difficult, if not impossible.

THEORIES OF MOBBING DUE TO ORGANIZATIONAL STRUCTURE AND PRACTICES

Because of what appears to be an increase in the frequency and severity of workplace bullying, an examination of organizational functioning and practices is both necessary and worthwhile. Glendinning (2001) addressed the need for a radical change in supervisor–subordinate relationships during an era of decreasing job markets. Glendinning claims that in spite of an ever-tightening job market, good employees continue to leave their employment prematurely, resulting in ongoing problems with recruitment and retention of qualified workers. Many studies of workplace satisfaction suggest that compensation is not the primary reason that employees decide to quit their jobs and that people who report to more considerate supervisors are less likely to leave their positions. By contrast, the presence of abusive supervisors, or *bully bosses,* will create unhealthy, unproductive work environments with higher staff turnover. In the Oliver Stone film *Wall Street,* an example of abusive supervisory attitudes can be found in the character Gordon

Gekko, who quotes passages from *The Art of War* and labels people as pawns. Michael Douglas portrays him as somewhat characteristic of the organizational downsizing that followed the boom of the 1980s. Although *Wall Street* was a fictional dramatization of life in the world of stock brokerage, real-world examples of attitudes like those portrayed in the film are not difficult to find.

In a 2014 article in *The Guardian*, Belgian psychology professor Paul Verhaeghe suggested that three decades of "neoliberalism, free-market forces and privatization" have transformed behaviors and norms in ways that reward psychopathic personality traits. These include such qualities as being able to win others over, being able to lie and feel no guilt, and avoiding personality responsibility for one's actions (Verhaeghe, cited in D. Yamada, 2014b).

Glendinning (2001) makes a good case for the difference between "tough" or "demanding" bosses and those who are bully bosses. While tough bosses try to produce high performance via setting high expectations for workers, bully bosses have another agenda. They use a management style that seems designed to cause physical or psychological torment. He also suggests that bully bosses' behaviors are not isolated outliers but that they occur with a high degree of prevalence.

The degree of bullying culture in an organization can depend on eight environmental conditions. According to Harvey et al. (2006), these include the following:

- standard operating procedures of the organization
- norms of behavior in the workplace
- rules of workplace conduct
- organizational values that are most significant
- symbols that represent the organization's most cherished virtues
- those symbolic and real organizational taboos or prohibitions
- people in the workplace most defining the character in the organization
- the ongoing emotional climate of the workplace

Several rational explanations for the increase in mobbing in today's work environment were cited by Harvey et al. (2009):

- Rapid global social change leads to high levels of uncertainty in most workplaces.
- Managers have increased time pressures to complete tasks and meet productivity goals.
- Workplace diversity continues to increase, creating more exchange of differences in workforce dynamics.
- Downsizing has left organizations and employees in those organizations uncertain about who will survive the next wave of reductions in workforce.
- Mid-level management is now often the target of downsizing initiatives, so organizations have become more "flat." Flat organizational structures create vulnerabilities for mobbing. Since there is no formal hierarchy in the organizational structure, members of the organization may compete openly or surreptitiously for organizational power and recognition in organizations that provide opportunity for neither.

- Bullies are more likely to act in organizations having poorly defined cultures and norms. Such lack of definition can typify many global and domestic organizations today.

Glendinning (2001) identified how organizations create conditions perfect for bully bosses and other bullies to thrive. Top-down management styles and top-down communication patterns create distance and insulation, clearly distinguishing subordinates from superiors. These styles may include managers who are authoritarian, who abuse power, who use overt and implied threats to maintain leadership control, and who behave in an intimidating manner with all subordinates. Another unfortunate feature of top-down or of hierarchical management structures is that managers themselves have limited rewards for good management. They may have been good as technicians or providers of direct services but may lack management skills and find no incentives for acquiring these needed skills. Other features of bullying environments include cutthroat competition, scarcity of true talent, and an organizational culture that is fear-laced (Glendinning, 2001).

Nonresponsive organizations can inadvertently encourage bullying when that lack of response is interpreted as lack of regard for the well-being of a targeted employee. Some organizations simply do not want to know about incidents of bullying. When appropriate standards for workplace behavior, such as respect, fairness, and safety, are not clearly defined, organizations are more vulnerable to abusive treatment of workers (Keashly, 2001). Namie and Namie (2003) claimed that while bullies single out their targets one at a time, witnesses usually observe the patterns of abuse. To thrive, bullies require secrecy, shame, and silence from observers.

Micropolitical behavior can be a helpful construct in understanding the dynamics of workplace bullying. The notion of micropolitics is based on the assumptions that organizations do not always have fully determined structures and processes. When structures and processes are less determined or unclear, organizations tend to expect workers to fill in the gaps by participating in decision making and process improvement. When employees are motivated by their individual goals for power and protection of their own status, collective needs suffer (Matthiesen & Einarsen, 2007).

The justice perspective is relevant in understanding workplace emotional abuse. Three dimensions of justice include *distributive justice, procedural justice,* and *interactional justice,* as discussed earlier in this work. Distributive justice refers to the fairness of distribution of outcomes. These may include rewards or consequences. Procedural justice refers to the fairness of work processes and procedures that underlie the distribution of outcomes. Finally, interactional justice refers to fairness in interpersonal treatment (Beugre, 2005).

This model offers insights to understanding workplace aggression that leads to mobbing. Being treated fairly is important to most people. Injustice may be a primary source of aggression, and the specific type of injustice a person experiences may influence who is to be the target of retaliation (Beugre, 2005). Procedural injustice may elicit aggression toward the organization, while interactional injustice may target an individual or that person's supervisor. By contrast, if people think they are being treated fairly, they may be able to subordinate their personal goals in favor of the needs of the group or the organization. Fair treatment tends to lead personal responses that are cooperative (Beugre, 2005).

A cognitive stage model of the perception of justice or injustice as proposed by Beugre (2005) may be relevant. Stage One is assessment involving two substages: (1) forming a justice judgment of an event and (2) assessing the degree of fairness or unfairness. Stage Two also involves two substages: (1) attributing blame and (2) developing aggression-induced cognitions. Finally, Stage Three involves (1) selecting a form of aggression for retaliation and (2) executing the aggressive response. This model assumes that retaliation following a perceived injustice is a complex process but that it starts with the occurrence of an injustice *before* attributing any blame.

The perception of injustice model might be helpful in understanding organizations at risk for emotional abuse. Organizations that are careless about the justice involved in their distributions, procedures, and interactions will logically be at higher risk for both creating and tolerating emotional abuse of workers.

A method of predicting mobbing in organizations is an assessment tool called the Val.Mob Scale (Aiello, Deitinger, Nardella, & Bonafede, 2008). This tool, both reliable and valid, measures power for predicting and preventing mobbing in a variety of occupational settings. Given the increase in global markets and the flexibility of labor forces, researchers suggest that an increase exists in *relational conflict*, or interpersonal conflict occurring in the relationships between people. The Val. Mob Scale measures relational conflict using seven thematic areas: (1) elements of discomfort, (2) threats and violence, (3) isolation, (4) communication, (5) horizontal and vertical social relations, (6) attachment or commitment to work, and (7) affective or emotional climate. Recommendations for preventing emotional abuse at work include changes in job design, changes in leadership style, changes in the social empowerment of workers, and improved ethical standards in the workplace.

In a study of Australian nursing personnel, Hutchinson, Vickers, Jackson, and Wilkes (2006) suggested that bullying is embedded in organizational structures that both conceal bullying and protect or even promote bullying. Data from that study also identified the existence of predatory alliances within workplace relationships facilitating bullying more than nonpredatory alliances. Hutchinson et al. suggested that bullying can become a disguised but legitimate institutional process. Themes identified in the Australian study focused on two key aspects of how these predatory alliances operate: (1) concealment of bullying, where protection is provided by the loyalty between bullying; and (2) promotion for the bully, in which abusive behavior is rewarded and tolerated within the organization.

In the context of this work, predatory alliances refer to small groups bound by secrecy, closeness, and agreed-upon rules. These small groups, mostly dyads and triads, operate within work teams, forming alliances with others more senior in the organization. It is not uncommon for members of these predatory alliances to be facilitated in their misdeeds via promotion and appointment. Because bullying can be masked or concealed for long periods of time, it may become embedded in the informal processes of an otherwise legitimate workplace (Hutchinson et al., 2006).

Management researchers Branch, Ramsay, and Barker (2007) suggested that while downward or horizontal bullying acts are most common, upward bullying does exist. Structured interviews of 24 previously upwardly bullied participants from a small sample of public and private institutions revealed that risks for mobbing can be found in the climate of current work environments, in organizations undergoing times of rapid change, and in organizations where power struggles occur. These authors made a distinction between power that is legitimate and power that is illegitimate, usually based on knowledge and skills, suggesting that managers lacking legitimate power are most vulnerable to emotional abuse, particularly if those managers do not experience support during times of rapid change.

Affective commitment refers to employee identification and psychological connectedness to an organization. It also refers to the emotional attachment an employee has with an organization. *Continuance of commitment* refers to a worker's awareness of the potential costs for leaving an organization, including loss of income, relocation, and concern for family well-being during a time of transition. *Organizational commitment* is a condition based on a person's experience within the workplace, such as how the person is treated and has been treated in the past (McCormack et al., 2006). Data collected from a sample of high school teachers in China suggest a positive correlation between worker satisfaction with supervisors and coworkers and the affective commitment those workers had toward their jobs. Data also suggest a negative correlation between dissatisfaction in those relationships and affective commitment to work. If these data are reliable and valid, then it would stand to reason that low job satisfaction may be linked to motivation for mobbing, since the perpetrator feels less connected to the organization and less invested in maintaining a positive environment.

In a 2008 study based on recent economic challenges, Swedish researchers examined worker health and organizational conditions (Oxenstierna, Widmark, Finnholm, & Elofsson, 2008). Because of systemic changes in the Swedish workforce in the 1990s, with unemployment jumping from 1.6 to 8.2 percent from 1990 to 1993, shareholder interests and production profitability grew in importance for Swedish industries. Since then, broad, sweeping workplace changes included leaner productivity, mergers, restructuring, global businesses, public-sector deregulation, privatization, and adopting purchaser-supplier business models. New institutional constructs have also emerged, previously unknown in Sweden's welfare-oriented state system. The results of such systemic changes have been dramatic. Unfortunately, research on job-related stress for the past 35 years appears to have been stagnant, examining few variables of workplace conditions and continuing to measure the same or similar phenomena as in times past. For these reasons, researchers examined the demand-control-support (DCS) model and the effort-reward-imbalance model as the most significant theoretical influences on employee stress. The DCS model is a psychosocial model of work environments that gives theoretical support to those workplace factors that actually cause problems and can be useful in predicting health outcomes, particularly cardiovascular disease (Tuckey, Dollard, Hosking, & Winefield, 2009). The model measured such concepts as the quantitative and qualitative aspects of one's workload, the degree to which a worker feels that the job requires input from him or her, and the amount of psychosocial support or emotional camaraderie one feels in the workplace. The following questions from Oxenstierna et al. (2008) were used in the DCS questionnaire to measure demands and controls:

- Does your job require that you do your work very fast?
- Does your job require you to work with much exertion to get the tasks done?
- Does your job require a high amount of input from you?
- Do you usually have enough time to get your work done?
- Does your job make conflicting demands on you—for example, the completion of contradictory tasks?

Although quantitative demands at work are highly sensitive to the demands of physical labor, several professions can be identified as high-demand jobs. The following items refer to the support scale applied by the DCS questionnaire:

- There is a spirit of unity and cooperation.
- My colleagues and I support each other.
- The atmosphere at work is pleasant and comfortable.
- People understand that anyone can occasionally have a bad day.
- I get along well with my superiors.
- I get along well with my coworkers.

Results from this questionnaire are useful for predicting other stress-related conditions such as pain, depression, and fatigue (Oxenstierna et al., 2008).

The effort-reward-imbalance model has been used to predict cardiovascular disease effects such as morbidity and mortality events (Oxenstierna et al., 2008). It is a psychosocial measure that identifies the degree to which one feels that the effort one invests is fair and proportionate to the reward one receives. Using the effort–reward theoretical orientation as a predictor of workplace bullying, when economic and political forces create added stress at work, organizations may be more vulnerable to employee emotional abuse if imbalances exist in effort and reward or in demand and control.

Bullies who actually meet the productivity goals of an organization could be the hardest for an organization to confront. If this is the case, a problem exists when the productive bully cannot distinguish between assertiveness in overseeing the work of others and aggressiveness in those tasks. Whereas aggression denies the rights and dignity of others, assertive behaviors are those with respect, openness, and trust as underpinnings (Townsend, 2008). When conflict exists, healthy organizations and healthy managers will look upon those situations as opportunities for transforming relationships. Assertive responses to conflict would include asking questions, asking for and receiving feedback, and having the ability to take emotional risks. Managers have the responsibility to ensure that their own communication is assertive and that they model assertive communications in their subordinates. Organizations that do not value and adopt assertive communication styles will be more at risk for emotional abuse of workers by managers and peers, while leaders who do promote a culture of mutual respect and shared responsibility minimize risks.

A 1995 American Red Cross study of emergency response workers in Northern California's East Bay Hills produced some notable and relevant results. It examined the stress responses of workers who were mobilized to respond to disasters and who experienced multiple stress responses. Although quantitative analyses were not plentiful, it was generally concluded among crisis responders that when multiple stress debriefing (MSD) techniques were implemented with these vulnerable groups, stress reactions were significantly ameliorated (Armstrong, Lund, McWright, & Tichenor, 1995). In group debriefing techniques in which group members are not considered ill but rather to have shared a common stressful experience, members can experience recovery by developing a common goal with other members. Although debriefing of emergency workers is a fairly recent practice, encouraging limited sharing about traumatic experiences for combat soldiers has been used with success for more than 80 years (Armstrong et al., 1995).

Survivors of stressful events can be helped to recover by identifying some of the positive outcomes that have resulted from experiencing a disaster together, such as greater camaraderie, appreciating the loving acts of others, feeling closer to family and friends, being able "to live for today," and having improved skills at letting go of that which is not important (Armstrong et al., 1995). Organizations undergoing massive changes such as downsizing, mergers, reorganizing, budget cuts, and production challenges may need improved skills at responding to the real sense of crisis or trauma that employees experience rather than ignoring it. Some variety of stress-debriefing activities could help workers to recover from crises at work.

One model for vulnerable organizations can be found in what was originally developed to study crime, the routine activities model. This framework suggests that for deviance to occur (such as mobbing or bullying), a motivated offender must come into contact with a suitable target in the absence of organizational constraints (Roscigno et al., 2009). If relational powerlessness is one of the core vulnerabilities in a potential mobbing victim and if relational power is one of the core advantages of a potential mobbing perpetrator, then the organization itself must also have an inherent culture that contributes to the emergence of bullies by failing to provide organizational constraints. Organizational constraints include protections such as the presence of labor unions, clear policies about conduct, clearly defined paths for career advancement within the organization, and management accountability to workers, especially about how that accountability is organized and processed.

For prevention of abuses created from relational powerlessness, the organization itself must have structures, values, a mission, a vision, explicit rules about interpersonal behavior, and sanctions for those who violate those rules (Roscigno et al., 2009). The two organizational qualities considered by Roscigno et al. (2009) were the use of close, direct personal supervision as a control strategy in the workplace and the presence of a chaotic organizational structure. The use of close personal supervision involves situations in which several managers are present in production areas during busy periods, noticing any and all periods of slacking off by workers. Workers then have less autonomy in pacing themselves throughout the day and feel more controlled. A chaotic organization involves lack of coherent organizational procedures needed for effective work and the maintenance of mutual respect among all. A chaotic organization is management's failure of one of its chief responsibilities: to provide a smooth and effective operation in which procedures are well coordinated. When such organization is lacking, chaos ensues.

As predicted, a review of literature (Roscigno et al., 2009) suggested that bullying is more frequently targeted at vulnerable workers and is more frequent where there is increased direct, personal supervision. Bullying will be less frequent where there are unions and bureaucracies and in employee-owned businesses; capable workplace guardians can help to mitigate bullying. The authors did admit, however, that although some strong unions are successful in protecting workers from abuse, sometimes the actual location of the unions prevents their effectiveness in protecting workers. Weak or ineffective unions offer even less protection.

Davenport et al. (2002) proposed a warning signals checklist that can indicate organizations at risk for mobbing incidents. Any combination of these factors may produce some risk, but the more warning signals present in the organization, the higher the risk for emotional abuse of employees. These eight warning signals included the following:

- Is one person being blamed for problems in a department?
- Is a person who is accused of substandard performance or some other unacceptable behavior someone who had a history of average performance?
- Are other employees, including management, not qualified for their positions?
- Are there sudden losses of key staff in the organization?
- Are staff members leaving at a higher rate than is typical for this organization?
- Are rates of absenteeism higher than normal for this workplace?
- Is staff morale extremely low? Is that usual or not for this organization?
- Have there been any recent changes in the organization, such as restructuring, new management, or new work procedures? If so, has there been time and training committed to helping all employees make adjustments? (Davenport et al., 2002)

Several studies have explored what situational factors might produce bullying. Rayner et al. (2002) cited situational stress as a major factor in organizations vulnerable to mobbing. In a German study, high demands combined with employees' lack of control of their own time were identified as risk factors. In Scandinavian studies, role conflict, leadership styles, and situations where workers have little control over their work all contributed to the risk for mobbing (Rayner et al., 2002). While any or all of these sources of stress may be part of high-risk environment, little evidence suggests that stress alone is a risk factor.

The role of conflict between work groups has also been examined. According to Czander (1993), organizational conflict is related to goal incompatibility, different decision-making philosophies, and differences in status and prestige. Organizational conflict is most apt to occur when there is competition for scarce resources. Conflict can have both functional and dysfunctional outcomes. Conflict generally precedes organizational change and may even be necessary for a change to occur. Conflict that is adequately resolved can be functional in that it can increase cohesion or bonding among members of a group or an organization. Efficiencies may also emerge from conflict. Evidence indicates that when one group is in conflict with another, each group, independent of the other, may quickly reach agreement on goals and strategies or tasks. Greater agreement can exist about rules, regulations, and procedures. Under these types of conditions, employees are less conflicted about authority and may even want strong leadership at certain points in in time. Effective leaders will involve themselves in continual monitoring of the needs for more or less hands-on management, depending on circumstances. When hate and aggression are projected outward, the risk of emotional abuse accelerates. A danger of scapegoating can emerge—that is, using an external object, person, or group to project hateful, aggressive impulses (Czander, 1993).

A two-part model for work satisfaction was cited by Baron et al. (2006). In this model, *organizational* factors affecting worker satisfaction included fair rewards systems, high respect for organizational leaders, an opportunity to participate in decision making, appropriate workloads, and comfortable (pleasant) work environments. Those *personal* factors that influenced worker satisfaction included one's status in the organization, the amount of seniority one has in the organization, the match between an employee's interests and the actual work that employee performs, and even genetic or temperament factors. Organizations at higher risk for worker emotional abuse may not be attending to either the organizational or the personal aspects of job satisfaction or both.

Leymann (1990) identified a number of risk factors in organizations vulnerable to employee emotional abuses, positing unresolved conflict as a necessary prerequisite in most mobbing situations. In addition to unresolved conflict, at-risk organizations tend to have a lack of an ethics-based conciliatory process for conflict resolution and lack of access to an impartial hearing, such as collective bargaining agreements. When such factors are missing from an organization, no mediation process is identifiable, and injured victims are not afforded any opportunity for redress.

Some evidence points to the wisdom of organizations moving beyond mere emergency responses to workplace bullying, where cases are individually handled as they occur, to instead having more proactive management practices. These practices need to include clear procedures, clear principles of respect and tolerance, clear discouragement and disincentives for bullying behaviors, clear methods for redress, improved top-down and lateral communication, and improved processes. The degree to which organizations ignore these practices will be in proportion to problems of workplace emotional abuse. During times of predictable increased stress, organizations need to be proactive in handling mergers, layoffs, reorganization, and budget reductions.

Factors That Enable Bullying

An important feature in determining whether people perceive a situation to be stressful is whether they believe they have the resources to cope with what is occurring and to respond appropriately. This perception is referred to as *secondary appraisal* (Keashly, 2001). Resources can be personal ones, including high self-esteem, high self-determination, and good conflict management skills. Resources can also refer to organizational resources, such as support from others, relevant workplace policies, and effective policy implementation.

The perception of solicitation (or provocation) of abuse by the victim has been found to be related to observers' judgments of harassment by a perpetrator. To the extent that a victim is viewed as provoking bullying in any way, observers are less inclined to evaluate the perpetrator's behavior as actually abusive (Keashly, 2001).

Finally, the issue of violation of standards of behavior is cited in much of the literature about emotional abuse at work. Most advocates would agree that employers and managers are obliged to treat employees with dignity and to respect their rights as human beings. Unfortunately, respectful treatment is often not clearly defined (Keashly, 2001).

Keashly (2001) studied 35 people self-identified as having been targets of mobbing who agreed to be interviewed about their experiences. In the 29 who completed the process, terms that frequently emerged were "subtle," "hidden nature," "very manipulative," "humiliated," "sort of picking at your mind," and "insidious." Many respondents used such terms as "unless you live it, you don't understand it." Some respondents felt that support from others depended on whether others had experienced or were currently experiencing similar treatment. Reponses tended to include three major themes: (1) the victim's past history with the perpetrator, (2) the effects on the respondent or target, and (3) the specific qualities of the abusive behavior.

In the Keashly study, none of the 29 respondents believed that the organization would be responsive to their plight. All respondents held that their organizations did not doubt or deny that the perpetrators had acted as the targets claimed they had. In fact, there was general acceptance that the behaviors had occurred, but the key organizational decision to take no action was based on the perception of who was primarily responsible. Categories of responsibility involve the organization's responsibility and the target's responsibility, as well as the perpetrator's responsibility (Keashly, 2001).

Salin (2003a) analyzed the key enabling features in a bullying process. First, necessary antecedents of bullying must exist. These are the enabling structures and processes present in an organization. Second, incentives for bullying colleagues or supervisors must also be present, including the motivating structures and processes in an organization. Finally, triggering circumstances must occur that set off or incite the bullying process. Bullying can be understood as the result of an interaction between these three groupings of enabling conditions. According to Salin, conditions in themselves may not lead to bullying but can serve as enabling factors if an additional motivator or trigger is present. Similarly, motivating and precipitating factors do not result in bullying unless the conditions are right. In addition, attention should be drawn to the double significance of enabling factors that simultaneously act as a foundation and a filter. The enabling factors can provide fertile soil for bullying. In addition, when motivating or precipitating structures or processes are present, the existence or lack of enabling conditions in the organization will affect whether bullying is possible.

Enabling structures and processes include those conditions that make it possible for bullying to occur. These conditions include, but may not be limited to, a perceived power imbalance between the possible victim and perpetrator(s), low perceived costs for the perpetrator, and dissatisfaction and frustration in the work environment (Salin, 2003a).

Another motivating structure or process can be found in the association between bullying and leadership style. A laissez-faire style of leadership, or "weak" or "inadequate" leadership, on higher levels in the organization seems to be conducive to bullying among colleagues (Einarsen, 1999; Einarsen, Hoel, & Cooper, 2002). Bullying seems to flourish when upper management does not assume responsibility and does not intervene in bullying (Salin, 2003a).

Incentives for bullying include low perceived costs when a perpetrator assesses the costs of bullying as relatively small. It can even be argued that bullying can actually be described as individually rational *rent-seeking behavior*—that is, actions that serve the individual by providing that person with a larger proportion of rewards (Krakel, 1997, in Salin, 2003a). Such a motivation would be based on an internal type of question: What will this cost and what are the potential payoffs? The costs involve such things as the risk of reprimand, the risk of dismissal, and the risk of social isolation and punishment by colleagues (Salin, 2003a). Benefits would be found in the reward system of the organization, such as higher pay, increased opportunities for promotion, and improved performance appraisals as a result of bullying others. The reward system may contribute to horizontal and vertical bullying by encouraging supervisors to get rid of very high-performing or very low-performing subordinates (Salin, 2003a).

The relationship between bullying and weak leadership can be also be understood in terms of low perceived costs. If it can be assumed that weak leaders are reluctant to intervene in bullying situations, weak leadership adds an incentive by reducing the risk of the perpetrator being sanctioned (Salin, 2003a).

Triggering circumstances can include such workplace changes as cost cutting, restructuring, and reengineering. Salin (2003a) contended that restructuring and downsizing led to the elimination of layers of management, reduction in the number of positions, limitations on promotional opportunities, increased workloads and internal competition, and lowered job security. These, in turn, led to increased pressures, increased stress, and lowered thresholds for aggression. In addition, downsizing and reengineering can result in general feelings of uncertainty and powerlessness (Salin, 2003a). During times when workers feel vulnerable and powerless, they are more likely to engage in behavior that is destructive or interpersonally deviant. This may increase a person's sense of power or control and can even serve to encourage employees to elevate their own status by lessening that of others through negative acts (Salin, 2003a). Bullying may be more prevalent during economic downturns and when organizations function poorly. Although destructive for the victim and ultimately for the organization, in the short term it can provide a number of self-enhancing functions for perpetrators who are at risk of being laid off or being forced into a lower position.

Systems Theory

Systems theory is another construct for understanding mobbing in the workplace. A cornerstone of social work theory and practice, systems theory assumes that individuals interact both with themselves and with their environments. A system is a set of units with relationships among them. A system is a whole composed of separate but interacting and interdependent parts. Large systems that function optimally achieve synergy or combined energy from the smaller parts. The combined energy or synergy is greater than the totals of those parts if the parts functioned independently. A boundary is that point at which one system ends and another system begins. Open systems are generally considered to be healthy systems. In open systems, members can accept energy from their interactions with the broader environment. Closed systems may not allow anyone in or out, so they may not allow for an exchange of energy with any outside systems or with the broader external environment. Over time, closed systems use up their own energy and develop *entropy*, or stagnation. This means they lose their ability to function. Interactions within and between systems occur continually (Ambrosino et al., 2005). The concept of *steady state* is also inherent in systems theory. Systems are not static but are constantly moving toward goals while maintaining order and stability. A system's natural trend toward maintenance of order and stability or equilibrium is that system's tendency toward a steady state.

Levels of the environment within systems thinking include *microsystem, mezzosystem, exosystem,* and *macrosystem*. The microsystem, or individual level, includes a person and all the other people and groups that incorporate the person's day-to-day life. The mezzosystem involves the relationships between two microsystems that are linked by someone who exists in both microsystems. The exosystem is the community, including those community factors that affect the way individuals or microsystems function. Finally, the macrosystem is society as a whole, including factors related to cultural attitudes and values as well as the infrastructures of that society (Ambrosino et al., 2005). Each interaction occurring within the micro-, mezzo-, and macrosystems that surround a person affects other systems in which the individual interacts. The systems approach allows one to deal with more data than other models and to create order from various disciplines by allowing for multiple influences, a range of risk factors, and several possible causes for phenomena. Concepts are equally applicable with a wide range of situations.

Some basic assumptions inherent in systems thinking are that actions assuring the survival of species (and organizations) are built into the organic evolution of the organism. These are called *adaptations*. People and environments contain structures and functions that may affect adaptation in a positive or negative way. Events that affect adaptation can be viewed as negative stressors or positive challenges. To the degree that an event is perceived as a negative stressor, it can evoke a stress response. Problem solving is a positive-challenge approach to an event requiring adaptation. Finally, to understand a person or an environment, one must consider all the relevant systems and subsystems of that person or environment (Germain & Bloom, 1999).

Systems theory, simply stated, emphasizes that context matters. An individual's perception of abusive behavior and the organization's response to that abuse are vital to that individual's personal response to the behavior. One consistent finding in literature about workplace abuse is that most people who report having been exposed to emotionally abusive acts at the hand of others in the organization choose to do nothing in response (Cox, cited in Keashly, 2001). The explanation frequently given is that the victim believes nothing would be done by the organization or that the victim fears retaliation or further abuse (Keashly, 2001). Victims generally believe that the organization will not believe them or will not support them or both.

Oshry (1996), a systems researcher, identified various forms of system blindness that can plague an organization's life. Several types can increase organizational stress: *conflict blindness, disharmony blindness, relational blindness,* and *process blindness.* Conflict blindness is spatial blindness, in which others are perceived not as they are but by the myths and prejudices of others. Disharmony blindness is temporal blindness, or the inability to see organizational history to help with understanding the processes and patterns that contribute to organizational problems. Relational blindness occurs in the life of a system or organization because humans are constantly shifting in their patterns of relating to each other. People tend to experience themselves as whole, autonomous beings rather than beings in relationship to each other. As a consequence, they can fall into unproductive and even destructive patterns with each other. When this happens, misunderstanding, opposition, and antagonism may ensue (Oshry, 1996).These outcomes indicate relational blindness. Finally, organizations can suffer from process blindness in which teams can get stuck in certain processes while neglecting others. Process blindness can make organizations vulnerable to turf warfare, alienation, and groupthink (Oshry, 1996). Groupthink is a tendency of members of highly cohesive groups to assume that their decisions cannot be wrong because all members support the group's decision (Baron et al., 2006).

Oshry offers a simple yet colorful understanding of systems and the stresses experienced within them. He simplifies the roles people occupy within systems as *tops, middles,* and *bottoms.* Tops (senior managers) are burdened by responsibility, with too much to achieve in too little time. Job demands require them to move quickly and respond rapidly to change, dealing with constantly unpredictable conditions. All this is required while tops deal with incomplete information and responsibility for the fates of many. They feel isolated and out of touch with much of the organization. They look to the middles (mid-level supervisors) for support but don't get it. Middles feel torn in their role between tops and bottoms. They are pulled in conflicting directions with conflicting needs and may appear as loners; they are seen by others as confused and lacking in authority. If they attempt to align themselves with tops, they alienate bottoms (workers, producers, service-delivery providers, and laborers). If they align themselves with bottoms in attempts to champion for them, they alienate tops. Middles do not receive positive feedback, either from tops or bottoms. Finally, bottoms feel oppressed by the system. Others higher up make all the decisions regarding work design, and bottoms feel unseen and uncared for. Tops are not visible at all to bottoms, while middles are not seen as having value, even though they may be well intentioned. Much of the energy of bottoms is focused on "them"—that is, anyone with greater authority in the organization.

According to this model, organizational difficulties result from conflicting work demands. All members of the organization feel disconnected, even from those within their own ranks. Executives become territorial and have turf struggles. Middle-group members become alienated from each other because of competition and powerlessness. Bottoms fall into groupthink, developing a "we" mentality that further separates them from middles and tops (Oshry, 1996). People do not see their own role in the problems, and no one sees the point of view of those in other positions. Ultimately, the customers suffer, with poor products, poor services, and inability to get their needs met by the system.

Systems Model of Organizations and Bullying

Senge (1990a) identified that organizations can have learning disabilities that include a number of irrational beliefs, including (1) "I am my position," (2) "the enemy is out there," (3) the illusion of taking charge, (4) a fixation on events, (5) the delusion of learning from experience, and (6) the myth of the management. Senge also cites in systems studies of organizational failure the parable of the boiled frog as an illustration of how gradually building threats to survival is pervasive. According to this metaphor, if you place a frog in a pot of boiling water, it will immediately try to jump out. But if you place a frog in water that is room temperature and gradually increase the temperature, it will stay put. When the water comes to 70 to 80 degrees, the frog will do nothing. It will even show signs of comfort. As the temperature rises, the frog continues to do nothing, until it becomes groggier and groggier and is unable to climb out of the pot. Though nothing is physically restraining it, the frog will sit there and boil to death! Why? Senge's answers that the frog's internal apparatus for sensing threats is geared to perceive sudden environmental changes, not gradual ones (Senge, 1990a). Organizations, and people, can be vulnerable to the same gradual threats to survival, and the learning disabilities cited above are the irrational beliefs that drive this organizational numbing. Bullying can result if the members of an organization are not aware that they are in danger, or "in hot water."

Organizational systems are complex. Systems are not static but constantly move toward goals while maintaining order and stability. A system's perspective shifts attention away from individual characteristics of the person or the environment and toward the "transactions" between parts of the system(s). It views people as actively involved with their environments and systems as goal-oriented. If systems require constant transactions between members for the system's survival, the purpose of any intervention is to provide and maintain such opportunities for transactions for all members and to work to reduce isolation of people and systems (Ambrosino et al., 2005). The systems approach for understanding workplace emotional abuse removes notions that individuals, change, or conflict are pathological and holds that instead, they are part of synergistic processes. Even so, organizations undergoing massive changes such as downsizing, mergers, reorganizing, budget cuts, and production challenges need to improve skills for responding to the real sense of crisis or trauma that employees experience rather than ignore it.

SUMMARY

Abusive workplace behaviors have many and varied roots. While no one theory perfectly captures the experience of workplace bullying and explains it within its context, many theories of social and individual behavior are relevant. A variety of personality types, patterns, and interactions can predict workplace bullying. Most important is that bullying is a problem at all levels of human functioning. Chapters 3 and 4 will examine the data and trends about vulnerable targets, perpetrators, and organizations.

3

Data and Trends in Workplace Emotional Abuse

This chapter provides an overview of research about bullying at work, both in the United States and around the world. Characteristics of people who are bullied, characteristics of those who bully others, and characteristics of high-risk work environments are described based on research findings and theoretical perspectives. On completion of this chapter, readers will have an understanding of the demographics of perpetrators and targets and of high-risk organizations, industries, management styles, and organizational structures.

In examining workplace issues, a number of perspectives are needed, including occupational choice and character style, problems with career success encountered by workers, task analysis, boundary issues, lines of authority, management changes, and interorganizational changes (Czander, 1993). This chapter will consider several questions concerning bullying and will attempt to address them from a number of perspectives. The most relevant questions are the following:

Questions Concerning Victims. A primary challenge in evaluating an alleged mobbing event is to determine whether the victim's psychological symptoms contributed to the mobbing, were created by the mobbing, or developed independently of mobbing. Can we identify preexisting psychiatric conditions or personality characteristics of those who are the victims of workplace mobbing? Is it reasonable to acknowledge that situational factors in the lives of victims may predispose them to victimization? What are the chances for rehabilitation and return to full professional functioning for victims, and what are best practices for treatment? Can we identify differences in those who recover favorably from emotional abuse at work from those who do not recover favorably?

Questions Concerning Perpetrators. Can we conclusively suggest that there are personality types that are correlated with being an abuser or perpetrator of workplace emotional abuse? Is it reasonable to acknowledge that situational factors may increase an individual's likelihood of bullying others at work?

EARLY ATTEMPTS AT RECOGNIZING AND DEFINING THE PROBLEM

A problem identified and labeled almost two decades ago in Scandinavia and Western Europe, workplace bullying, or mobbing, involves aggression toward a targeted employee in the workplace and subjecting him or her to psychological harassment, generally over a long period of time. Although the terms are interchangeable, mobbing usually refers to more than one perpetrator, whereas bullying can be perpetrated by one person or many. Such harassment may result in psychological and occupational consequences for the victim. In other contexts, a mob might be defined as a large, disorderly crowd or even as an organized gang of criminals or hoodlums.

The verb "to mob" means to jostle, to attack, or to annoy, but mobbing in the context of this book has an interesting origin. As mentioned earlier, Austrian ethologist Konrad Lorenz used the term to describe behavior that animals sometimes use to scare away a predator. Weaker animals may band together to display threatening behavior toward an animal they perceive as a threat (Davenport et al., 2002).

When animals that have been "mobbed" are later observed, they demonstrate a demoralized, sulky demeanor (Gravois, 2006). Peter-Paul Heinemann used Lorenz's term "mobbing" to emphasize the seriousness of the bullying behavior that can drive a victim to isolation, despair, and even suicide (Davenport et al., 2002). Gang bullying or mobbing in the workplace is much like the attack by animals on another animal in nature or like the bullying of children toward other children.

Although recognized for decades as workplace emotional assault in most of the developed Western world, mobbing is only very recently being recognized as an injurious activity in the United States; and while most Western countries have protected workers from mobbing in both policy and practice for many years, laws protecting workers in the United States have been slow in development.

PREVIOUS ATTEMPTS AT UNDERSTANDING WORKPLACE EMOTIONAL ABUSE

Previous literature has addressed definitions, prevalence, assessment, etiology, prevention, and outcomes of the harm created by mobbing. However, to date an integrated framework has not been developed that would provide strategies for prevention and intervention at the micro level (individual), the mezzo level (social interactions), and the macro level (larger institutional, social systems). Most notably, nothing has yet appeared in social work literature to address this evolving concern.

This chapter analyzes the causes, effects, treatment, and prevention of emotional abuse, or mobbing, in the workplace from three perspectives: an organizational behavior perspective, a clinical assessment and treatment perspective, and a social work intervention perspective. Finally, this section addresses public policy implications and pending legislation.

Perspectives about the causes of workplace mobbing and characteristics of victims and perpetrators are examined. Data regarding employees who may be predisposed to victimization or targeting and those who may become perpetrators of abuse are presented, along with an exploration of some theories of predisposing individual psychopathologies for both actors and victims. Examination of the reactions and symptoms of emotionally injured workers follows, accompanied by suggestions for best practices for treating victims. Brief case histories of individuals who have experienced emotional abuse of varying degrees are provided. Names and identifying data have been changed or omitted for confidentiality.

An analysis of preventative measures in conflict-resolution processes, management skills, leadership strategies, and organizational policies and practices are examined. Data are presented on the effectiveness of sound leadership practices and organizational structures to prevent and quell the spread of this epidemic. Clinical recommendations for treatment are provided from best-practices perspectives. Social work's response to workplace victimization and suggestions for social work's role in addressing these problems are examined. Finally, emerging trends, including recent and pending legislation, provide implications for future preventative and remedial action.

A growing body of relevant literature and data already exists in various disciplines, including organizational behavior, business, occupational health, HR, and social psychology. Ethical research practices ensuring prevention of harm to human subjects preclude conducting controlled studies to measure actual cause and effect, yet many existing studies have been able to quantify the degree, severity, and scope of mobbing across cultures. This work provides a basis for developing a model of the role and function of social work in identifying, intervening in, and preventing emotional abuse in the workplace. It also provides a way to understand social work's imperative to address these issues from a public policy perspective. Data from more than 300 studies and books that examined the prevalence and severity of workplace emotional abuse are included in this chapter.

CHARACTERISTICS OF PEOPLE WHO ARE BULLIED IN THE WORKPLACE

Comparing information on strengths and vulnerabilities can be challenging for a number of reasons. First, data-collection methods on victimization rely primarily on self-reports. Like other types of victimization data, best estimates are that victims or targets seriously underreport their experiences. Many reasons can account for this trend. Victims might simply leave the workplace early. They might not fully understand the scope and nature of the problems they are experiencing. They could fear that they will not be believed or be taken seriously. Like most recent victims of abuse, mobbing victims often do not understand that the acts for which they are targeted might be illegal. Einarsen et al. (1994, in Mayhew et al., 2004) suggested that victims perhaps see themselves as lacking the ability to cope with or resolve bullying situations and perhaps lack self-esteem or belief in self-efficacy. Studies have suggested that identifiable characteristics of victims may evidently lock the victim into the bullying situation (Zapf & Einarsen, 2003, in Mayhew et al., 2004). These characteristics can include

- victims' inability to defend themselves or to leave,
- remaining "dependent" in the situation due to the interplay between personal and situational factors,
- personality type,
- position, and
- power in the organization (Niedl, 1995, in Mayhew et al., 2004).

External factors such as the labor market and economic conditions can increase the risks for being unable to leave an abusive work environment.

A difficulty lies in the effort to identify antecedents of workplace bullying because almost all currently available data were gathered *after* a person experienced some degree of emotional abuse. Identifying antecedent variables and distinguishing them from consequent variables in the existing literature is therefore problematic. Independent variables cannot be easily separated from dependent variables and spurious correlates in such retrospective studies. Abusive incidents are likely to be underreported, reported much after the abuse process, or not reported at all. A study from Finland suggested that 64 percent of people who had experienced emotional abuse at work did not report the bullying by two years later (Mayhew et al., 2004).

For some, bullying may be sporadic rather than chronic, or it may mean that some victims manage to cope effectively with the situation (Kivimäki et al., 2003). Finally, like other forms of victimization, until a problem is identified and labeled by claims-makers, victims may have no frame of reference or context in which to understand what they are experiencing. Many victims whose lives have been affected by workplace bullying are surprised and relieved to learn that there are both a name and identifiable symptoms to describe what they have experienced.

People develop a subjective understanding of the world and their place in it. Rayner et al. (2002, citing Janoff-Bulman, 1992) defined an event as *traumatic* when it challenges three basic assumptions previously held by the injured person:

- The world is a benevolent place.
- The world has meaning.
- One (that is, the self) is a worthy person.

Applying this model to bullying at work often means that targets of bullying find themselves in situations where they feel someone is out to get them. They feel hounded, let down, and puzzled about why the abuse happening to them (Rayner et al., 2002). If victims have invested greatly in their work, it may be hard for them to conclude that the world is anything *other* than meaningful. Many victims therefore adopt an attitude of self-blame and self-condemnation, whether or not it is deserved.

Einarsen (1999) suggested that in many cases, perpetrators feel some envy for their targets of bullying, and Zapf (1999) argued that organizational problems don't directly harass workers, but rather employees in organizations do. According to Zapf, people manifest mobbing behavior in response to leadership problems and organizational problems. Mobbing is an extreme reaction to the stress created by the lack of leadership and chaotic organizations. Zapf (1999) identified mediators of stress that may be absent for targets of bullying. First is the ability to predict stress. In general, the less predictable a stressor, the greater will be the reaction to the stress. Second is the person's belief that he or she can exert some control over the stressor and can lessen the stress outcome. Finally, the individual coping skills of the person will greatly influence reactions. Thus, the person's interpretation of stressors will predict the impact of those stressors and will influence the person's behavioral reactions to stress. From this perspective, Zapf suggested that both victim and perpetrator live out their roles in response to organizational stress coupled with their own reactions and coping styles and skills.

Several theorists, including Lutgen-Sandvik (2003), have defined bullying, or *employee emotional abuse,* as repetitive, targeted, and destructive communication by more powerful members toward less powerful members in the workplace. Less organizational power might be considered one of the general qualities of victims. Some individuals may be at higher risk for being victimized by provoking the hostility of potential perpetrators, a concept referred to as *victim precipitation* (Elias, cited in Tepper, Duffy, Henle, & Schurer-Lambert, 2006).

The notion of victim precipitation suggests that targets of hostility may participate to some degree in their own victimization. For example, in studies of peer bullying in school children, Olweus (2002) found that victims tend to be anxious, insecure, and vulnerable to aggressive behavior because they demonstrated little ability to defend themselves against attack. Adults may also precipitate bullying by the presence of their own negative affect and display such emotions as anger, hostility, sadness, or fear (Tepper et al., 2006). These types of people may be submissive victims who are anxious, insecure, and passive and may demonstrate little ability to protect themselves against mistreatment. Their characteristics may include anxiety, distrust, dissatisfaction, submissiveness, insecurity, vulnerability, and little ability to protect themselves.

While some might consider the consequences of treating others aggressively, victims may become weaker but safer targets for supervisors' own frustrations (Tepper et al., 2006). Abusers may feel less risk of consequence from a person who already displays high negative affect. Supervisors may be inclined to bully because subordinates who already have a high degree of negative affect and frequently experience emotional distress anyway. Periods of emotional distress may result in rules violations or performance problems to which others respond with hostility. If this presumption is correct, workers who violate rules or who perform poorly would then be less likely to receive aid from coworkers, making the vulnerable victims even more submissive and safer targets.

Randle (2001, in Magnuson & Norem, 2009) posited that the target's personal or professional strength or lack of it is not a factor in whether they get bullying or mobbed. Targets may be self-assured, skilled, bright, independent, cooperative, ethical, just, and kind, according to Namie and Namie (2003). Targets may have strong work histories that include commitment, integrity, and high levels of productivity (Duffy & Sperry, 2007, in Magnuson & Norem, 2009).

Targets are often ashamed that they have been weakened by the aggression of a manager or coworkers (Duffy & Sperry, 2007, in Magnuson & Norem, 2009). Targets might not readily admit that bullying has occurred. They often fear retaliation and their confidence in the ability of others to protect them—that is, administrators or administrative structures—may be weak (Magnuson & Norem, 2009).

Westhues (2002) suggested that those workers most vulnerable to becoming targets are those in formerly secure employment. If this is correct, then mobbing would be more predominant in bureaucratic organizations, particularly those that have traditionally been gender segregated, such as public welfare, police and defense forces, and health and educational programs. Westhues (2005a) also posited that academics who are ganged up on in university settings are characteristically more trusting, naive, and politically inept but also high achievers. He states that in many cases, victims are partially responsible for what happens to them, paradoxically by being principled people who do not go with the flow (Westhues, 1998).

Crawford (cited in Davenport et al., 2002) suggested that individuals can become victims no matter who they are, how old they are, or how devoted or loyal to the organization they may be. One can become a victim regardless of professional experience, organizational skills, levels of responsibility, and degree of workplace initiative. Even good team players can become victims. Subjects interviewed in the Crawford study all had in common a high degree of loyalty toward their organizations and were highly identified with their work or by their work. Crawford also suggested that creative individuals might be subjected more often to mobbing because of their ability to promote new ideas that are challenging.

In their landmark 2003 publication *The Bully at Work: What You Can Do to Stop the Hurt and Reclaim Your Dignity on the Job*, Namie and Namie listed reasons people are bullied. They suggested that targets may share these features:

- They may tend to refuse to be subservient.
- They are often people whom the bullies envy.
- They tend to have good social skills and positive attitudes.
- They tend to be ethical and even whistle-blower types.
- They have integrity.
- They prize equity and justice.
- They have nonpolitical and therefore impractical expectations about how organizations should work.

Unfortunately, targets of bullying may be publicly or privately vulnerable because of personality or life-situation issues (Namie & Namie, 2003).

Gender and Age

Gender and age differences in victimization are not easy to analyze. Data by Rayner et al. (2002) suggest that women are statistically more likely than men to report being bullied, but it is unknown whether women are actually bullied more than men. By contrast, a closer examination of the relationship between bullying and gender reveals that more complex patterns exist than just the gender differences. Men are more often bullied by male superiors. Women report being bullied by both superiors and colleagues, and by both women and men (Salin, 2003b). Salin's work indicates that only women reported being bullied by subordinates. Salin's data also suggest that male line workers and supervisors report higher rates of victimization than their female counterparts, but the pattern reverses for middle and senior managers. That is, female middle and senior managers report victimization at higher rates than do their male counterparts.

Hoel and Cooper (2000) examined age and gender differences in bullying. They sent surveys to 12,350 employees in more than 70 organizations in the public, private, and voluntary sectors across Britain, and received 5,288 responses that could be tallied to study workplace mobbing. The average (mean) age of respondents was 43. A near-even gender split was reflected: 53 percent of the respondents were male, and 47 percent were female. More than 97 percent identified themselves as white. A total of 85 percent respondents worked full-time; 15 percent worked part-time. At the time of the study, the sample reflected employment norms in Britain.

Results were mixed. Not all respondents had been bullied. Women respondents reported a higher frequency of bullying experiences than did men. Younger employees (that is, those between the ages of 16 and 24) reported the highest levels of bullying, followed by those in the 35–44 age range. Those 55 years and older appeared to be less likely to be bullied. A relevant caveat, however, was that the duration of the bullying was correlated with the age of the victim. Older people experienced longer durations of bullying. Only 9 percent of respondents ages 16 through 24 reported being bullied for more than two years, but 51 percent of those 55 and older had been bullied for two years or longer (Hoel & Cooper, 2000).

For more than a decade the WBI's research director, Gary Namie, has conducted regular data collection and analyses that are published annually. For example, in his 2007 survey, data from 7,740 respondents indicated the following: Thirty-seven percent of workers in the United States have been bullied at some time in their work lives. Most bullies were bosses. Sixty percent of bullies were women. Women targeted other women 71 percent of the time. Bullying was four times more prevalent than illegal harassment—that is, anything protected by civil rights statutes or workplace sexual harassment laws. Sixty-two percent of employers ignored the problem. Forty-five percent of targets suffered stress-related health problems. Forty percent of bullied individuals never told their employers. Only 3 percent of victims filed lawsuits (Namie, 2007).

Because bullying or mobbing is underreported, it is extremely difficult to obtain conclusive information on age and gender. Nonetheless, the studies to date have provided some descriptions. Similar to victims of intimate-partner violence and sexual harassment, targets of abuse frequently blame themselves for the experience and have trouble creating coherent story lines that persuasively and succinctly convey their situation (Tracy et al., 2006).

Cross-Cultural Considerations

Considerations of workplace bullying in the United Kingdom began to appear in the mid-1990s. Although mobbing was not widely understood by that time, a question about whether bullying in schools carries over to the adult workplace was explored by Rayner and Cooper (1997). Part-time students at Staffordshire University participated in a widespread study of workplace bullying. A total sample of 1,137 anonymous surveys was collected. Gender balance was considered good (52 percent men and 48 percent women). Respondents were asked about their "worst working situations" and then asked if they had been bullied or not. A surprising 53 percent responded that they had been bullied at some point in their work lives. In this sample, men were rarely bullied by women, but women were bullied equally by men and women. Bullies were most often managers or senior managers (Rayner & Cooper, 1997). A high proportion were bullied in groups, while only 19 percent were singled out and targeted alone. No statistically significant differences were found for sector or gender balance of organizations. Authors concluded that anecdotal evidence can be found in most organizations but that bullies tended to select their targets, that they vary in their motivations and the targets they select, and that anyone could become a target.

In the Spanish university study referenced in chapter 1 by Lopez Cabarcos and Vazquez Rodriguez (2006), data suggested that a malevolent atmosphere at work or unresolved problems—but not physical appearance, nationality, or ability to adapt to the groups—were the primary conditions for bullying. The most common abuses were inadequate information to do the work, extreme criticism, public devaluation of employees and their efforts, and lack of promotional opportunities.

In the previously mentioned study of Australian nursing personnel in New South Wales (Hutchinson et al., 2008), only 102 of 500 survey recipients responded (20 percent). However, researchers used their data to examine allegations of attacks on reputation, personal attacks, and attacks through work tasks. Women accounted for 92 percent of the respondents. The qualitative results suggested that attacks on reputation might be a strategy to render a person "more deserving" of overt bullying (or less deserving of protection). If this is true, it would hint at some explanation for the lack of response or intervention by any observers or onlookers. The New South Wales study was limited in sample size and was further limited by its self-report survey method and self-selection in responding.

In the previously mentioned study by Bilgel et al., white-collar Turkish workers were surveyed in 2006 to determine the nature and extent of workplace bullying in 25 primary health-care units in three municipal areas of the metropolitan city of Bursa, Turkey. A 20-item survey assessed the effects of bullying, utilizing the following measures available within Turkish HR departments:

- Job-Induced Stress Scale (House & Rizzo, cited in Bilgel et al., 2006)
- The Hospital Anxiety and Depression Scale (Zigmond & Snaith, cited in Bilgel et al., 2006)

- The Job Satisfaction Scale (Quinn & Stains, cited in Bilgel et al., 2006)
- The Propensity to Leave Scale (Camman et al., cited in Bilgel et al., 2006)
- Bullying Inventory (Quine, cited in Bilgel et al., 2006)
- Support at Work Inventory (Bosma, cited in Bilgel et al., 2006)

Of the 1,200 surveys distributed, 79 percent (944) were returned. Of those returned, 877 (92 percent) were used for analysis, with the others omitted due to missing data. Fifty percent of respondents reported having been bullied. Another 50 percent reported having witnessed bullying. Data suggested that the likelihood of bullying increased by 60 percent when respondents had managerial responsibilities. In 44 percent of the instances, the perpetrator was a superior, and in 26 percent the perpetrator was a colleague on the same status level. Thirty-seven percent of the cases reported that the bully was a male, and in 25 percent of cases the bully was a female. Both sexes were involved in the remaining 38 percent. In 50 percent of cases, the bully was the same gender as the victim. In those cases that did report the age of both perpetrator and victim (294), 49 percent reported the perpetrator as older than the victim, 195 reported the perpetrator as similar in age, and 32 percent reported the perpetrator as younger. Of those who reported bullying, 60 percent reported making some response when the behavior occurred, but 23 percent were not satisfied with the outcome. Most frequent responses included ignoring the bully or talking with friends and relatives (Bilgel et al., 2006). The Turkish study suggests that more passive or indirect methods were used more than confrontation or formal reports.

Mona O'Moore, director of the Anti-Bullying Centre, School of Education, Trinity College, Dublin, Ireland, and fellow researcher Jean Lynch reported in 2007 on a national survey of the workforce of Ireland. Six percent of the 1,057 respondents claimed to have been bullied "frequently," while another 17 percent admitted to having been bullied "occasionally" in the previous 12 months. Seventy-two percent of the nonbullied reported that their work environments were friendly, but only 49 percent of the bullied sample reported a friendly workplace. A hostile work environment was claimed by 39 percent of the bullied respondents. The results implicated leadership styles, working environments, working conditions, and staff relations as correlates of bullying. In particular, the greatest difference between the bullied and nonbullied was the level of satisfaction with immediate supervisors' abilities to resolved conflict (O'Moore & Lynch, 2007).

Data from a Finnish study (Kivimäki et al., 2003) suggested that bullying occurs in the medical and nursing professions between 5 percent and 6 percent of the time, based on 5,432 respondents from a sample of 10,949 medical professionals surveyed. Of those who reported having been bullied, 64 percent did not report bullying two years later, suggesting that bullying may be sporadic rather than prolonged. Data from the study implied that exposure to bullying predicts the onset of depression in a dose–response gradient (that is, the more exposure, the greater both the likelihood and severity of depression). Prolonged bullying was also associated with cardiovascular disease.

A 1997 study of 464 Norwegian marine industry workers revealed that 7 percent of respondents admitted to having been severely ridiculed, insulted, teased, verbally abused, or the target of gossip (Einarsen & Raknes, 1997). The survey sample included workers, supervisors, and managers. Ninety-five percent of respondents were men, but the marine industry in Norway is heavily male dominated. While most respondents (89 percent) reported experiencing at least one of the negative acts in the previous six months, as many as 22 percent reported being subjected to one or more of the bullying behaviors in the preceding month, and almost 7 percent had experienced the negative acts on a weekly or daily basis. While bullying acts were common, findings suggested a correlation between the experiences of being bullied and psychological health and well-being impairment. Effects on bullied workers included frustration, stress, helplessness, alienation, lowered self-esteem, low productivity, and poor work-unit cohesiveness.

In their 2001 study, Voss et al. studied a group of 1,557 women and 1,913 men, all employees of the Swedish postal service, for their use of sick leave as correlated with bullying. Analysis of 150 different workplace variables was conducted using multivariate models. Some of the variables included workplace size, teamwork, proportion of men to women, working hours, noise and lighting conditions, indoor climate/temperature, support and encouragement from workmates and managers, justice in the workplace, availability of information, and the quality of social relationships. Bullying was reported by only 15 percent of the respondents but was associated with a twofold increase in the risk of high use of sick leave.

Bullying seems to cut across many professions, including the medical profession. In southern India, workplace bullying is becoming recognized as a serious and significant issue in health-care settings because it can ultimately impair patient care (Bairy et al., 2007). A total of 102 male and 72 female health-care workers were asked to participate in a study about workplace bullying: 89 (51 percent) reported having been bullied. Bullying targets were most often under 30 years of age. Bullying was likely to occur in the form of comments by seniors staff on the failure of their junior colleagues to meet expected standards of competence. According to respondents, 95 percent of bullying incidents went unreported, most often because those bullied did not know how to complain or were afraid of the consequences of reporting.

A 2009 study from the United Kingdom suggests that tendencies toward bullying start in schools among children and then can carry over into the adult world of work (Whittaker, 2009). This study indicated alarm that the stories of bullying in the United Kingdom have increased and that intimidation of workers, especially by managers, is getting more prevalent and more severe. According to Whittaker:

> Bullying can happen to anyone, and even the most robust can fall prey to this form of abuse as it can be subtle, such as exclusions from meetings, being cut out of the loop of important decisions or meetings, and added emails as an afterthought, which undermines authority and destabilizes [a person or] a department. (p. 16)

While awareness of the problem of workplace emotional abuse is growing worldwide, it has garnered less attention in emerging economies. As Harvey et al. (2009) suggested, to the degree that cultures rely only on standard operating procedures (with no allowance for exceptions to rules), when rules of conduct are strictly stated and enforced, when organizational values do not honor dignity or respect, when symbols of power are highly visible, when taboos—both symbolic and concrete—exist, when heroes or key personalities define the nature of the organization and those definitions endorse abusive behaviors, and when the daily climate of an organization is not civil, trouble will ensue.

To summarize, although it is not practical to survey all cultures and report on similarities and differences, features of the 21st century global work environment appear to contribute significantly to the increase in the incidence and prevalence of workplace mobbing. As organizations evolve into global entities, one could expect an increase in both frequency and severity of emotional abuse for a number of reasons (Harvey et al., 2009). Mobbing is a workplace malady not limited to highly industrialized societies. It has been studied in almost every part of the world, in spite of differences in economies, professions, degrees of economic development, and governmental infrastructures. It seems to be getting worse. Evidence to date suggests the following:

- Workplace diversity is increasing with global operations.
- Foreign assignments can be remote, and management surveillance can be reduced as a result.
- Legal environments between countries vary greatly.

Occupational Risks

A relevant question for consideration is whether or not mobbing is more prevalent in some professions than others. Authors Davenport et al. (2002) asserted that mobbing can occur in all types of industries and organizations but that it may be more likely in small companies, in government organizations, and in nonprofit organizations. As mentioned in chapter 1, precipitating climates often include those where there are fewer protective mechanisms in place.

In the 1998 book *Eliminating Professors,* Westhues identified academia as a high-risk environment. Data from a random sample of 1,535 university employees (11 percent of that institution's workforce) suggested that of 810 respondents, 23 percent met the criteria used to define workplace mistreatment (Spratlen, 1995, in Westhues, 1998). The highest proportion of those abused were professional staff, who were considered to serve "at will," rather than faculty or classified staff, who may have had the formal protection of labor organizations.

Data examined by Keashly et al. (1994) suggested the highest incidence of abuse occurs in medical schools, where students are targeted with verbal abuse and humiliation. Academic or institutional settings were cited as the second most frequent setting for abuse. Abusive behaviors in academia include such offenses as unfair evaluations, inappropriate or unreasonable workloads, and the assignment of unpleasant tasks as punishments (Keashly et al., 1994).

Abuse of teachers by principals was examined by Blase and Blase (Geffner et al., 2004). In face-to-face interviews with 50 teachers in the United States who had reported emotional abuse by principals, researchers identified varying levels of abuse and a range of responses. Abuse ranged from indirect, moderately aggressive behavior to direct and escalating aggression, to direct and severely aggressive behavior. Teachers reported feeling shocked and humiliated, having their decision making impaired, and claimed to have experienced psychoemotional problems.

Keashly et al. (1994), citing Cox (1991), discussed a survey examining the prevalence of verbal abuse in the nursing profession in the United States. The study was based on 1,100 responses to a nationwide survey distributed via the journal *Nursing Manager* in 1988. The results were significant. In response to the question "In your workplace, have you ever had an experience in which you had been verbally abused?" a surprising 97 percent of staff nurses and 97 percent of nursing managers responded, "Yes" (Keashly et al., 1994). Respondents in that study reported an average (mean) incidence of five verbal abuse incidents per month. The primary perpetrators of verbal abuse were physicians for both nurses and nurse managers.

Gary and Ruth Namie (2003) conducted the U.S. Hostile Workplace Survey 2000, one of a series of multiyear surveys, with analysis of data from a sample of 1,335 individuals from a variety of employers in the United States. At the time of the study, the sample was believed to be the largest of its kind in the world. Work environments and education levels were as follows: Thirty-five percent were corporate employers, 33 percent government employers, 13 percent small or family-run businesses, and 19 percent nonprofit organizations. Sixty-three percent of respondents reported having college degrees or some college, 17 percent held graduate degrees, and 4 percent had PhDs, MDs, or law degrees. Women made up 50 percent of the bullies, and those women targeted women 84 percent of the time. Almost all bosses (81 percent) had the power to terminate their targets at will. Bullying was far more prevalent than illegal discrimination. In 77 percent of the bullying instances, the victim was not protected as a civil rights–designated status group. The data from the 2000 study suggested that mobbing occurs not just with less powerful, unskilled, low-wage earners but that mobbing is more prevalent within corporate or governmental organizations. The 2000 data also suggested that perpetrators of bullying are not limited to dominant men and that bullying is not limited to what would be known as discrimination against a protected status group. In a more recent version of the U.S. Hostile Workplace Survey (Namie, 2008), 95 percent of 400 respondents identified themselves as victims of workplace bullying. Government workers represented 28 percent of respondents, 31 percent were from for-profit corporations, 11 percent were from nonprofit organizations, 19 percent worked in education (K-12 through university levels), and 8 percent worked in health care.

Other than academia and health care, the best substantiations of high-risk professions seem to be found in *organizational characteristics*. These include policies, practices, values, structures, communication patterns, and decision-making norms. Organizational characteristics are not limited to specific professions or disciplines. Ohio State University researchers Roscigno et al. (2009) focused on routine activities of abusive employment environments. These environments tend to be characterized by high proportions of women and minority staff providing personal services at low wages without the benefit of "guardians" of the workplace. Guardians might include unions for employee redress, bureaucratic controls, and accountability practices. Harvey et al. (2009) suggested that contextual factors of the global workplace stimulate or elicit bullying, including deficiencies in work designs, deficiencies in leadership behavior, a socially exposed position of victims, and low moral within the department or organizations.

Davenport et al. (2002) highlighted the following high-risk organizational traits:

- poorly managed organizations
- highly stressful work environments
- repetitive or boring tasks
- reluctance of management to acknowledge that bullying occurs
- organizations or subgroups involved in unethical practices
- organizations with little opportunity for advancement (that is, flat organizations)
- rapid organizational changes

A study of risk assessment in 12 Italian organizations cited risk factors other than profession or industry. These included poor team atmosphere, role ambiguity, procedural injustice, poor social climate, negative work conditions, leadership deficiencies, lack of innovation, and confusing rewards systems (Giorgi, 2009).

A 2007 study in Denmark (Ortega, Høgh, Pejtersen, Feveile, & Olsen, 2009) suggested no significant gender differences, however. Unskilled workers reported the greatest prevalence of being bullied (11 percent), and managers/supervisors reported the lowest prevalence (5 percent). In addition, those workers who worked with "things" rather than with "people" (clients, customers, consumers) were more at risk. The authors did conclude that bullying from supervisors and managers is lower in Denmark and Scandinavia in general than in the United Kingdom, the United States, or Australia. This is in part because Danish and Scandinavian workforces are characterized by lower power distance between superiors and workers. Power difference is related to the structure of the workplace and the relative presence or lack of power between managers and their subordinates. Scandinavian workplaces tend to be more egalitarian, possibly suggesting national characteristics rather than industry-specific traits.

While not identifying specific professions or organizational settings most at risk for workplace emotional abuse, some researchers have identified risks inherent in social-class status and occupational position, suggesting that workers who are poorly paid are easy targets for disrespect and bullying by supervisors (Roscigno et al., 2009). In contrast, other evidence suggests that abuses are more likely to occur between peers than from managers or supervisors toward subordinates (Neuman & Baron, 1998).

Not surprisingly, a mobbed target may actually have characteristics that seem favorable to the organization, but managers may be more dependent on the group of bullies than on the target (Zapf & Einarsen, 2002). Belgian psychology professor Paul Verhaeghe (D. Yamada, 2014b) suggested that at a macro level, political climates influence the prevalence of bullying. He suggested that a trend toward neoliberalism, privatization, and free markets have all influenced the workplace so that psychopathic personality traits are actually rewarded. Some of these include skill at persuasion, a tendency to avoid responsibility or ownership for winning people over, the ability to lie and not feel guilty about it, and the inclination to avoid responsibility for personal actions.

Of the thousands of workplace mobbing cases studied by Heinz Leymann, universities were among the most represented locations (Gravois, 2006). Years later, they continue to be risk environments for bullying. Some of the dynamics for this abuse are examined later in this chapter. While no agreement seems to exist about the highest-risk professions for mobbing, researchers do agree on the nature of organizations that are at highest risk for emotional abuse of staff. Unlike the view of Max Weber (one of the founding fathers of modern sociology) that bureaucracies are the living embodiment of procedural rationality, mobbing is an indication of procedural irrationality (Westhues, 2005b).

Data on Vulnerable Personalities

Although Leymann (1990) rejected the idea that a target's personal characteristics play any part in the development of bullying at work, not all would agree. Davenport et al. (2002) claimed that anyone can be victimized, no matter who they are or how old they are. Victims may be devoted to their work, creative, organized, committed, and responsible. One thing that does seem to stand out in descriptions of victims is a high degree of identification with their work and loyalty to the organization. They tend to be politically naive and trusting but principled. In fact, the authors reported that the subjects interviewed had histories of professional accomplishment, with strong characteristics of intelligence, competence, creativity, integrity, and dedication.

By contrast, Olweus (2002) characterized school victims of childhood bullying as passive or submissive, having problems asserting themselves, being anxious or inattentive, and lacking concentration. Olweus suggested that targets may even be provocative in their behavior. In adulthood, victims may be those who find it difficult to integrate into a work group. In top-down bullying (that is, manager or supervisor to subordinate), the victim may represent a threat to the supervisor or manager. Victims may have low social skills, low performance, or may be considered to be "difficult," and they may view themselves as deficient in conflict-resolution skills, social competence, assertiveness, and self-esteem (Zapf & Einarsen, 2002). Hazler, Carnay, and Granger (2006) suggested that victims have less effective interpersonal skills, tend to be socially isolated, may have underlying fears of personal inadequacy, and may have poor self-concepts.

Djurkovic and McCormack (2006) collected data on neuroticism and the psychosomatic model of workplace bullying. The goals of the study were to determine whether the effects of bullying on negative affect were independent of, or were moderated by, neuroticism. Neuroticism in this example pertained to a tendency to experience negative mood states. Cross-sectional, self-reported data from 127 research participants suggest that neuroticism does *not* moderate the relationship between bullying and negative affect. Findings were that (a) although neuroticism predisposes victims to negative affect and that (b) being exposed to bullying increases negative affect, there was not a significant relationship between neuroticism and negative affect in those bullied.

An extensive study from Norway in 2009 examined personality profiles among targets and nontargets of workplace emotional abuse. Data were collected from 496 employees in seven nursing homes in Bergen, Norway. Using the Norwegian translation of the NEO-Five Factor Inventory (NEO-FFI), the study questioned them about their personality styles as related to neuroticism, extroversion, openness, agreeableness, and conscientiousness. Findings were that neuroticism was negatively correlated with extroversion and conscientiousness. Extroversion was positively correlated with openness, agreeableness, and conscientiousness. Conscientiousness was correlated with agreeableness. Results suggested that there was no significant correlation between the NEO-FFI scores and exposure to bullying, contradicting any suspicion that the causes of bullying are specific characteristics of the person being bullied. The surveyed nursing home employees in this study were mostly female (and so were not a representative sample of professions), but they represented only those employees who were still working. Consistent with other researchers, the authors cautioned that many targets of workplace emotional abuse become ill and leave the workplace or the workforce (Lind et al., 2009).

In a study of supervisor–subordinate dyads in the National Guard of the United States, Tepper et al. (2006) identified negative affect in victims as a correlate of being targeted for abuse. Negative affect included anxiety, distress, dissatisfaction, submissiveness, insecurity, and poor ability to protect oneself. What is not known about the victims surveyed in the Tepper et al. study is whether the negative affect preceded the bullying, was created by the bullying, or existed independently of the bullying.

RELEVANCE OF MMPIs IN EMPLOYEE ASSISTANCE PROGRAM SAMPLES

As stated in the previous section, a primary challenge in evaluating an alleged mobbing event or process is to determine whether the victim's psychological symptoms contributed to the mobbing, were created by the mobbing, or developed independently of mobbing. Because of the frequent suspicion that bullied targets are employees who have emotional problems that preceded their victimization, two studies provide a more objective source of information about victims. The first was published in a 2009 issue of *Victims and Violence* and involved 107 workers who had sought mental health services because they saw themselves as victims of mobbing (Balducci et al., 2009). A psychologist saw the workers a minimum of two times and conducted testing at the second session. The study investigated the relationship between the experience of mobbing as compared to personality traits and symptom patterns using the MMPI-2. As most professionals in social sciences know, the MMPI-2 consists of 567 true–false questions that can be answered by an adult with a sixth-grade education. It is easily administered and is the most widely used instrument in forensic evaluation, including cases involving personal injury, emotional harm, workers' compensation, pain, and disability (Girardi, Monaco, Prestigiacomo, & Talamo, 2007). The sample was balanced by gender (45 percent women) and age (the mean age was 42.7 years, *SD* = 9.2 years). Of these, 57 percent were married, 36 percent never married, and 7 percent were divorced. Regarding education, 2 percent had an elementary school education, 11 percent had completed secondary school, 59 percent had high school diplomas, and 28 percent had a college degree or postgraduate qualification. Most (83 percent) were full-time employees or worked on a permanent contract. Three scales critical to interpreting the validity of the test include the L (lie) Scale, a measure of impression management; the F (infrequency) Scale, a measure of symptom exaggeration; and the K (subtle defensiveness) Scale, a correction measure with which to take account the tendency of some people to deny problems.

Of the 100 tests that checked valid and reliable for analysis, 65 percent of respondents perceived themselves as being exposed to mobbing at least daily for the past six months; 19 percent claimed to have been mobbed weekly, 11 percent claimed at least monthly victimization, and 5 percent admitted to having been targeted occasionally. Four of 10 scales indicated elevated scores: Scale 1 (Hs), Scale 2 (D), and Scale 6 (Pa) indicated that respondents were experiencing severe psychological distress. The combination of high scores on Scales 1, 2, and 3 suggests that participants might have a tendency to convert psychological distress into somatic symptoms (that is, a "neurotic" profile). The elevation of Scale 6 suggests pronounced paranoid ideation. Results for this study of mobbing victims supported a previous view that after the bullying experience, victims show features of a neurotic style of psychological functioning, especially when under stress, that they may not have clarity about the causes of their problems and that they may be prone to utilizing dysfunctional defense mechanisms such as somatization (the tendency to experience emotional distress with physical health symptoms), denial (disbelief), and repression (unintended forgetting). In addition, elevation on Scale 6 (paranoia) indicates a tendency to be suspicious of others and to blame others for misfortune. Surprisingly, only about half of the participants showed the actual severity of PTSD symptoms indicative of a full diagnosis of PTSD, so findings did not support a previously held view that PTSD is a typical reaction to mobbing. In 48 percent of the cases, PTSD symptoms were subthreshold, so they could be better reflected with a diagnosis of adjustment disorder. This study was a good response to the much-stated claim that mobbing causes or results in PTSD. While that does occur in some instances, the rate at which PTSD results from a mobbing process is somewhat low. Sixty-five percent of victims reported significant depressive symptoms. Findings indicated a significant relationship between exposure to mobbing behaviors and depressive-suicidal ideation and behavior. Seven participants (7 percent) had already attempted suicide at the time of testing. While it might be tempting to interpret these findings as supporting a notion of a personality *vulnerable* to mobbing, the profiles of mobbing victims tend to be similar to profiles of a control group of people self-referred to mental health services for other problems. The only difference between the groups is the elevation of Scale 6 (paranoia) in the victims of mobbing. From this study it is impossible to say whether the tendency toward paranoid ideation is a cause, a consequence, or merely a correlate of mobbing. What is known is that MMPI-2 profiles do not differ from those of other self-referred clients requesting mental health treatment.

The other source of useful information came from meta-analysis of clinical data collected from intake assessments by EAPs who assessed the personalities of 146 randomly chosen individuals from an original pool of 535 participants exposed to mobbing from 2001 to 2004. Although 160 were originally selected for study, 14 were omitted for incomplete or inaccurate test results, including high scores on the F Scale (infrequency) or high scores on the VRIN Scale (variable response inconsistency). Researchers used validity, clinical, and content scales of the MMPI-2 and the MINI, a short, structured interview designed for diagnostic purposes (Girardi et al., 2007). Two major clinical dimensions emerged among those exposed to mobbing: (1) depressed mood, difficulty making decisions, change-related anguish, and passive-aggressive traits; and (2) somatic symptoms, including a need for attention and affection.

Respondents indicated elevated scores on the HS Scale (somatization), the D Scale (depression), the HY Scale (hysteria), and the PA Scale (paranoia) but relatively *lower* than average scores for the FAM Scale (family problems). The low family scores suggested that the difficulties the subjects were experiencing did not appear to be related to any problems in bullied targets' home lives (Girardi et al., 2007).

Elevations in victim scores were found in the HS (somatization), D (depression), HY (hysteria), and PA (paranoia) Scales, but no clear cause-and-effect relationship was discerned. As was found in the Balducci et al. study (2009), scores from Girardi et al. (2007) tended to be low for family problems (FAM Scale) but were slightly higher for single women than for other victims. Victims emerged as having difficulty making decisions, experiencing change-related anguish, being introverted, and having a tendency to behave passive-aggressively. Again, it is unclear whether the personality profiles of mobbing victims or the psychological damage resulting from mobbing is a cause or an effect or exists independently from the mobbing experiences. Only a longitudinal study with a control group could delineate a clear cause-and-effect relationship (Girardi et al., 2007).

Based on those two fairly extensive studies, no consistent evidence indicates a personality style more vulnerable to mobbing. While clinical data and test outcomes suggest evidence of symptoms of psychiatric distress and perhaps some relationship between personality and victimization, no clear cause-and-effect relationship is evident. Many theorists even posit that victims tend to be better than average in their work performance and have higher than average EI.

Clearly, not everyone is a target. A study by Nielsen, Matthiesen, and Einarsen (2008) suggested that a "sense of coherence (SOC)" is a protective factor. In a study of 560 participants in a Norwegian support association for targets of bullying, questionnaires were distributed by mail, and 221 were completed and returned (39 percent). One question asked: How comprehensible is your world? Responses to this question were compared to symptom severity. Findings suggested that SOC is most protective when bullying is *mild;* however, these protections lessen as bullying becomes more severe.

While no cause-and-effect relationship regarding bullying can be verified, a question might remain about general vulnerability to being the target of bullying. Like studies of family violence, discerning preexisting personality traits or vulnerability to reactive psychological disorders is difficult because we generally know victims' traits after the bullying has occurred. Future studies are needed, perhaps of a longitudinal type, to follow participants over time to determine whether some workers are more likely to become targets at work.

CHARACTERISTICS OF PERPETRATORS OF BULLYING AND MOBBING

Understanding how people become bullies is critical to being able to reduce the chances of it occurring in the first place. However, it is difficult to gather accurate data on perpetrators because, as for other acts of aggression between people who know each other,

- incidents tend to be underreported;
- perpetrators are highly unlikely to self-identify as bullies or self-report;
- complaints are generally made from the victims, not the perpetrators;
- unlike abusive parents or partners who perpetrate intimate-partner violence, bullies are not usually forced/compelled into receiving treatment, so we have even less opportunity to study characteristics, histories, and traits; and
- because of the negative outcomes to targets, bullies are more likely to remain in the workplace undetected and unexamined.

General Perpetrator Qualities

While concluding that general qualities information and data on personality traits are difficult to obtain, Field (1996, in Stevenson, Randle, & Grayling, 2006) provided a relevant definition of the workplace bully. Bullies refuse to acknowledge their mistakes or deficits. They tend to deny responsibility for their actions and the effects on others. If the bully is in a leadership role, that leader may defend against any legal or moral authority for the well-being of others (Field, 1996, in Stevenson et al., 2006).

In answer to the question of who are bullies, Rayner et al. (2002) suggested that bullying has likely existed as long as people have had power over others. These authors lamented that the study of bullying is generally absent from textbooks in management and leadership. Unfortunately, much of the information gathered has been from the target's point of view. Keeping in mind the inherent difficulties in gathering relevant and useful data, this section will address a number of qualities that can help identify bullies. Namie and Namie (2003) suggested that people become bullies in at least three different ways: through their own personality development, by being acutely aware of signs of competition on the job, and simply by accident. They also contended that chronic bullies are prone to dominating others in multiple domains, not just work, and that bullies are motivated by their own failures to confront deep feelings of personal inadequacy. To defend against admitting their own shortcomings, bullies invent, and then attack, flaws in others (Namie & Namie, 2003).

P. R. Johnson and Indvik (2006) claimed that anyone can become abusive under the right circumstances. According to those authors, men and women are equally likely to be verbal abusers, and factors such as personality, stress, family background, and special events can play roles in verbal abuse. The authors also posited that many abusers are bosses who have the freedom to fire their employees (rather than needing to go through a structured process). Are these statements correct? This section explores the questions of who are bullies, how and why they emerge these traits, and what may be done to identify them before they act.

According to Namie and Namie (2003), chronic bullies are among the most mean-spirited people in the workplace, and they tend to be skillful at manipulating others. A small number of them are even sadistic and enjoy harming others. The Namies categorize bullies as "opportunistic," "accidental," and "substance abusing." Opportunistic bullies are most likely to be encountered at work. They tend to be climbers in the organization, well connected up the chain of command, and shielded from punishment by those in power. Accidental bullies tend to be benign and unaware of the effects of their actions. They tend to be blind to the rest of the world and can be awkward or childlike. When confronted, the accidental bully is likely to retreat and apologize. Finally, substance-abusing bullies are dangerous and threatening because they are not always in control of their behaviors. When alcohol or drugs enter the picture, rationality and logic are too often lost. Chronic bullies are those who engage in constant criticism, passive aggression, and gatekeeping (controlling access to people, information, or resources). Those who control through fear and intimidation can be considered chronic bullies (Namie & Namie, 2003).

The 2003 Workplace Bullying Inventory (WBI) (Namie, 2003) was an online, self-report survey querying respondents who visited a Web site seeking information on or solutions to their problems of bullying. Results from 1,000 respondents revealed the following: Only 25 percent of the time was a target a member of a protected status group; women were more likely to be targets; bullies were higher ranking than targets for 71 percent of respondents; women experienced more "bottom-up" bullying (that is, from subordinates); when women bullied, they tended to target multiple victims; and bullies enlisted help from others 77 percent of the time and acted alone much less often (23 percent).

Roscigno et al. (2009) suggested that for deviance, like bullying, to occur in a workplace, the right combination of "motivated offenders" must converge with "suitable targets" in the absence of "capable guardians," so bullying does not occur in a vacuum or in isolation. They further stated that the victim who occupies a structural position in the workplace with little power will be at greatest risk. In addition, perpetrators can be enabled by characteristics of the work environment. In such organizations, the workplace does not adequately guard against or prevent bullying.

SCHOOL-AGE BULLIES AND ADULT BULLIES

Is adulthood bullying related to childhood bullying? Do childhood bullies become adult bullies? According to most studies, the simple answer is "yes."

According to Magnuson and Norem (2009), bullying may be the most prevalent form of violence in American schools and is most likely to affect the greatest number of students. Unfortunately, reaching adulthood does not always reduce one's tendency to behave hurtfully toward others, and society is developing awareness that little bullies grow up to be big bullies. According to Dilts-Harryman (2004, in Magnuson & Norem, 2009), change a few of the age-related descriptors, and adult bullies are simply once-young bullies who terrorized other children. Olweus (1993, in Magnuson & Norem, 2009) suggested that children who engage in bullying during childhood continue to behave in aggressive manners at work and at home in adulthood. In fact, correlations have suggested that children who behave as bullies during childhood are more at risk for involvement in the adult criminal justice system later in life.

Einarsen et al. (2002) examined the characteristics of typical school-age bullies and suggested that bullies can be identified by aggression toward peers. While some mental health professionals claim that people with aggressive behaviors are deeply anxious or insecure, Einarsen et al. (2002) found no evidence of this in those they studied. Although bullies in school may not be popular, they do not seem to be as unpopular as those whom they target. Data suggest that over time, bullies are more likely to abuse alcohol and engage in criminal behavior. Data also indicated that 60 percent of boys who were bullies in grades 6 through 9 were later convicted of at least one crime by age 24, compared with a control group with only a 10 percent conviction rate.

Olweus (1993, in Magnuson & Norem, 2009) suggested that children who bully continue to demonstrate elevated aggression in adult life—in intimate relationships, at work, and in family relationships. Bullies may threaten, humiliate, intimidate, shout, and throw objects. They may also engage in indirect activities, such as hiding things and ignoring phone calls or e-mails. In adult bullying, power imbalance seems to be a key feature (Magnuson & Norem, 2009).

PERSONALITY TRAITS

Brodsky (1976, in Seigne et al., 2007), one of the first to study bullies' characteristics, identified bullies as being aggressive, driven by power, sadistic, and bigoted. Olweus suggested that being a bully is a stable condition and that psychosocial experiences can influence a bully's development (Olweus, 1973, in Seigne et al., 2007). While there may be a paucity of evidence that concludes a personality profile of the bully in the workplace, a large study of 2,200 employees in Norway (Einarsen et al., cited in Seigne et al., 2007) indicated that 5 percent of bullies identify themselves as both highly aggressive and hostile.

Clinical narrative studies by Randle (1997, 2001, in Seigne et al., 2007) suggested personality traits of serial/recidivist bullies at the extreme as being diagnosed with personality disorders. Personality disorders, according to the DSM-5 (APA, 2013), are

> enduring patterns of inner experience and behavior that deviate markedly from the expectations of the individual's culture. The pattern is manifested in two or more of the following areas: cognition . . . , affectivity . . . ,

interpersonal functioning . . . , and/or impulse control. The pattern is inflexible and pervasive across a broad range of personal and social situations. The enduring pattern leads to clinically significant distress or impairment in social and occupational functioning. The pattern is stable and of long duration. Its onset can be traced back at least to adolescence or early adulthood. (p. 231)

McCarthy (2001, in Seigne et al., 2007) described bullying managers as sadistic, psychopathic, and sociopathic. These managers are also described as autocratic, having aggressive leadership styles, and associating with positions of power (Quillan, 1996, in Seigne et al., 2007). For the most part, these descriptors are largely opinion rather than the result of data collected in any systematic manner.

Abusive supervisors in a blue-collar setting were described by Bamberger and Bacharach (2006). Multisource data on 1,473 blue-collar workers employed in 55 different work units examined the relationship between abusive supervision and employee problem drinking. The goal of the study was to determine whether drinking problems were initiated or exacerbated as a function of workplace conditions of abusive supervision. Abusive supervision correlated with problem drinking in subordinates, and some work groups had higher incidence of problem-drinking employees when the supervisor was abusive, but the study was inconclusive about actual causal factors. In fact, researchers admitted that abusive supervision might even be the *result* of drinking problems in employees. Nonetheless, specific characteristics of abusive supervisors were identified. Abusive supervisors were described as coercive, quick-tempered, intimidating, arrogant, and assuming that employees were "guilty until proven innocent" when rule infractions were alleged (Bamberger & Bacharach, 2006).

Chong et al. (2003, in Matthiesen & Einarsen, 2007) examined data from self-reported bullies. A sample of 19 percent of 288 respondents who were members of various work groups indicated that they had subjected others to bullying. This somewhat high percentage of bullying decreased to 3 percent when the role as perpetrator was more strictly and operationally defined as a combination of peer-reported and self-reported. The 3 percent included those people who admitted to bullying others and had the confession validated by at least two colleagues. Zapf and Einarsen (2002) have suggested three central precursors of bullying related to the bully's characteristics, including threats to the bully's self-esteem, the bully's lack of social skills, and what is termed *micropolitical behavior,* such as rivalry or competition.

In a cross-sectional survey by Matthiesen and Einarsen (2007), respondents were selected randomly from six Norwegian labor unions and the Norwegian Employers' Federation. The labor groups, all from the area surrounding Bergen, Norway, represented a convenience sample that reflected diversity in work environments, increasing the validity and reliability of the data. A total of 4,742 labor union members and representatives from employers responded from an original sample of 10,616, a 47 percent response rate in which 53 percent of respondents were male (2,513) and 47 percent were female (2,229). Personality traits of respondents were addressed via Likert-type scale questions adopted from research by Olweus (1987, 1991, in Matthiesen & Einarsen, 2007) on schoolyard bullying:

- *Aggression after provocation* was measured by three items.
- *Aggression against superiors* was measure by two items.
- *Aggression against peers* was measured by three items.
- *General self-esteem* was measured by one item.
- *Social anxiety* was measured by four items that were broken down into *perceived incompetence* and *anxiety in social situations.*

About 8 percent of the sample reported having been the target of bullying at work. An additional 2 percent could be defined as *provocative victims,* both anxious and aggressive in their reaction patterns. Another 5 percent of respondents admitted to bullying others at work. Respondents who had experienced being neither a target nor a perpetrator were used as a comparison (control) group. Perpetrators scored significantly higher on levels of aggression compared to the comparison group. Perpetrators also described themselves as more aggressive after provocation than did controls. Perpetrators indicated higher levels of aggression against superiors, compared to the mean scores of the other three groups—that is, higher levels of aggression against superiors than the victims, the provocative victims, and the controls (Matthiesen & Einarsen, 2007).

The term *predatory bullying* refers to cases where the victim has done nothing provocative to elicit the bullying. In such cases the victim is inadvertently in a situation where a predator is demonstrating power or trying to exploit an accidental victim (Magnuson & Norem, 2009). A distinction can be made between predatory bullying and bullying occurring as result of conflict-related experiences (Einarsen, 1999). Predatory bullying is most common in a climate where hostility and aggression are common and in organizational cultures already tolerant of bullying. Conflict- or dispute-related bullying occurs because of escalations in interpersonal conflict. Reliability analyses using Cronbach's alpha were conducted to investigate the prediction that perpetrators have a high but unstable sense of self-esteem (Einarsen, 1999). Perpetrators were found to have higher but less stable (more fragile) self-esteem than the comparison group. According to Einarsen, results of unresolved conflict can take three forms:

- aggressive behavior as a struggle tactic in interpersonal conflict
- malingering as a tactic
- resentment to perceived wrongdoing or unfair treatment

Role conflict was also examined as a causal factor in bullying: Do perpetrators, victims, and provocative victims have elevated levels of role conflict and role ambiguity? Results indicated that all three bullying groups (bullies, victims, and provocative victims) did experience elevated role stress, and perpetrators experienced significantly more role stress in terms of role ambiguity than did the comparison group (Matthiesen & Einarsen, 2007). Perpetrators in general appear to manifest a more aggressive behavior pattern in the workplace than do others if work roles and duties are ambiguous or if lines of authority are unclear. This aggression has been described as "petty tyranny" by Ashforth (1994, in Matthiesen & Einarsen, 2007).

Bergman, McIntyre, and James (cited in Geffner et al., 2004) described the aggressive personality as having both a *need* component and a *cognitive* component. The aggressive person has a need, desire, or motive to forcefully overcome opposition. That person will fight, engage in revenge, injure, or attack others with the intent to injure or forcefully punish them. Implicit and explicit cognitions that influence aggression are part of those motives. The authors suggested that aggressive people are characterized in the following ways:

- They often view aggression as a method for tolerating frustration.
- They generally dislike their victims.
- They want to cause some type of harm to those they persecute.
- They do not have adequate control over their aggressive behavior.

James, James, and Mazerolle (2002, in Geffner et al., 2004) suggested that individuals who are aggressive tend to respond to evocative situations in a more hostile manner than do others and that they use different analytical processes to understand the world than do those who do not respond aggressively. Specifically, nonaggressive people have reasoning processes influenced by cultural norms and values that define acceptable social responses. These processes are shaped by inferences that nonaggressive people make about what constitutes reasonable social behavior. The conclusions reached by nonaggressive people are generally consistent with cultural norms and values and would be viewed as sensible, rational, and socially appropriate.

By contrast, aggressive people use analytical cognitive processes that are guided by different values, those that are consistent with a more malevolent intent as the explanation of others' actions (Anderson, 1994; Crick & Dodge, 1994; Dodge & Cole, 1987; Tedeschi & Nestler, 1993; and Toch, 1993; all cited in Geffner et al., 2004). Aggressive individuals tend to view themselves as victims of the exploitation or oppression of others. Those beliefs of the harmful intent of others tend to guide aggressive people into searching for evidence to confirm their beliefs that they are victimized, thus justifying their aggressive responses to their perceived victimization (Averill, 1993; Finnegan, 1997; Tedeschi & Nestler, 1993; and Toch, 1993; all cited in Geffner et al., 2004). Aggressive people also have a tendency to characterize targets of their hostile acts as immoral, untrustworthy, or in some way deserving of the hostile treatment those aggressive people will inflict (Averill, 1993; Gay, 1993; and Toch, 1993; all cited in Geffner et al., 2004).

Aggressive people may believe that their hostile actions are an indication of strength and bravery and may be attempting to gain respect from others. They may also believe that *nonaction* is a form of weakness (Baumeister et al., 1996, in Geffner, 2004).

Given the difficulties in gathering good data, what could one reliably conclude from a research perspective? The next section will attempt to address this question and provide *some* insight, if not actual conclusions.

THE BULLY AS ARCHETYPE AND METAPHOR

The American Heritage Dictionary, Second College Edition (1983) defines "archetype" as "an original model, after which other similar things are patterned." "Metaphor" is defined as "a figure of speech in which a term that ordinarily designates an object or idea is used to designate a dissimilar object or idea in order to suggest a comparison or an analogy." Can the concept of "bully" be used metaphorically, or can it be conceptualized as an archetype?

Harvey et al. (2007) noted that leaders do not always have the best interest of the organization in mind when they make decisions. Throughout modern history, many actions of leaders such as John D. Rockefeller, Henry Clay Frick, Henry Ford, Armand Hammer, Harold Geneen, and Ivan Boesky, to name only a few, have been shown to be destructive. Harvey et al. (2007) also suggested that the study of destructive leadership has examined both personal and situational characteristics that promote or allow the development of leadership abuses. Situational variables present in many of the histories of destructive leaders might include alienation, nonsupportive families, negative role models, life stressors, competitive pressures, exposure to negative superiors or negative peer groups, and financial need (Gessner et al., 1995, in Harvey et al., 2007). One obvious category of destructive leaders in an organization is that of the bully. Bullying behaviors that emerge in leaders in an organization can include envy, destructive narcissism, fear and antisocial behavior, and negative life themes (death of parents, presence of a lasting deformity, poverty, or physical harm). Finally, the bully may continuously inflict a highly negative quality on another for pleasure. The bully may have a quality of "evilness" as a cardinal trait, as if the bully's conscience has been "switched off."

Davenport et al. (2002) described bullies as "evil personalities using power to destroy the spiritual growth of others for the purpose of defending and preserving the integrity of their own sick selves" (p. 59). According to those authors, bullies may act by their own notion of "divine right." They may struggle with threatened egotism and inflated self-appraisal. They may suffer from what is known in clinical literature as narcissistic personalities, harassing others not because of who they are but because of what they represent to the bully.

Finally, in her accounts of personal experiences of being bullied in academia, researcher Margaret Vickers (2001) identified bullies as evil and sociopathic, with characteristics that include disturbed and maladaptive social relationships, clearly reflecting antisocial behaviors. Vickers portrayed bullies as being controlling of others, humiliating of others, interpersonally aggressive and exploitative, needing to dominate others, and demonstrating themselves as powerful (Vickers, 2001). While Vickers's accounts are personal and subjective, she does make a case for negative features in many people who may be described by others as bullies. The concept of bully, then, can be understood as both a *description of a type* of person who engages in a type of behavior and as a myriad of *emotionally aggressive and harmful scenarios.*

Vickers (2001) suggested that perpetrators are "evil," although she conceded that not all bullies are intentionally bad, because some do not seem to know that what they are doing is wrong. Seigne et al. (2007) examined the issue of premeditated aggression in the workplace in Dublin, Ireland. Results suggested that respondents who admitted to bullying others did tend to use more assertive responses to situations. They also concluded that correlations exist between aggression and independence, between impulsivity and moodiness, and between aggression and hostility. Independence, impulsivity, moodiness, and hostility, then, may all be risk factors for aggressive acts.

P. R. Johnson and Indvik (1994) examined the impact of unresolved trauma on career management. While their findings specifically addressed childhood trauma such as sexual abuse, physical abuse, emotional abuse, and neglect, they also found that low self-esteem and low trust for others are outcomes of childhood abuse. These findings are relevant to discussions of abuse at work because people with unresolved issues with parents and siblings are more likely to have problems with employers and coworkers. When sibling rivalry remains unresolved, coworker behavior can remind the affected employee of the sibling relationship and can evoke hostility, withdrawal, and even depression. Certainly the issues of childhood experience can be relevant to discussions of conflict and rivalry at work, particularly those events that result in emotional abuse.

Workplace bullies may represent a "type" of person: ill intentioned, self-absorbed, power seeking, and aggressive. While few data sources can confirm this, viewing a bully through the lens of metaphor or archetype can help with one's understanding of bullying behavior. Whereas social work's emphasis on systems theories of human functioning and on "person-in-environment" will likely preclude reducing bullying behavior to mere "badness" on the part of perpetrators, considering aberrant behavior from micro perspectives may have some value.

CONDITIONED REASONING TEST OF AGGRESSION

The relationship between aggression and Conditioned Reasoning Test of Aggression (CRTA) scores can provide some insight about aggression and learned behaviors. James (1998, in Geffner et al., 2004) suggested that people who act aggressively are usually not aware of their cognitive biases and offered a concept of "justification mechanisms" (JMs) to identify implicit cognitive processes that guide and shape aggressive responses. Because these JMs are implicit and hidden, they cannot be assessed by self-report measures. The CRTA is a measurement instrument based on the assumption that aggressive people use their thought processes to justify their aggressive actions, especially if those actions are intended to injure or harm (Geffner et al., 2004). Developed by James and McIntyre (2000, in Geffner et al., 2004), the CRTA is based on a type of inductive-reasoning problem that asks respondents to determine which general conclusions follow from a set of premises. This measurement is constructed to make respondents believe that a multiple-choice CRTA question is about a simple true-or-false response. In fact, the measurement is really about the logical conclusions drawn from self-justifying thinking and actions. The self-justifying cognitive processes and JMs are those that would allow a potential perpetrator to act aggressively and to think and feel that aggressive behaviors are justifiable.

A typical CRTA problem designed for entry-level jobs is as follows:

The old saying "an eye for an eye" means that if someone hurts you, then you should hurt that person back. If you are hit, then you should hit back. If someone burns your house, then you should burn that person's house. Which of the following is the biggest problem with the "eye for an eye" plan:
  This approach:

  a. Tells people to turn the other cheek
  b. Offers no way to settle a conflict in a friendly manner
  c. Can only be used at certain times of the year
  d. Tells people they have to wait until they are attacked before they can strike (Bergman et al., cited in Geffner et al., 2004)

Two solutions exist for this problem. Alternative D is the logical conclusion based on JMs that justify aggression, a conclusion that intuitively appeals to aggression-prone people because it promotes retribution as being preferable to reconciliation. It is also grounded in an unstated assumption that powerful individuals will dominate those less powerful unless the less powerful ones strike first. Alternative B is the nonaggressive counterpart to aggressive JMs. It is preferred by nonaggressive people because it is a more prosocial alternative and provides a counterbalance to the tone of Alternative D (Bergman et al., cited in Geffner, 2004).

As respondents use analytical skills to identify the most logical conclusions, their reasoning is led by their implicit beliefs about what defines rational actions. What they judge to be the best answers are conditioned on whether underlying biases, JMs, implicitly influence their problem-solving processes (Bergman et al., cited in Geffner et al., 2004).

The CRTA resists response distortions, unlike traditional personality tests that are self-report in design, so it is a true inductive-reasoning test with respondents finding the most logical answer. Respondents try to find the right answers to a reasoning test rather than the socially desirable answers to a test measuring personality. Scoring with the CRTA is interpreted so that higher scores mean that the JMs for aggressive behavior are more central to shaping a person's reasoning. Results suggest that it is possible to identify those individuals who are more inclined to perceive others as more deserving to be the targets of aggressive acts.

How could a test like the CRTA be relevant to the study of workplace mobbing? Research in the workplace has suggested, for example, that both nuclear facility operators and shipping-package handlers with higher CRTA scores will tend to have higher absenteeism. Temporary workers with higher CRTA scores might be more likely to refuse their work assignments or fail to report for work. New restaurant workers with higher CRTA scores are more likely to quit within 30 days of hire. People with higher CRTA scores are more likely to steal office supplies from their employer after receiving criticism or negative feedback about their work performance (Bergman et al., cited in Geffner et al., 2004).

Findings suggest that the CRTA can provide a valid and efficient method for identifying those people who are prone to act with direct or indirect aggression at work. Findings also suggest that aggressive personality traits do underlie hostile actions at work. Does the CRTA actually predict aggressive acts? Not necessarily, but it has been used effectively in identifying people prone to aggression and also in predicting indicators of behavior, so it might be useful in screening out job applicants who are prone to committing hostile workplace acts, including bullying (Geffner et al., 2004).

SUMMARY

As suggested in this chapter, risk factors can be identified across professions, personalities vulnerable to bullying, and characteristics of perpetrators. Readers must remain mindful that risk factors or correlations do not imply causation. Some professions that would seem likely to be risky have low rates of bullying. Some people with risk profiles for victimization may never find themselves as targets of bullying. Individuals with risk profiles for perpetration may never inflict emotional harm on others at work. Some childhood bullies do mend their ways and change behavior by adulthood. Some become responsible and responsive individuals with abilities at relating well to others. However, many, whether due to lack of insight, lack of empathy, or lack of external motivation, take their abusive tendencies to the adult world of work. When allowed to go unchecked, their behaviors can be the cause of misery, illness, and disability.

The next chapter will examine at-risk professions and environments, leadership practices, and organizational risk factors that may add clarification to what seems on the surface to be a varied and somewhat confusing picture.

4

At-Risk Professions, Environments, and Organizational Functioning

This chapter attempts to answer a number of questions about at-risk professions, environments, leadership styles, and organizational practices. These include the following:

- Can we identify characteristics of work environments or workplace dynamics that might place an organization at risk for increased incidence of mobbing? If so, are some professions at higher risk than others for bullying to occur?
- Could preventative measures such as training, conflict-resolution skills, strategic planning, change management, and timely interventions reduce the likelihood of workplace mobbing, thereby reducing employer risks?
- What do we know about leadership style and organizational bullying?

SYSTEMIC REWARDS AND COST–BENEFITS FOR PERPETRATORS

A rational model of rewards and benefits for perpetrators concerns the risk of detection, apprehension, and consequences versus the benefits to be gained by the behavior. Boyett and Boyett (1998) identified the mechanisms for influencing behavior, borrowing from the now well-established field of behavioral psychology.

Two broad opportunities exist for managing behavior: antecedent conditions and consequent conditions.

Antecedents are signals or triggers for getting a behavior started. According to Daniels (1994, in Boyett & Boyett, 1998), trying to manage triggers does not tend to work well or for long. People may temporarily change their behavior, but when authority or controls are not in place, temporary behavior changes are likely to revert to previous behaviors. Antecedents alone might get behavior change started, but they generally cannot sustain it. Lasting changes are influenced much more by consequences—that is, by systemic rewards or punishments. Consequences are those forces that keep a behavior going or prevent it from continuing. From behavioral theory, one can understand various forms of consequence:

- **Positive Reinforcement:** Popularly called the "carrot." This approach offers rewards for desired behavior.
- **Punishment:** Popularly called the "stick." As a consequence of doing an undesirable behavior or failing to do a desired one, a person may receive as a consequence something aversive or may have something desirable taken away.
- **Extinction:** The "ignore it and maybe it will go away" approach is also ineffective.
- **Negative Reinforcement:** Can be understood by taking away something negative to increase the likelihood of desired behavior.

Each of these strategies has utility and applicability as management tools, but in the instance of workplace mobbing or bullying, the *wrong behaviors* may be rewarded by the system, and *sanctions* or *punishments* for undesirable behaviors may not be forthcoming or consistent. In any analysis of behavior that is the target of change, the enabling factors and the restraining/rewarding features need to be clearly identified. Because so much of workplace emotional abuse is covert, it may be difficult for the organization to identify it and address it. To prevent or remediate bullying, organizational infrastructure and the organization's mission, vision, and values must also be included. Along with these, explicit and implicit rules for corporate behavior need to include directives for ensuring emotional respect of others in the workplace.

Salin (2003a) suggested that the necessary antecedents of bullying are enabling processes and structures present in a work environment, along with motivating structures and processes and precipitating (or triggering) processes. These costs and benefits must all be examined and understood. Low perceived costs to perpetrators are among the prerequisites for bullying to occur. The costs of the risks of getting caught, reprimanded, dismissed, or socially punished by management or colleagues must be assessed. Einarsen and Skogstad (1996, in Salin, 2003a) and Leymann (1990, in Salin, 2003a) have emphasized that the size, length, and formality of decision-making processes in some organizations make an individual less visible and thus reduce the risks that a perpetrator might be caught and punished. This would suggest that larger, more bureaucratic organizations could be at greater risk because of the slowness of processes. Salin (2003a) also suggested that bullying might be rational or individually rewarding because of such conditions as

- high internal competition,
- a politicized organizational climate,
- an organizational reward system that contributes to bullying by rewarding or promoting someone who has manipulated or harmed a colleague, and
- income or remuneration for work performed that is based on the relative ranking of employees.

Sabotaging the work of others may therefore be an incentive for a bully, and bullying can be a means of establishing status within the organization.

Einarsen (1999, in Harvey et al., 2009) hypothesized that bullying will take place only if the bully feels he or she has permission or support from superiors and other coworkers to behave in this manner. Anderson and Pearson (1999, in Harvey et al., 2009) posited that if the tolerance for bullying in the organization increases, the socially accepted norms for workplace behavior can change quickly too.

Lewin (cited in Covey, 1991) is credited with modern-day understanding of the forces that depict the dynamics of change in a process. Driving forces are those facts and influences that motivate behavior, while restraining forces are those influences that prevent the change in behavior. To simplify, mobbing can be created by driving forces that are not sufficiently met with restraining forces. Organizations that go through cycles of driving forces met with restraining forces in response to crises or changes will soon become cynical (Covey, 1991). Force field analysis—that is, examining driving and restraining forces—could be a helpful construct in considering the motivating and preventative influences for emotional abuse at work.

HIGH-RISK PROFESSIONS

High-risk professions may or may not be easily identifiable. Kok (2006, in Ozturk, Sokmen, Yilmaz, & Cilingir, 2008) suggested that job stress, pressure for productivity, violation of ethical principles, poor management and leadership styles, role conflict, role vagueness, and social atmosphere all predispose an organization to mobbing. While these traits can exist in any setting, and while data from all types of work environments do not exist, some professions have emerged as appearing to be at high risk. These are nursing, medicine, human services, education, and other high-stress professions. Highlights of studies in these domains will follow.

Nursing

Nursing, medical schools, and health-care system studies have strongly suggested that mobbing is prevalent within these settings and professions. A six-month study in Turkish university nursing schools by Ozturk et al. (2008) collected data via a 60-item mobbing scale, a questionnaire containing six questions about demographics and 10 about nurses' opinions about mobbing. The study's goals were to develop a mobbing scale for academic nurses about the prevalence and severity of bullying in nursing schools. Respondents were 162 academic nurses, average age of 33.2, with an average of 7.2 years on the job. Ninety-three (57 percent) were married, 93 (57 percent) did not have children, 102 (63 percent) were research assistants, and 91 (56 percent) had PhDs. Ninety-eight (61 percent) noted that they were exposed to mobbing at some time during their academic careers. Of these, 33 (34 percent, or 20 percent of all respondents) were actual mobbing targets. Of those who had been bullied, 49 percent were still experiencing the abuse, 67 percent had been exposed for three years or more, and 39 percent believed that they had been targeted because of their job achievements (Ozturk et al., 2006).

Another Turkish nursing study surveyed 346 teaching staff at participating nursing schools (Yildirim, Yildirim, & Timucin, 2007). Participants included 33 professors, 43 associate professors, 59 assistant professors, 35 instructors, and 176 research assistants. The response rate was very good at 69 percent (n = 210). Findings suggested that the type of mobbing behaviors most typically encountered were those involving attacks on personal status in the organization (85 percent) and attacks on personality (82 percent). Being blamed for things that were not the responsibility of the target was also reported by 56 percent of respondents. Other mobbing behaviors were frequent complaints of respondents, including having decisions and recommendations criticized or rejected, having untrue things said about them, making them feel that their work was being "inspected," and constantly finding mistakes. Yildirim et al. (2007) also found that in 68 percent of instances, the abuser was a manager or supervisor of the target. Another 27 percent of respondents claimed to have been abused by a colleague of equal status. Only 5 percent in the Yildirim et al. study reported being abused by subordinates.

An interesting caveat appeared in both of the Turkish studies cited. Only women can work in the nursing profession in Turkey, due to national regulations. If Salin (2003b) was correct, and women are more vulnerable to targeting for bullying, then nurses in Turkey would by definition be a high-risk group. Allan (cited in Yildirim et al., 2007) stated that the mobbing behaviors described by Yildirim et al. "resonate" with the British experience of abusive relationships within the National Health Service. British studies have suggested that women and minorities continue to be at highest risk.

Verbal abuse of nurses by physicians in a hospital setting was examined by Simms (2000). According to this researcher's findings, hospitals breed workplace verbal abuse that can be partially attributed to feelings of grief and loss experienced in health-care cultures when patients do not heal or recover. Hospitals may frown on open expression of grief when treatments fail and patients die. As a result, unexpressed grief can emerge as anger. It is Simms's position that hospitals do not always provide professionals with adequate emotional support, and physicians and nurses may in turn fail to provide support for grieving peers (Simms, 2000). Nurses also struggle with "failure" and "no cure" and may blame themselves for not meeting patient and family needs. This sense of failure, along with a sense of lack of control over patients' conditions, can lead health-care professionals to be increasingly critical and controlling. Simms suggests that these behaviors will be exaggerated if the professional has had previous exposure to abuse at home or at school.

Stevenson et al. (2006) conducted a study of nurses in the United Kingdom. Four hundred second- and third-year nursing students from a large university school of nursing received surveys about their mobbing experiences. Return rate was very good ($n = 313$, or 76 percent). Fifty-three percent of respondents had experienced one or more bullying incidents during their training. This is considerably higher than an earlier study suggesting that 38 percent of health-care workers in a community health trust were being bullied (Quine, 1999). The most frequently reported negative behaviors from the study by Stevenson et al. (2006) were being ignored or excluded, being inappropriately criticized, having efforts devalued, and being humiliated or ridiculed in front of others. The least frequent negative behavior experienced by the students was the threat of physical harm, an offense reported by only 3 percent of the sample. Researchers suggested, however, that the 3 percent sample was significant because more than seven people actually felt physically threatened. Other problem behaviors included more passive behaviors such as lack of appreciation, poor communication, and being denied learning opportunities.

A smaller but more complex and comprehensive study was conducted by Australian researchers in 2006 (Hutchinson et al.). In a sequential, mixed method of study, nurses who had been bullied agreed to participation and interviewing. They were asked about the nature and effects of their bullying experiences, what their perceptions were, what action they took, and how the organization responded procedurally. None of the participants reported having any history of performance problems before the bullying experiences. Most (75 percent) had been employed for more than four years by their current employer. At the completion of the interviews, six "themes" emerged. These suggested the ways in which bullies worked together (mobbed) to control nursing teams by using a variety of techniques, including insisting that those who were targets were silenced and "invisible." Bullying caused considerable harm to those who were targets. Two startling themes focused on key elements of the outcomes of those bullying alliances. These were concealment of bullying, where the loyalty between bullies provided them with protection from consequences, and bullies were protected and promoted, where abusive behaviors were both tolerated and rewarded within the organization.

While bullying is undoubtedly harmful to the individuals who are targeted, another social problem can be identified as both an outcome and a correlate of workplace bullying in American health care. A landmark 1999 Institute of Medicine report called *To Err Is Human* stated that workplace bullying extends far beyond issues of performance and civility to patient safety and well-being (Leape & Fromson, 2006, in Martin, 2008). Martin further posited that health-care leaders and managers must be diligent in viewing bullying not only from a labor perspective—that is, a legal and ethical point of view—but also from a hospital safety point of view. In fact, the Joint Commission on Accreditation of Hospitals (JCAHO) adopted the 2009 Leadership Chapter Standards that require hospital leaders to create protocols for managing disruptive work environments to maintain a safe atmosphere. According to JCAHO, disruptive behaviors include those associated with bullying of any hospital personnel (Martin, 2008).

D. Yamada concluded that bullying is a very relevant concern within health care. Citing a study at the Vanderbilt University School of Medicine (Swiggert et al., 2009), D. Yamada (2009) reported that Vanderbilt created a procedure that could serve as a model. The Vanderbilt response to bullying appears to deal with cases in a fair and responsive manner but avoids the temptation to merely dismiss the possibility for working with the offending person for behavior change. This can be accomplished by sending a message in the workplace that bullying is not acceptable. It requires HR professionals and departments to handle bullying situations in a very direct manner. Effective prevention and remediation measures are key to the success of this process. Multidisciplinary teams are encouraged to address organizational risk factors. Teams should include experts in education, law, management, HR, and occupational health, organizational experts, and psychologists from clinical and organizational domains (D. Yamada, 2008). D. Yamada (2000) also emphasized the need for status-blind processes in which bullying can be addressed no matter what the organizational position of either the victim or the perpetrator. While dismissing bullies may be indicated, it might not be required as the first response. D. Yamada concluded that left unchecked, abusive treatments at work can multiply and repeat. Medical schools and health-care systems are not immune.

While no conclusive evidence indicates that medicine in general or medical schools and health-care services organizations, specifically, are at higher risk than other employment domains, much of the literature has focused on bullying within health care. Certainly, risks do exist in these settings. It might be that the traits inherent in many typical American work environments identified by Davenport et al. (2002) are the very traits that, when exaggerated, may contribute to bullying in health-care environments. These can include focus on competition and success; an individualistic orientation rather than a collectivistic one; communications that are open, direct, and goal-oriented; independence; emphasis on independent thinking and action; and relationships that can tend to be short-term.

As with the results of studies of victims and perpetrators, it might be that organizational factors are the greatest determinants of workplace bullying. Physician Jacqueline Randle (2005) wrote that nurses often do not want to acknowledge bullying as an issue because it conflicts with their image as caring professionals. She argued that traditional approaches to nursing education have helped to entrench bullying within the profession so that each new generation of nurses is socialized to accept it as a normal part of nursing practice. Randle concluded,

> Bullying and its effects on self-esteem are perpetuated by practices within nursing. The situation will only be changed if nurses and educators transform their practice and the context in which bullying occurs. Otherwise, each new generation of nurses will continue to be socialized into negative practices which undermine both their own feelings of self-worth and standards of nursing care. (p. 16)

Are health-care professions at high risk for emotional abuse in the workplace? Do the stresses and strains of job requirements put undue burdens on health-care staff members that result in incivility between employees? No clear answers exist.

However, given the attention to bullying within the health-care professions, it is apparent that health-care students and professionals are in one of the high-risk groups for workplace emotional abuse.

Human Services

Human services would not be where one might expect mean-spirited behaviors between employees or between employees and their managers. D. Yamada, cited in Davenport et al. (2002), explained that because "emotional labor" is required in human services–type environments, the psychological consequences of work are easily exaggerated. Although many human services organizations prefer professional social workers, with at least BSW degrees and preferably MSW degrees, it is not uncommon for positions to be filled by staff with less education or by those with education in professions not in social work. This trend can result in poor understanding of human behavior and poorly developed skills in dealing with difficult clients and their problems. Davenport et al. (2002) posited further that bullying is most prevalent in environments where employees are deeply committed to their work and loyal to the organization. Human services organizations easily fit that description, as workers there are generally not motivated by wages or fame. Nonprofit organizations may be particularly vulnerable due to lack of formal labor organizations representing workers—that is, lack of unions. Faith-based organizations can also be vulnerable to these types of risks.

Social work theorists Gummer and Edwards (1995, in Ginsberg & Keys, 1995) described the politics of human services administration. Human services organizations can be understood politically from at least three perspectives: the public social-policy perspective; the ends-and-means perspective; and the interest groups' perspective.

The public social-policy perspective requires human services organizations to pursue goals over which there may be widespread disagreement. Some of these goals include distributive justice for poor people, people of color, and other groups of oppressed people. Many times, the public's response to these issues is influenced most by political power and influence rather than knowledge and expertise (Gummer & Edwards, 1995, in Ginsberg & Keys, 1995). Public welfare services might be a good example of this policy-versus-power-versus-expertise dilemma.

The ends-and-means perspective, even when consensus is finally reached by social policy and politicians, creates further challenges. Since funding sources want to be assured that expenditures and investments are producing the outcomes they are designed to produce, both assessing the need for service and evaluating the effectiveness of services are increasingly important. The processes of determining needs and measuring outcomes create significant organizational pressure and significantly affect organizational dynamics.

The third perspective, interest groups' perspective of human services organizations, can be understood from a political vantage point. Until the 1960s, what are now human services agencies were referred to as "social services" (Gummer & Edwards, 1995, in Ginsberg & Keys, 1995). While this may seem like a small distinction, social services agencies really meant *social work agencies,* because the type of work done was *social work* and the staff members who performed the work were social workers. While not all staff members in those days were professionally trained as social workers, a considerable number of administrators and lead workers held MSW degrees, and the policies and practices of the organizations were strongly influenced by the *Code of Ethics of the National Association of Social Workers* (hereinafter NASW *Code of Ethics*) (NASW, 2008).

Unfortunately the antipoverty programs initiated during the Lyndon B. Johnson administration and since have tended to view social workers as part of the problem instead of part of the solution (Gummer & Edwards, 1995, in Ginsberg & Keys, 1995). How did this affect social services/human services? By the mid-1990s, fewer than 20 percent of human services administrators had social work training. The other 80 percent identified themselves as educators, managers, attorneys, public administrators, and health-care professionals (Gummer & Edwards, 1995, in Ginsberg & Keys, 1995). Along with the shift in professional identity, human services organizations have faced a need to develop a clearer understanding of the politics of organizational functioning and the appropriate uses of power. Neither of these perspectives has been easy to adopt. The trend toward understanding the use of power has necessitated human services leaders to develop knowledge and skills in the areas of

- thinking, behaving, and working politically;
- diagnosing interests and assessing power;
- controlling agendas and decision alternatives;
- enhancing communication skills and building networks;
- playing by the rules;
- performing a useful function; and
- managing impressions.

Having addressed some of the challenges of human services systems, human services work environments have distinctive characteristics that create pressures for staff. Some of these include the following:

- Emphasis on productivity. Groups are greatly affected by the degree of this emphasis.
- Emphasis on tasks rather than relationships. Groups have shifted from focus on processes to focus on accomplishing tasks.
- Emphasis on time, which may shift focus away from the traditional social work practice that understood that reaching goals with clients can take time to accomplish. When time limits are imposed, outcomes may not always be as favorable as desired. Social work values would suggest that timelines for client goals should be determined by the client's needs, not by organizational timelines.
- Emphasis on managing large client loads, which creates a dilemma: Whose needs are primary? The client's, the workers', and the organizations' needs often do not match well. (Siegel, cited in Ginsberg & Keys, 1995).

Given the pressures in today's human services organizations, the lack of literature and data addressing workplace bullying is somewhat surprising

A survey of 2,780 clinical social workers in Florida in 1992 examined the role of stress and professional burnout (emotional exhaustion) in the lives of social workers providing direct clinical services (Um & Harrison, 1998). Results suggested that burnout increases when perceived role conflict increases but that role ambiguity itself is not related to burnout. Findings also suggested that when social support is available and utilized, burnout decreased. The study identified that worker training and adequate supervision, especially for newly recruited workers, are an integral part of organizational prevention strategies. While the study did not specifically examine the effects of burnout, social support, role conflict, and bullying, it could well be that mediating the effects of high-stress work organizations would help to reduce risks of bullying.

Max Weber's definition of *bureaucracy* may suggest other organizational risk factors for mobbing. These include limitations in the scope and authority of each position; top-down control; centralized recordkeeping; high levels of employee specialization; positions in the organization requiring full-time commitments and generally representing career paths; recruitment of new staff based on the skills of applicants and those of the position being sought; functions and behavior governed by strict rules; and clear separation between private and public lives of employees (Netting et al., cited in Dewees, 2005).

While admitting that a bureaucracy is more a theoretical concept than an actual structure, bureaucratic characteristics, even while providing safeguards and guardians, might also contribute to risk for emotional abuse because of rigidity and rules. Many if not most public social services are administered and delivered from within some sort of bureaucratic structure, so by definition they may have increased risk.

Is bullying prevalent in human services organizations? The earlier commentary about human services would logically suggest that bullying does occur; however, this question remains unanswered. Social work researcher Tracy Whitaker's 2012 study "Social Workers and Workplace Bullying" surveyed 111 social workers in the Washington, DC, area to determine bullying prevalence using two survey tools, the Workplace Harassment Scale and the Coping Response Scale. Whitaker's aim was to determine whether workplace bullying is prevalent within social work and also to identify targets' preferred coping mechanisms. A startling 58 percent of those respondents whose surveys were used ($n = 64$) had experienced bullying more than once within the previous year. Those bullied were most often direct service workers (35 percent) or administrators/managers (29 percent). Women were identified as the bullies in 67 percent of the responses, more than twice the rate of male perpetrators (33 percent). Other outcomes were consistent with data about health-care professions.

Given the stresses of human services organizations in today's economy, human services agencies and social work professionals are not immune to bullying. More research is needed about public services in general and public human services in particular.

Education

Education is by far the most frequently examined profession in the mobbing litera-ture. Studies from the United States, the United Kingdom, and Canada all indicate that workplace emotional abuse has grown in frequency and severity in public educational systems and in universities. Universities were among the most highly represented in the cases studied by Leymann (Gravois, 2006).

Blase, Blase, and Du (2008) studied 172 American elementary, middle, and high school teachers to understand their perceptions of the major sources and intensity of workplace emotional abuse. While no conclusions could be reached about the abuse always being the principals' and other administrators' behavior toward teachers, the authors did suggest that administrators are the perpetrators in anywhere from 50 percent to 90 percent of instances. Examining the scope of mis-treatment of teachers by principals, the effects of the mistreatment, and teachers' coping strategies, the authors collected data via a self-administered questionnaire asking the following questions:

- What types of abusive behaviors do teachers in American schools experience?
- What levels of harm from principal mistreatment do teachers perceive?
- What are the perceived effects of principal mistreatment?
- Do teachers of various demographic backgrounds report different effects from principal maltreatment?
- What are the frequencies and intensities of harm of specific principal mis-treatment behaviors for participants?
- Do teachers of varying demographic backgrounds perceive different levels of frequency and intensity of harm from specific principal mistreatment behaviors?
- What are the most harmful principal mistreatment behaviors for teachers of various demographic variables?
- What are teachers' perceptions of factors that contribute to principal mistreatment?

Outcomes for Blase et al. (2008) were as follows: Seventy-eight percent of respondents reported at least moderate harm to themselves from principal mis-treatment, and 49 percent reported the harm to themselves as serious or severe; 75 percent rated harm to their work as at least moderate, and 49 percent rated harm to work as serious or extensive; 58 percent reported at least moderate harm to their families, and 31 percent reporting serious or extensive family harm. In response to the question about how teachers cope, 80 percent indicated that they avoided their principal. Seventy-seven percent stated that they relied on others for support. Sixty-one percent said they simply endured the mistreatment by their principals. Senior teachers were more likely to assert themselves with their principals, and the oldest group was most likely to involve their unions or associations. Tenured teachers were more likely to report abuses than nontenured. No differences in coping strategies were found among teachers holding various degrees, in various school levels, or of different racial or ethnic groups. A total of 77 percent of all respondents indicated that principal mistreatment markedly undermined teaching. The five most frequent types of abuse were

- failure to recognize or praise for work achievements,
- favoring "other" teachers,
- trying to intimidate,
- failure to support in difficult interactions with parents or students, and
- ignoring or snubbing.

These data should cause concern. More than three quarters of respondents stated that they would leave their teaching positions because of harm caused by their principal's mistreatment. Of even greater concern, almost half (49 percent) wanted to "leave teaching altogether" because of the mistreatment (Blase et al., 2008). This is an ominous trend, because even though the recent job market in the United States has been tight, the shortage of well-trained, committed, and effective teachers is an ongoing problem.

Another study by Blase and Blase (2006) examined the physical symptoms of teachers who had been emotionally abused by principals in work settings. Symptoms included sleep disorders, headaches, backaches, fatigue, exhaustion, illness, hyperactivity, weight changes, alcohol or other drug use, ulcers, skin problems, irritable bowel syndrome, heart arrhythmia, and suicide. The types of mistreatment included insensitivity to the feelings of teachers, lack of support, withholding needed resources, denying opportunity for advancement, flagrant favoritism, lack of professional conduct, thwarting teachers' work efforts, boundary violations, outright stealing, making unreasonable demands on teachers' time, unwarranted disciplinary action, unfair evaluations, explosive anger, racism, sexual harassment, forcing teachers out of jobs, and preventing teachers from leaving. The 2006 data suggested that the harm from principals affects teachers, students, the schools' reputations, and education as a whole (Blase & Blase, 2006).

A danger of spillover exists when bullying occurs in educational environments. Students and faculty members are negatively affected by an organizational environment that is overly permissive (McKay, Arnold, Fratzl, & Thomas, 2008). Recommendations for prevention or remediation include protections such as antibullying policies, education and training for employees and administrators about workplace emotional abuse, protocols on civility, and modifying the organizational culture.

A landmark work by Kenneth Westhues titled *Workplace Mobbing in Academe: Reports from Twenty Universities* (2005a) compiled essays, research studies, and case histories. Westhues identified a major difference between academics and other occupations in the institution of tenure at universities. Tenure is a lifelong job contract that is typically very difficult for an employer to break. It exists to ensure academic freedom, but it can be the very dynamic that perpetuates mobbing in academia. Westhues suggests that it might be that tenure is at least a correlate, if not a contributor, to mobbing. Employers and peers may want a faculty member to leave but cannot force departure on the tenured faculty person. Mobbing may be seen as an indirect but effective method of ensuring early termination of otherwise secure employment for the targeted victim.

A number of primary mechanisms for removing tenured faculty from their academic posts exist. A few of these are *cover-up, devaluation, reinterpretation, official channels, intimidation,* and *bribery.* Westhues (2005a) likened the cover-up for academic bullying to the cover-up that occurs when police officers use excessive force against alleged perpetrators:

> For getting rid of an academic without repercussions, the cover-up is a powerful tool. If few people know about the reasons, the processes, and the outcomes, then the potential for generating outrage is minimal. Many academics cooperate in a cover-up because they are ashamed by the criticism of their performance and because they are not accustomed to seeking publicity. (p. 320)

Academic staff members may sue for wrongful dismissal from employment. Unfortunately, however, participation in the cover-up may also draw the legal system into participating in the cover-up, extending the abusive behavior from the job alone into multientity mobbing. Courts might participate in the cover-up by forcing the coerced academic to reach an agreement with the university or educational system. This form of legal cover-up of mobbing can include payment to the academic upon acceptance of a silencing clause or a conditional settlement that restricts further public scrutiny of the situation (Westhues, 2005a).

Devaluation is another form of bullying that can escalate into mobbing when attacks become systemic and are viewed as legitimate to a broad audience. History has shown countless examples of devaluation, from South Africa to Nazi Germany, to the Rodney King police beating, to the more recent incidents of police shooting of unarmed African American men in New York, Cleveland, and outside of St. Louis. These occurrences or processes then get supported by the legal system and the media. Devaluation of academics can occur in similar instances through general attitudes (Westhues, 2005a). When the devaluation process operates with bullied academics, very little moral outrage may arise, similar to the lack of moral outrage when other less powerful groups are bullied by those with more power. Westhues (2005a) cited an example in South Africa in the 1960s. Black South Africans did not enjoy equal protection under the law and were not treated as equal, so when police shot and perhaps killed a hundred black protesters, the event did not create as much uproar as if the police had shot and killed only a few white protesters. Because bullied academics have less power than administrators and boards, their mistreatment may be less noticed and less protested.

Reinterpretation occurs when attackers interpret a situation in a way that does not present them as unjust. Reinterpretation is a form of remaking of history. Academics, through their research and teaching, develop experience in interpreting and reinterpreting actions and motives. The mechanism of reinterpretation may serve this type of "defense mechanism" in perpetrators of academic bullying.

Use of official channels relates to the "just world belief" discussed in chapter 2. Just world beliefs are deep and hard to budge (Lerner, 1980, in Westhues,

2005a). Many whistle-blowers or others lodging legitimate claims against improprieties expect that their concerns will be taken seriously and investigated. They are shocked when they themselves come under attack instead (Westhues, 2005a).

Although heavy-handed techniques such as physical intimidation are uncommon in industrialized countries, more subtle forms of bullying can occur when academics are threatened by individual administrators with loss of jobs, grants, respect, peer groups, and good standing with superiors. Intimidation tactics like these are often then supported by institutional mechanisms (Westhues, 2005a).

Bribery can work in a similar but reverse manner, where the academic might be offered promotions, access to resources, or other organizational benefits in exchange for silence. In the end, such institutional responses constitute mobbing. These features inherent in academia may help explain why so much emotional abuse in academia goes unchecked and unchallenged.

Canadian researchers S. Yamada and Cappadocia (2014) highlighted the problem of bullying of psychology graduate students by their supervisors, identifying both the individualistic, competitive nature of academia and the power imbalance of the student–supervisor relationship as risk factors. Bullying behaviors included

- destabilization, including shifting goal posts without notice, changing duties without notice, undervaluing the students' efforts, and efforts at demoralization;
- isolation, including withholding needed information, ignoring or excluding the students, or attempt at restricting non-school-related activities;
- overwork, including undue pressure to produce work with impossible deadlines;
- threats to personal standing by behaviors such as sarcasm, undermining of personal integrity, teasing, inappropriate jokes, verbal and nonverbal threats, and violence to students' property; and
- threats to professional status, such as persistent criticism, overmonitoring of the student's work, belittling comments, public humiliation, and the use of intimidation for discipline.

A point–counterpoint type of argument appeared in a somewhat recent issue of the American Federation of Teachers' publication *AFT on Campus*. In response to the question posited by the article's title, "Is Higher Education Soft on Workplace Bullies?," associate professor Corliss Olson of the University of Wisconsin responded with a resounding "YES." Olson suggested that bullies are creative, manipulative, and charming, so administrators fail to see their culpability during grievance procedures (Olson & Agina, 2009). Olson further posited that bullied targets come to resemble victims of domestic violence, internalizing negative messages and becoming unable to act in their own defense (Olson & Agina, 2009). Union of Rutgers Administrators and American Federation of Teachers steward Ines O. Agina disagreed. She argued that bullied academics can call upon a union representative to discuss bullying behavior before it escalates and that further antagonism can be stemmed (Olson & Agina, 2009). Agina further suggested that union members help each other through difficult times on the job by challenging inappropriate behavior. It is likely that both of the realities presented in the AFT journal are valid and hold true part of the time, but they might not be equally operational in every academic setting.

Finally, Westhues (cited in Gravois, 2006) stated, "Tenure is supposed to protect scholars from outside control, but it does a lousy job of protecting them from one another!" (p. 10). Westhues suggested that to estimate one's risk of being mobbed in academia, one need only look at the many ways that one "shows others up," including "publications, teaching scores, social connections, eloquence, wit, writing skills, athletic skills, computer skills, family, age, class, pedigree, looks, house, clothes, spouse, children, and sex appeal. Any of these will do!" (Gravois, 2006, p. 10). Westhues concluded that academic cultures need to be developed so that members of academic communities are aware of the competitive in themselves and others because many of these tendencies can be harmful and destructive to peers.

Other Risk Professions

Even though data are slow to emerge and difficult to locate concerning mobbing in other professions and arenas, one extensive study of employees including human services and civil service workers was conducted in Denmark in 2004–2005. Goals of the study (Ortega et al., 2009) were to estimate the prevalence of bullying and to identify risk groups in a population. Job classifications were divided into 13 major groups:

- academics
- teaching professionals
- technicians
- health professionals and health-care workers
- social work professionals
- managers
- clerks
- shop and market sales workers
- service workers (housekeeping and restaurant)
- protective service workers (fire, police, prison guards, military)
- skilled industrial workers
- unskilled industrial workers
- drivers

A total of 15 industrial groups were identified:

- agriculture, fishing, and quarrying
- manufacturing
- electricity, gas, and water supply
- construction
- wholesale and retail trade
- hotels and restaurants

- transport, post, and telecommunication
- financing and insurance
- letting (leasing) and sale of real estate
- public administration
- education
- human health care
- social work in institutions
- social work with noninstitutionalized clients
- others (for example, associations, culture, and waste disposal)

Unskilled workers and industrial workers were the most likely workers to have been bullied (9 percent). The comparative lower prevalence of bullying from superiors was interpreted to be a function of the low power-distance and feminine values that may characterize a Scandinavian workplace (Einarsen, cited in Ortega et al., 2009). About 7 percent of social work professionals reported experiencing bullying at some time in the preceding year, lower than the average for the entire group. No significant gender or age differences were found in the prevalence of bullying, but significant differences in occupational status and work processes were found. Some of these included the following:

- Unskilled workers reported the highest prevalence of bullying.
- Managers and supervisors reported the lowest prevalence of bullying.
- People working with things (that is, male-dominated professions) and people working with clients (that is, female-dominated professions) reported higher levels of bullying than those who worked with symbols or customers (Ortega et al., 2009).

The most likely age ranges targeted for abuse seemed to be those respondents from 40 to 49 years of age (31 percent) and from 50 to 59 years of age (30 percent). These risk-age ranges are somewhat consistent with earlier references showing older workers to be more at risk. This is inconsistent with findings from at least one other study that suggested younger, entry-level workers in low-level positions are more at risk.

A limited study of public-sector employees in New South Wales by Shallcross, Sheehan, and Ramsay (2008) examined the experiences of workplace mobbing. Unlike many survey methods to determine the prevalence and extent of workplace bullying, the Australian researchers conducted a qualitative analysis of members of a small support group that met regularly over a 12-month period. All eight participants had been forced to exit from their positions. Data were obtained through intensive interviews that lasted from one and a half to two hours and were transcribed with the consent of the participants. Five themes reflecting the experiences of mobbing emerged in the interviews, including the culture of public-sector jobs, abuse that was displayed in a covert or passive manner, actual mobbing that led to expulsion from the workplace, serious impacts on coping strategies ultimately affecting health, and workplace policies or procedures that were unfair or objectionable.

The most common theme was that of public-sector culture, characterized by inadequate staffing and high turnover. Employees reported that the public agency to which they reported was often called upon to justify its services, and staff felt that the services were not valued (Shallcross et al., 2008). The list of grievances reported by participants included the devaluation of cultural differences, unfounded accusations, management perpetuation and condoning of flawed appointment processes, and abuse of both power and position. Responses from participants would seem to support the position of Gummer and Edwards (1995, in Ginsberg & Keys, 1995) that the politics of public service organizations create inherent stresses that can place the organization at risk. The small sample size and the qualitative features of the study provided some inherent limitations; nonetheless, the information helps to round out the portrayal of work life in the public sector.

HIGH-STRESS ORGANIZATIONS CAN PRESENT ADDITIONAL RISKS OF MOBBING

Many work environments are high-stress ones. However, emotional bullying does not occur in all of them. What then, is the relationship between stress and bullying?

Davenport et al. (2002) suggested that people in high-stress environments can be mobbed at every level of the organization if they are not able to keep up with the demands placed on them. Supervisors may be perpetrators of mobbing if demands from higher administration are unreasonable. Subordinates may bully each other or may bully someone who supervises them if they believe those supervisors are responsible for increased workplace stress.

Salin (2003a) highlighted the role of stress in current work environments that are typified by restructuring, downsizing, layoffs, compressed promotional opportunities, increased workloads, internal competition, and lowered job security. These types of stress tend to lower individual and collective thresholds for aggression and can increase the perceived benefits of bullying others for both relief and personal gain.

Stewart (2007) proposed an integrative framework for understanding workplace stress and workplace aggression. The author suggested that although speculation about the causes of workplace aggression can be found throughout professional and lay literature, few theoretical orientations had previously provided an understanding of the antecedents of workplace aggression. Stewart's framework divided the precursors of aggression at work into four categories:

- *Individual characteristics* include self-attributed aggression, attitudes toward revenge, locus of control, type A personality, and negative affect.
- *Situational stressors* include organizational constraints and quantitative workload, role conflict and role ambiguity, organizational injustice, and psychological contract violation.
- *Cognition characteristics* include conditional reasoning and JMs.
- *Affect characteristics* include frustration, job dissatisfaction, arousal, and anxiety.

Social psychology authors Neuman and Baron (2002) identified social ante-cedents of bullying and aggression from a "social-interactionist" perspective. They suggested that a number of workplace norms will all serve as antecedents of workplace bullying. These included reciprocity (do unto others as others have done to you), perceptions of injustice, norm violations, distributive and perceived injustice, and frustration. Neuman and Baron (2002) also addressed the issue of stress and its relationship to aggression and physical violence. In a 1998 study, they collected data suggesting that individuals who reported having been treated unfairly by their supervisors were much more likely to engage in some sort of workplace aggression than were those who reported being satisfied with the treatment they received. In addition, the aggression was likely to be directed against the source of the perceived injustice. For example, if an employee was unhappy with outcomes controlled by the organization, such as job security, pay, benefits, and general work conditions, that person would be more likely to behave aggressively toward the whole organization (for example, engaging in theft or vandalism). However, when the dissatisfaction was with a particular manager or boss and involved such things as respect, fair treatment, support, or guidance, aggrieved workers were more likely to behave aggressively toward that manager or boss.

An attempt at identifying and reducing workplace stress was used via an extensive multiyear study of the U.S. Department of Veterans Affairs (VA). The study (Kowalski, Harmon, Yorks, & Kowalski, 1998) examined the role of macro-level (that is, organizational-level) stress and its relationship to aggression. Earlier that year, a VA central-level employee-relations specialist had hypothesized a rela-tionship between discrimination complaints, grievances, workers' compensation claims, stress, and workplace violence. Prior to that time, the VA had not addressed the root causes of these concerns. A research team developed a statistical model from prior survey data (archival data), identified issues affecting daily business activities within the VA, and then examined the relationship between daily busi-ness to both stress and aggression. Surveys were distributed to 7,000 workers at 11 worksites, with workforce numbers ranging from 30 to 3,000 per site. Offending behaviors were inventoried, including such things as "the silent treatment" and "glaring." Although many staff had not previously considered these actions as aggressive, they were able to acknowledge how upset they felt when they were the targets of these actions. Eight work-climate factors were identified as the root causes of stress, aggression, turnover, use of sick leave, and costs of service delivery, as well as job satisfaction:

- involvement
- goal alignment
- creativity and improvement
- information and communication
- supervisory trust and supportiveness
- development
- respect and fairness
- structures of work tasks

The VA study was a very practical field study designed to address and correct problems in the organization's functioning rather than attempt to establish academic evidence. The intervention proposed was to develop and deploy action teams within the VA that worked on improving organizational functioning at both the local and national levels. The success of this intervention is discussed in a later chapter on workplace interventions, but it can be said at this juncture that actions teams are known to be helpful.

Social workers have been involved in MSD teams for the past few decades. As previously mentioned, group debriefing can be useful in helping emergency response staff to recover from the aftermath of a disaster (Armstrong et al., 1995). In the MSD model, group debriefing is provided to emergency workers who are not considered ill but who have a common goal. These workers are encouraged to share their experiences in a group setting, and leaders or facilitators may be more or less directive. Social workers very typically provide these MSD services after a disaster has occurred. What may be equally relevant but much less examined is that social workers and other interventionists could also be helpful in aiding organizations to recover from the disaster of emotional abuse of its employees. This could be accomplished by helping the surviving work group to identify their common experiences, to gain support from each other, and to learn from what has happened.

Is workplace stress related to workplace bullying? Is it a causal or antecedent condition? Is stress an organizational consequence of emotional abuse of members of the workforce? Or is it correlative only? These questions have not been definitively answered, but one could certainly conclude that workplace stress and employee bullying are related. Whatever the relationship, theorists and practitioners alike would agree that there is a need for intervention and prevention.

ETHICS AND RISK ENVIRONMENTS

Ethics and risk environments can be synonymous when assessing a workplace for potential for abuse. Einarsen (1999) suggested that whether a behavior is understood, tolerated, or accepted ultimately depends on the culture of the organization where the behavior occurs. Davenport et al. (2002) stated that

> when unethical activities, such as endangering employees, client, or the environment, or conducting shady financial transactions are being exposed by employees, they may be mobbed for whistle-blowing. Rather than openly and truthfully dealing with the problem, a company fears primarily for its reputation and the short-term bottom line, and less for the harm it might inflict. (p. 68)

It is generally inferred from available literature that culture and climate of an organization are significant variables in workplace bullying. A study published in the *Journal of Business Ethics* (Bulutlar & Öz, 2009) examined the effects of bullying behavior upon the relationship between ethical climates and organizational commitments. Climates refers to practices and procedures that are shared among organizational members. They represent organizational variables, not individual or psychological ones. Moran and Volkwein (Bulutlar & Öz, 2009) defined climate as a product of member interaction that represents a collective perception of autonomy, trust, cohesiveness, support, recognition, innovation, and fairness. Climate helps a person to interpret situations. It reflects prevalent norms of the organization and is a major influence upon shaping behavior.

Various climates exist in the workplace. One of these is the climate of organizational ethics (Martin & Cullen, cited in Bulutlar & Öz, 2009). Ethical climates will influence decision making, conflict-resolution strategies, and behavior standards. Ethical climate refers to those perceptions of typical organizational practice and procedures that have ethical intent (Bulutlar & Öz, 2009). Three dimensions of ethical reasoning were proposed by Victor and Cullen (Bulutlar & Öz, 2009): *egotism*, *utilitarianism*, and *deontology*. Egotism means self-interest in behavior. Utilitarianism, or benevolence, considers the most good for the greatest number of people. Finally, deontology, or principle theory, deals with rules, law, codes, and procedures that specify decisions and actions for the good of others. These concepts provide explicit ethical guidelines for decision making.

Martin and Cullen (2006, in Bulutlar & Öz, 2009) proposed five more guidelines for assessing ethical climates: instrumental, caring, independence, laws and codes, and rules. These five constructs serve as implicit guidelines for ethical decisions, rather than the more explicit ones discussed earlier, suggested by Victor and Cullen (1988, in Bulutlar & Öz, 2009). As Martin and Cullen indicated, a climate in which people act from an egoistic perspective, with workers doing anything necessary to maximize their own benefit without consideration for others, will be a fertile environment for harming others to increase one's own status. When such a climate exists, it is normal for people to act without consideration for the well-being of others, placing their self-interest first at any cost. When bullying behavior is not tolerated by any formal or informal norms or rules, bullying is far less likely to occur.

Wimbush and Shepard (1994, in Bulutlar & Öz, 2009) posited that a close link exists between employee behavior and the ethical climate of the organization. In particular, ethical climate is a predictor of unethical behavior, deviance, or both (Peterson, 2002, in Bulutlar & Öz, 2009). Ethical climates that promote self-interest above organizational health and social responsibility are far more likely to have bullying problems.

A 2009 study designed to examine ethics was conducted in Turkey by Bulutlar & Öz. The educational levels of respondents suggested that bullying targets are *not* just employees with low skills and low education. Over two-thirds of bullying targets who responded held undergraduate degrees, and almost 25 percent held graduate degrees, which indicated that higher education is *not* a protective factor. Results of the study indicated a relationship between ethical climates, affective (that is, emotional) commitment, and bullying in the workplace. Findings suggested that people with higher stages of moral development tend to behave more ethically. Those at lower stages of moral development will more likely behave unethically (Bulutlar & Öz, 2009). Other researchers have posited that unethical behavior among individuals will be limited if their relationship is of long duration.

Logically, the longer the relationship, the *greater* the degree of accountability people will tend to have to each other (Harvey et al., 2009).

Global organizations seem to be at greater risk for ethical breaches precisely because of this lack of accountability. Foreign assignments might be located in remote regions in the world where legal environments are still in development. An example is that the "rights of workers" is an evolving concept in many, if not most, emerging economies around the globe (Harvey et al., 2009).

According to Wornham (2003), school systems are surprisingly high-risk environments for ethical violations, suggesting that the pressure to produce results and pressures to demote the rights of teachers are commonplace in educational work settings. The recent conviction of educators in Georgia for manipulating student test scores is an example. Competition between schools and between districts adds to the pressure. The workplace in the 21st century is typified by long working hours, continuous change, and increased workload. All these factors can increase the likelihood of teacher harassment. Although teachers are expected to set good examples for children and students, their own rights might be minimized so that ethical treatment is not guaranteed. According to Wornham, as of 2003, bullied victims in the United Kingdom believed that perpetrators would rarely be sanctioned and that management would not take action in cases of bullying. They also thought that an absence of direct legal protection for those suffering workplace victimization contributed to stress-related injury related to work.

Ethical considerations were examined by a group of 40 new Polish MBA graduates who had completed a course sponsored by the Poznan University of Economics in partnership with Georgia State University, Atlanta (Ryan, 2006). Although the study collected opinions of ethical issues within HR management (HRM) in Poland, a large number of literature citations gave validity to this qualitative analysis. Many respondents commented on how the recent history and rapid cultural changes of the former Soviet Bloc nations had affected the field of HRM, itself a very new discipline and field of academic study. The Ryan study is an opportunity to look at the evolutionary changes as a country shifts from socialist, outside rule to an autonomous and mostly capitalistic system.

To describe recent (20th century) cultural attitudes, Wasowicz (cited in Ryan, 2006) explained that Poland as a nation has historically been very bitter while it was governed by others. According to recent history, for more 100 years Poles chose passive resistance, which was reflected in attitudes toward work. Regarding Polish attitudes toward the law, especially after World War II and Polish socialism, Ryan's interviewees said, "Their laws were 'their laws, not our laws.' They were unjust laws and one is not obliged to observe unjust law" (Ryan, 2006, p. 278). A game-type strategy developed in Polish communities in which people were invested in circumventing the law but went to great lengths to avoid detection. Unfortunately, 45 years later, when a democratically elected parliament passed new laws that were distinctly Polish laws, the practice and motivation to resist laws persisted (Ryan, 2006). Under Soviet influence, "there were *never any incentives* for the workers, managers, and companies to improve their performance, as long as they met production quotas" (Dobruc, cited in Ryan, 2006, p. 278). In addition to the job security most Poles enjoyed under Soviet domination, most workers enjoyed additional human services supports, including cash loans from employers for household goods, holiday parties, access to vacation property, and gifts for children of workers. During these years, HR departments were not engaged in managing HR—they handled only administrative functions, including record keeping. HR staff workers were required to have only low-level skills, and their duties revolved around keeping intricate and accurate records of employee data, demographics, and activities. For many years, during the socialist era, HR departments collected and maintained data records *against* people that could be retrieved at any moment. These records could have a significant effect on social well-being for state-approved permissions, such as for purchasing an automobile or home, receiving a passport, and traveling. During those years, HR departments were useful to socialist aims, sometimes denouncing people to legal authorities when information was obtained (Ryan, 2006).

Only recently have Polish organizational and governmental leaders begun to understand the impact of HR practices on organizational functioning and profits. Like other economies favoring employers over workers during bad economic times, high unemployment rates in all but the large urban centers of Warsaw, Poznan, and Kraków in the 1990s left workers vulnerable. Polish labor laws began to address worker protections and rights. Revised in 1997, they protected workers against a number of potential workplace abuses, yet the Ryan (2006) study highlighted some specific ethical areas in which "ethics in business are still developing" (Josefowski, cited in Ryan, 2006):

- Ethical issues in recruiting candidates for jobs—procedures not transparent. Family, friends, and political connections still favored.
- Ethical issues in hiring—discrimination in hiring women. Unmarried women face ongoing personal questions about their marital plans and plans for childbirth.
- Age discrimination.
- Ethical issues in job status—employers often prefer to contract for labor rather than hire employees and incur fiscal and social security costs.
- Ethical issues in performance evaluations and opportunities for promotion.
- Abuses of authority.
- Mobbing, a term introduced in Polish labor law under socialist rule in 1974.

Like other definitions of mobbing, Polish definitions include the notion that

> mobbing describes actions relating to the employee or directed against the employee, which consist of persistent and sustained harassment or intimidation of the employee, resulting in the employee's feelings of diminished professional usefulness, causing or aimed at humiliating or ridiculing the employee, isolating or placing him outside the workers community. (Article 94.2, Polish Labor Code, 1974, in Ryan, 2006, p. 288)

The law also declares that it is the employer's obligation to protect workers from mobbing and to take action if and when it occurs. In addition, in January 2004 the following was added to the code: "When mobbing is the cause of an employee's health disorder, the employee can demand compensation for pain and suffering from the employer" (Article 94.3, cited in Ryan, 2006, p. 288).

The Polish Labor Code also specifies that when an employee leaves an employment situation or contract on the grounds of mobbing, then the affected employee can demand compensation from an employer. The amount of the compensation to be awarded cannot be lower than the minimum salary described in other provisions of the law. Compensation guidelines are written into code, and an employee cannot be offered or expect to take a compensation amount than is less than what is dictated by law (Ryan, 2006).

In addition to the ethical deficits described earlier, Ryan (2006) cited corruption, bribery, misrepresentation (that is, lying) on job applications, inflating productivity and sales information, and false documentation for illness as areas of additional ethical breaches. Analysis of the data from the opinion surveys in the Ryan report concluded that because the future for HRM will necessitate change and new technologies, ethical considerations might be easily overlooked but that ethical problems continue to emerge. These need remediation. Mobbing prevention has been part of Polish labor law for over 35 years, but the problem has persisted and perhaps *worsened* as the Polish economy shifted from state-managed to privately managed organizations. While things were not better under Soviet domination, ethical concerns, including mobbing, have stayed the same or worsened since the breakup of the Soviet Union.

Are poor, low, or ineffective ethical practices always a risk for emotional abuse at work? Perhaps not, but if the workplace culture tolerates or supports bullying while failing to limit bullying, it will be more likely to occur. Whether the organization's ethical practices are whole and transparent or questionable, the fact that bullying may have become "normalized" makes it hard for the victim to challenge it (Stevenson et al., 2006).

D. Yamada (2009) commented that policies and procedures are necessary to address ethics in general and mobbing in particular. Citing Felblinger (2009), this study concluded that there are no ideal or proven models. Lamenting that there is minimal research to guide creating and implementing good programs for prevention and remediation, D. Yamada (2009) cautioned that those who embrace the challenge of program development need to act inclusively and transparently and take advantage of the wisdom of experienced stakeholders.

HIGH-RISK ORGANIZATIONAL STRUCTURES, TRAITS, BEHAVIORS, AND DYNAMICS

High-risk organizational structures, traits, behaviors, and dynamics are examined by a number of theorists. Well-loved author, academic, and theorist Stephen R. Covey (1991) emphasized the importance of understanding *driving* and *restraining* forces, or those influences that push and resist action. A debate persists about best practices for healthy organizations. Is it better to increase driving forces or decrease restraining forces? The answers may not always be clear.

Wornham (2003) suggested that the 21st century workplace, with its long hours and constant change, can lead to increased risk for harassment. A French study in 2008 (Niedhammer, Chastang, & David) examined psychosocial work factors on general health outcomes. In this large study of over 24,000 employees, the use of sick leave and long sickness absence were all associated with low decision latitude, high psychological demands, low social support, and the prevalence of bullying.

Theorists are not in agreement about the organizational features related to workplace bullying. Koonin and Green, cited in Geffner et al. (2004), highlighted several organizational factors associated with the perpetuation of mobbing. These included dynamics such as office politics, lack of clear performance expectations, outright dishonesty, failure to provide needed information so employees can do their jobs, rude or discourteous responses to workers, acceptance of poor work quality, and lack of appreciation for staff.

Einarsen (cited in Heames & Harvey, 2006) suggested that workplace and organizational stresses will make bullying more likely. Leymann (1990) identified deficits in leadership practices to be one of the primary factors in workplace bullying. Several significant issues must be confronted when dealing with workplace bullying, including how the workplace responds to bullying when it occurs, how the workplace tolerates or prohibits bullying, how bullying affects the culture or the organization, and the organization's reputation when tolerating or prohibiting bullying (Heames & Harvey, 2006).

Skogstad, Matthiesen, and Einarsen (2007) suggested a number of organizational and leadership features of risk environments, including role conflict, employees' lack of control, work pressures, job insecurity, a competitive and critical organizational climate, and destructive leadership styles, such as autocratic and laissez-faire leadership.

A relationship between bullying and organizational change has been suggested by Baron and Neuman (cited in Skogstad et al., 2007). In a study of 178 full-time employees, correlations were found between a number of organizational changes and an increase in workplace aggression. Some of the changes included use of part-time staff, pay cuts or freezes, management changes, increased diversity, and increased monitoring of employees (Baron & Neuman, cited in Skogstad et al., 2007). Leymann claimed that the four common factors in creating a work climate at risk for emotional abuse are deficiencies in work design, deficiency in leadership behavior, a socially exposed position of the victim, and a low moral standard of the workplace (Leymann, 1993, in Einarsen, 1999).

Roscigno et al. (2009) hypothesized that bullies will emerge in organizations where chaos is prevalent but will emerge less frequently in organizations where "guardianship" is established by rules and governed by laws, including bureaucratic procedures and union agreements. Findings from a team of four researchers who examined the dimensions of workplace bullying, organizational characteristics, and dynamics of group interactions suggested that bullies do tend to emerge in organizational environments typified by chaos, especially when few capable "guardians" (as defined earlier) exist. These findings point to a serious lack of agreement about organizations at risk. In spite of this lack of certainty, a number of workplace characteristics have been studied. Several are discussed here.

HIGH-RISK EMOTIONAL CLIMATES IN WORK ENVIRONMENTS

What is known about the emotional climate of work environments that are most at risk? While structure and practice create risk from a work-design perspective, one can reasonably assume that workplace climate and culture also contribute to the likelihood of bullying. Climate and culture refer more to what it *feels like* to work in an organization. What are some of these qualities?

Davenport et al. (2002) suggested that a number of factors contribute to risk, the most significant being management's excessive bottom-line orientation, poor communication channels, poor teamwork, and insufficient diversity education. Other risk factors include stress-intensive environments, monotonous tasks, disbelief by managers, organizations involved in unethical activities, and flat organizations in which ambitious people have few opportunities to excel. Factors in the life cycle of an organization can be risks as well. Events such as downsizing, restructuring, acquisitions, and mergers can also be times of organizational vulnerability.

Processes including workplace deficiencies and scapegoating are identified as risk conditions, as are low perceived costs for bullying behavior. Formal and informal power differences are risk factors for bullying, along with high internal competition, a politicized climate, and certain types of reward systems (Salin, 2003a). Tepper et al. (2006) suggested that when employees have high levels of negative affect and supervisors have low "procedural justice" (that is, perception of fairness), abusive supervision is more likely to occur.

A number of theorists posit that workers are more likely to behave aggressively if they perceive that an injustice has occurred. This is particularly true if perpetrators, including bullies, feel their aggression is justified (Beugre, 2005). Another fairly obvious workplace trait would be organizations in which high degrees of conflict exists.

While context is not the only determinant of individual behavior, it does matter. Namie and Namie (2011) identified a number of factors correlated with high bullying risk, including fund scarcity, cutthroat cultures, a personality mix including those with narcissistic or exploitative traits, and lack of employer response or responsibility. If aggression is rewarded, it will persist.

PSYCHODYNAMICS OF ORGANIZATIONS

Czander (1993) examined organizational structures of decision-making systems, control systems, political systems, and informational systems. He suggested that structure becomes the skeleton for providing needed order in organizations and helps the organization meet its goals. From a psychoanalytical perspective, danger and anxiety are lessened when a structure is established that contains minimal *denial* or *projection* and that the functions of the organization are *not* designed merely to fulfill unconscious wishes of its members. Czander suggested that the psychodynamics associated with authority will affect many aspects of organizational

functioning, including communications, decision making, understanding moti-
vational factors of subordinates, and understanding employees' capacities for
cooperation and compliance. He further stated that the allocation and structural
arrangements of authority in an organization have an impact on organizational
practices and effectiveness and, in most cases, operate ineffectively. Czander identified three types of authority "constellations" found in organizations:

- highly controlling and assertive constellations, where freedom from fear
  is promised via perfect compliance with the superior's directives
- maternal "nurturance" and support constellations, where the superior
  gains some gratification through processes of giving and receiving affection
- friendly, egalitarian constellations, where the superior's behavior appears
  to be more permissive and open but in actuality creates suspicion and
  covers fears of reprisals

While all of these modes can present challenges, Czander claimed that the
most puzzling practice of supervisory behavior is when the supervisor uses his or
her position to psychologically play on the emotional vulnerability of a subordinate to increase the supervisor's own psychological gratification. The experience
of authority under the best conditions generally still leaves subordinates with
anxiety about the limits of the relationship (Czander, 1993). Such would be the
case with an emotionally abusive leader. Subordinates have limited comfort in
most supervisory relationships, but discomfort increases significantly with abuse
of power.

HIGH-RISK MANAGEMENT AND LEADERSHIP STYLES

Management and leadership styles are the subjects of students and experts in
organizational psychology. Risk-prone leaders and risk-prone leadership styles
simply ignore basic tenets of good leadership, but there may be more specific
characteristics to consider.

Valle (2005) has suggested that it may be possible to predict the extent to
which supervisors will engage in abusive supervision. Abusive supervision takes
many forms, but is usually an ongoing series of hostile treatment toward employees (Tepper, cited in Valle, 2005). Another theorist described abusive supervisors as
demonstrating "petty tyranny" (Ashforth, 1997, in Valle, 2005). According to both
Tepper and Ashforth, tyrannical supervision is associated with lower job and life
satisfaction, lower work commitment, work–family conflict, and increased job stress.

In a study of U.S. National Guard members and military supervisors, Tepper
et al. (2006) examined supervisor–subordinate dyads via survey instruments. Variables examined abusive supervision, perception of procedural injustice by supervisors, and negative affect in subordinates. Findings suggested that when employees
have high negative affect—that is, high levels of anxiety, distress, dissatisfaction,
submissiveness, insecurity, and little able to protect themselves—they are more
likely to be targeted for emotional abuse. Supervisors were more abusive if they

perceive low levels of *procedural justice* and if they experience depression. Measures of procedural justice included statements such as "My organization uses procedures that collect accurate information to make decisions" and "My organization makes decisions in an unbiased manner." Supervisors who experience depression as a *result of procedural injustice* were more likely to abuse subordinates in the field. An example of such procedural injustice might be an incident where a supervisor uses due process in the discipline of a subordinate, then has the discipline overturned by a more senior administrator. These data contrast with those from other studies that suggest depression as an effect and not a cause. In supervisory bullying, it may be that abusive supervisors are triggered by a perception that procedures in their organizations lack fairness and objectivity.

Davenport et al. (2002) cited examples of bad management that are likely to contribute to, or allow for, mobbing to persist. These include excessive emphasis on profits and outcomes with little regard for the people doing the work, hierarchical workplace infrastructures, lack of communication channels, inadequate conflict-resolution practices, lack of clear grievance procedures, poor leadership, poor teamwork, little diversity education, and a scapegoat mentality.

Landmark work by Salin (2003a) identified bullying from a power-imbalance perspective and suggested that formal power imbalances are a prerequisite of bullying. Without such an imbalance, the author suggests that the target might be able to resist an attack. Salin also posited that "petty tyranny" by leaders may not be limited only to vertical aggression (that is, top-down) and that power imbalances can exist between peers.

Boyett and Boyett (1998) identified leadership practices likely to produce failure. These include short-term "fixes" to organizational problems, allocating resources based on greed, overemphasis on competition in the workplace, ignoring organizational gridlock, addressing problems rather than the sources of problems, drift of organizational goals, limiting organizational success, and failure to plan for investments.

Namie and Namie (2003) stated that "good employers purge bullies, bad ones promote them" (p. 33). Sadly, this is often true. To the degree that employers ignore or reward inappropriate behaviors, bullies can rise within an organizational hierarchy. Characteristics of management behaviors that ignore bullying include denial of the existence of bullying, confusion about the nature of bullying or how to deal with it, a focus on external appearances instead of quality organizational functioning, management's inability to acknowledge that it does not have all the answers, disregard for employees' feelings, lack of ethics, poor communication practices, and muddied thinking about prevention or remediation (Namie & Namie, 2003).

Koonin and Green (cited in Geffner et al., 2004) posited that laissez-faire leadership practices and lack of accountability for corporate culture are those organizational conditions most likely to ignore or even support bullying. Abusive supervision, then, is a phenomenon that can be identified between an employee and supervisor or between several employees. Results of a study of Dutch police officers suggest that conflict-management styles, along with qualities of agreeableness, can be measured for effectiveness in attempts at persuading others. Outcomes suggested that people use a whole range of complex problem-solving methods, even within a single incident or event, to persuade others. The effectiveness of any one technique was generally determined by a combination of approaches.

Managers must be cautious about counseling or confronting managers who bully their subordinates, because bullying managers are not easy for *anyone* to approach or tolerate, regardless of hierarchy or leadership styles in organizations (Westhues, 2005b). There is also an unspoken notion that one must not interfere with a peer's parallel territory. People also generally do not want to get involved with subordinates not under their direct command. Most people would rather the organizational infrastructure take care of employee matters. An organizational leader who condones aggressive tactics will contribute to the likelihood that bullying and mobbing will become entrenched behaviors within the organization (Westhues, 2005b).

Covey (1991) identified characteristics of principle-centered leaders—that is, good leaders—as follows:

- They are continually learning and developing new skills.
- They are service oriented by thinking of others and seeing their life work as a "mission."
- They are positive, optimistic, and upbeat.
- They see potential in other people and believe in the ability for others to grow.
- Their own lives are balanced and full.
- Because their security comes from within, they view life as an adventure to be enjoyed and savored.
- They are productive in creative and innovative ways.
- They exercise their bodies, minds, spirits, and emotions to keep them alive and functioning.

Covey held that it is likely that risk-prone leaders and risk-prone leadership styles ignore these basic tenets of good leadership. In contrast to principle-centered leaders, risk-prone leaders or ineffective leaders tend to be reactive and self-doubting. Instead of owning responsibility for outcomes, they tend to blame others. Instead of being proactive and planful, risk-prone leaders work without clear goals and objectives. Rather than looking for optimal outcomes for all, risk-prone leaders think "win–lose." Risk-prone leaders respond with a need to be understood rather than understanding others. Finally, poor leaders generally have a deep fear of change (Covey, 1991).

One of the most significant conditions present in most bullying situations can be leadership deficiencies (Leymann, 1996, in Heames & Harvey, 2006). The specific leadership deficiencies resulting in emotional abuse in the organization include a high tolerance for negative, hurtful behavior. A 1997 study in the United Kingdom found that 73 percent of workers surveyed believed that management was fully aware of bullying situations but remained "inactive"—that is, did nothing (Wornham, 2003). Deficiencies in leadership practices, including tyrannical leadership styles, are obvious flaws that can be part of a process of emotional abuse. The same could be said about insensitive or arrogant demeanor in the treatment of employees (Giorgi, 2009). What may not be as obvious, however, is that a laissez-faire style has also been associated with emotional abuse at work. Leadership's reluctance to recognize or take action when bullying is reported gives the impression that bullying is tolerated in the organization (Giorgi, 2009). Skogstad et al. (2007, in Giorgi, 2009) suggested that leadership's failure to mediate in role conflict, role ambiguity, and conflicts between coworkers is associated with bullying.

Valle studied high-risk leadership traits in a sample of 77 full-time employees at a medium-sized university in the southeastern United States. Respondents were self-selected as part of a university-wide call for research subjects and completed online surveys about supervisor–subordinate relationships. A seven-item Leader–Member Exchange (LMX) Scale (Scandura et al., 1986, in Valle, 2005) included examples such as "My supervisor understands my problems and my needs" and "My working relationship with my supervisor is extremely effective." Items were scored using a five-point Likert-type scale, with responses ranging from 1 = strongly disagree to 5 = strongly agree. The LMX Scale was analyzed for internal consistency. A number of supervisory profiles emerged from the data. The Cronbach's alpha internal consistency reliability estimates were as follows:

- demeaning behavior: 0.83
- denying behavior: 0.81
- delaying behavior: 0.85
- lying behavior: 0.83
- harassing behavior: 0.17

Job satisfaction and intent to leave were also measured. The conclusions indicated that poor supervisor–subordinate relations lead to a perception of emotional abuse in the supervisor–subordinate dyad and an intention to leave the job (Valle, 2005).

In a study conducted by Hauge et al. (2011), more than 10,000 Norwegian employees were surveyed using self-report questionnaires. The predictors of workplace bullying in this study included domains such as leadership practices (fairness in task assignment and treatment), leadership support (availability of supervisors to assist staff with work-related problems), and role conflict (lack of clear goals and objectives within job descriptions). As predicted by researchers, workplace bullying was largely explained by work-environment conditions, including the lack of fair and supportive leadership, role ambiguity, and generally stressful work conditions.

A construct for understanding leadership styles was defined by Bruch and Ghoshal (2002). Conceptualizing the influence of both *focus* (or concentrated attention) and *energy* (or vigor fueled by personal commitment), the authors suggested that both are positive traits but that neither alone can result in a purposeful organization or a purposeful leadership style. Using combinations of the traits, they described the four types of managers as:

- low focus, low energy—the *procrastinators*
- high focus, low energy—the *disengaged*

- low focus, high energy—the *distracted*
- high focus, high energy—the *purposeful*

Procrastinators will perform routine tasks, but when an important decision or action is needed, they hesitate until the moment for action has passed. In extreme instances, procrastinators can be chronically passive. About 30 percent of all managers are actually procrastinators (Seligman, cited in Bruch & Ghoshal, 2002).

Disengaged managers have high focus but low levels of energy. Some are exhausted and cannot reenergize themselves. They may have strong reservations about tasks they are asked to perform. Disengaged managers use a type of "defensive action," convincing themselves that problems do not exist rather than addressing them. They may refuse to take action even when it is clearly needed. Disengaged managers account for about 20 percent of all leaders (Bruch & Ghoshal, 2002).

Distracted managers can have good intentions and high energy but are unfocused. They may confuse appropriate action with chaotic activity. Since they do not generally slow down to reflect on their actions, they have trouble creating new and adaptive strategies as new problems emerge. By far the largest group, distracted managers make up more than 40 percent of all managers. "Distracted mangers feel a desperate need to do something—anything. That makes them as dangerous as the proverbial bull in a china shop" (Bruch & Ghoshal, 2002, p. 9).

Finally, purposeful managers have both energy and focus. They put effort into work but also achieve critical milestones more than other types of managers. Purposeful managers take organizational needs seriously but also invest themselves with personal responsibility for accomplishment. In addition to high levels of productivity and accomplishment, purposeful leaders seem to find ways to manage their stress and recharge themselves when energy levels are depleting. In fact, they tend to be effective in conserving and channeling their energy and that of others (Bruch & Ghoshal, 2002). Unfortunately, purposeful managers make up only 10 percent or less of those in leadership positions.

Can leadership practices and profiles contribute to or mediate the presence and long-term effects of workplace emotional abuse? Clearly the answer is "yes." D. Yamada (2009) concluded, "We need ethical leaders who will stand against psychologically abusive workplace behaviors, even when it is not convenient to do so" (p. 36).

SUMMARY

While this is not an exhaustive review and analysis of high-risk organizational characteristics, some patterns appear to exist that predict the likelihood of workplace bullying. The notion of high-risk personality types who are targets for bullying does not seem to be substantiated by the literature or studies included in this chapter. While the bullies themselves may share some characteristics, it is not at all clear that there is a personality "type" for bullying. It appears, then, that as in most other human interactions, context matters.

Organizational dynamics might be the best predictors for the emergence of bullying. Organizations at high risk are those that

- value profits above people,
- do not encourage longevity on the job,
- make increasingly difficult demands on workers, and
- severely limit employee autonomy and freedom and foster dishonest practices.

While it may not be possible to prevent all of these organizational vulnerabilities, the presence of guardians, safeguards, and controls may help to minimize risk exposure. Some of these will be explored in chapter 7.

5

Reactions of Victims to Emotional Abuse at Work

Diagnostic criteria for several psychological disorders have been found to result from or co-occur with workplace emotional abuse. This chapter addresses the initial response to abused workers by clinical professionals. It includes risk assessment, crisis management, medical referrals, ensuring safety and survival, and creating a therapeutic alliance with an injured worker. This chapter will help readers understand the initial approaches treatment professionals should utilize when working with targets of emotional abuse at work and the array of relevant diagnoses when a person is the victim of workplace mobbing.

TARGETS' RESPONSES TO BULLYING

Why do targets feel such deep hurt in response to workplace mobbing? It is because targets of workplace humiliation are often good employees who do their work well and have a strong commitment to jobs (Davenport et al., 2002). Employees who are good at their professions are also often very committed to the workplace and may try harder for a longer period of time to survive their circumstances, no matter how intimidating or even brutal. This effort to hang on can add to confusion and feelings of betrayal.

Typical reactions to bullying include feeling isolated, confused, and even paranoid. Initial symptoms can include symptoms such as poor concentration, sleep or appetite problems, and irritability—all symptoms of mild to moderate depression. When bullying persists, more pronounced psychophysiological symptoms develop, including hypertension, digestive disorders, more severe sleep problems and appetite disturbances, extreme fearfulness, and even substance-use disorders. Finally, in the most severe and persistent instances, panic attacks, severe depression, accidents, and even heart attacks and suicide can be the outcome (Davenport et al., 2002).

In a study examining individual experiences and responses to workplace bullying (Buttigieg, Bryant, Hanley, & Liu, 2011), a small sample of workers who had been emotionally injured at work and who had filed complaints at an Australia-based legal center underwent a series of in-depth interviews. To obtain insight about the subjective experiences of bullying, a qualitative method using semi-structured interviews looked to themes within the context of respondents' values and experiences. Respondents identified the types of bullying as verbal abuse, unfair management practices, unfair dismissals, unfair workloads, having needed information withheld, oppressive monitoring, social ostracism, and practices that reduced take-home pay for workers.

Because targets usually feel social isolation in response to their experiences, self-blame is a common reaction. If peer witnesses, institutional "helpers," and senior managers side with the bully or bullies, victims can feel hopeless and begin to doubt themselves for not being able to avoid or resolve their situations. Studies in social psychology suggest that observers watching the bully tend to hold the victim responsible for what is happening to them. Even with no preexisting biases, observers often tend to side with the bully. In addition to the ability to garner support for bullying behaviors, bullies may be skilled at creating chaos in an organization, further wearing down the ability of a target to respond with constructive action (Namie & Namie, 2003). This state of "exhaustion" is consistent with what is known in crisis response theory about the alarm, reaction, and exhaustion process of normal responses to perceived threat.

So far in this text, the information about responses to bullying has been general and largely anecdotal. But what do the data actually suggest about the symptoms and responses of victims? The next section will examine this question via various studies form around the globe.

THE INJURY OF VICTIMIZATION

Heinz Leymann's original work on victimization (1990) cited immediate and grave psychophysiological effects of mobbing. It identified the following symptoms of injury:

- loss of coping resources
- feelings of desperation
- feelings of helplessness
- hyperactivity
- depression
- compulsions

Leymann estimated that from 10 to 15 percent of suicides in Sweden in any given year were committed by victims of mobbing (Leymann, 1990). Emphasizing mobbing as injury, not illness, Davenport et al. (2002) linked physical and psychiatric symptoms to the stage and degree of mobbing. According to their study, the degrees of mobbing are based on the severity of symptoms:

- *Mobbing in the first degree* can produce bouts of crying, sleep disturbance, irritability, and poor concentration.
- *Mobbing in the second degree* is linked to hypertension, gastrointestinal problems, depression, weight gain or loss, substance misuse, and uncharacteristic fearfulness.
- *Mobbing in the third degree* can be typified by severe depression, frequent panic attacks, severe heart problems, vulnerability to accidents, suicidal behavior, and, in severe cases, violence directed at others.

Namie and Namie (2003) highlighted a long list of symptoms typically experienced by targets. Of these, emotional damage included shame, isolation, hypervigilance, mood swings, and disturbed sleep. Physical health effects can be many, but a few of these included poor immunity, stress headaches, hypertension, increased allergies, menstrual difficulties, and, in severe cases, heart attacks. Examples of financial damages included income loss through short-term or long-term disability, loss of housing, depletion of savings, unpaid leave via the Family and Medical Leave Act (FMLA), and exhaustion of sick leave and vacation leave balances. Social relationship costs can include coworker resentment, wavering support from family and friends, abandonment by outside friends, strain on spouses and children, and, in severe instances, separation and divorce.

DATA FROM AROUND THE GLOBE

The effects on mental health created by stress can become overwhelming when one is the target of workplace emotional abuse (Koonin & Green, cited in Geffner et al., 2004). A study of 50 teachers who had been emotionally abused by principals found that the teachers reported feeling depressed, helpless, hopeless, devastated, broken, defeated, humiliated, and desperate, along with other reactions (Blase & Blase, cited in Geffner et al., 2002).

Other data regarding victim responses to bullying vary across cultures and can sometimes be conflicting. Additional research from Scandinavia, for example, suggests that prolonged bullying at work can be correlated with the onset of cardiovascular disease and depression, as well as increases in risk behaviors such as overeating, smoking, overuse of alcohol, and use of other drugs (Kivimäki et al., 2003). Vartia (2001) concluded that targets of bullying suffer from low confidence, poor goal clarity, stress reactions, and errors resulting from haste.

Einarsen (1999) demonstrated that bullying at work can cause stress and severe psychological trauma, including PTSD, and that victims can suffer from extreme anxiety as a result of the social humiliation occurring on a regular basis. Hazler et al. (2006) made a case for including biological measures in research on bullying. They examined the role of the endocrine system in responding to chronic stress, including the stress of being the target of bullying. Citing literature about the relationship between peer abuse and biological processes at the time of puberty, the researchers examined how hormones produced by the endocrine system have a reciprocal relationship with the environment. In children, peer abuse is generally believed to have an impact on biological processes and vice versa. Cortisol is a hormone that regulates the fight-or-flight response, activity of the immune system, sensory acuity, and some aspects of memory and learning. In adults, as in children, the endocrine system produces cortisol and other hormones in response to environmental stress. Chronic stress, like the stress of being bullied, can have lasting influence on the patterns of hormone production (Hazler et al., 2006).

Spanish researchers Meseguer de Pedro, Soler Sanchez, Saez Navarro, and Garcia Izquierdo (2008) studied 396 workers using a self-response questionnaire. The questionnaire included the following measures: a Spanish adaptation of the Negative Acts Questionnaire, the Psychosomatic Complaints Questionnaire, and a measure of absenteeism. The study addressed the relationship between workplace mobbing and psychosomatic symptoms. Twenty-eight percent of respondents suffered from stress-related symptoms, including sleep disturbances, migraines, gastrointestinal complaints, fatigue, overeating, low libido, muscle tics, and shortness of breath. To validate the effects of work-related bullying and psychophysiological symptoms, researchers categorized the sample into "cases of stress" and "no stress." This data categorization was modeled after the criteria established in surveys about work conditions in a 2004 national survey by NIOSH. In that study, any employee who presented a combination of three or more psychosomatic symptoms was considered a possible case of stress (Ministry of Work and Social Affairs, 2004, in Meseguer de Pedro et al., 2008). A contingency table was then set up, examining the victims and nonvictims of mobbing. Only 22 percent of the nonvictim participants could be categorized as "cases of stress," compared to more than *twice* as many (48 percent) of the mobbing victims being categorized as "cases of stress." Surprisingly, no relationship was found for either group between stress, mobbing, and absenteeism (Meseguer de Pedro et al., 2008).

Two 2014 studies conducted at the University of South Australia examined the relationship between bullying and both job and personal resources, focusing on the mediating role of emotional exhaustion. Data suggested that workplace bullying depletes emotional reserves, self-efficacy, and optimism via emotional exhaustion (Tuckey & Neall, 2014). A 2008–2009 South Australian study by Bond, Tuckey, and Dollard (2010) examined the relationship between bullying and symptoms of PTSD in police officers. Of particular interest was the notion of psychosocial safety climate in the organization. Findings suggested that chronic stressors, such as ongoing bullying, could be sources of posttraumatic stress and that workplace bullying might be related to PTSD through a process of classical conditioning, where environmental cues in the workplace come to be associated with feelings of danger or threat.

Another study based on data collected during face-to-face interviews with 800 Australian workers employed in tertiary education, health, and long-distance transport concluded that victimized workers can experience extreme levels of stress, anxiety, emotional exhaustion, and burnout. In the Australian study, the intensity of the symptoms increased in proportion to the severity and duration of the inappropriate behavior (Mayhew et al., 2004).

Davenport et al. (2002) cited Leymann's symptoms linked with the prolonged distress and anxiety that result from mobbing. These conditions, when experienced over time, can lead to lasting physical symptoms and illness. The symptoms include symptoms of muscular tension, various stress responses from the autonomic nervous system, and tension related to being in a hyperalert state. When allowed to persist without treatment, symptoms of PTSD can develop, including flashbacks, exaggerated startle response, fatalistic outlook on life, emotional numbing, persisting anxiety, nightmares, insomnia, poor concentration, uncontrolled acting out, panic attacks, and suicidal or homicidal ideation (Wyatt & Hare, cited in Davenport et al., 2002).

A longitudinal study of nursing students in the United Kingdom over a three-year educational period strongly suggested that a high proportion of nursing students in the United Kingdom experienced bullying. Both the Tennessee Self-Concept Scale (TSCS) (Roid & Fitts, 1988, in Stevenson et al., 2006) and the Professional Self-Concept Nursing Inventory (PSCNI) (Arthur, 1992, in Stevenson et al., 2006) were used to measure participants' experiences. Quantitative findings indicated that the process of becoming a nurse was highly distressing and that participants' levels of self-esteem (measured by the both the TSCS and the PSCNI) *declined dramatically* over the three-year study. By the end of the training, 95 percent of respondents reported below-average self-esteem (Randle, 2003, cited in Stevenson et al., 2006). The findings of the study were significant because all of the participants had reported average or above-average self-esteem at the start of their educational process. One respondent stated the following:

> I wouldn't do it over again. . . . If I knew what it was going to be, I definitely wouldn't do this again. I never thought nurses could be so *bitchy.* I'm a grown woman and they've made my life hell. . . . My daughter's at school and she's had less bullying than me. They're just bullies, to other nurses and to the patients as well. (Randle, 2003, in Stevenson et al., 2006, p. 5)

Excerpts like this one strengthen the opinion that student nurses often experience negative physical and emotional reactions to emotional abuse during their training. While no mention of preeducation emotional status was specified, and while no clear cause and effect could be substantiated, the symptoms reported at the termination of the training process seemed to be an outcome rather than a cause of it (Randle, 2003, in Stevenson et al., 2006).

The injury of victimization from mobbing is real. In addition to organizational dysfunction and low worker morale when mobbing exists and persists in an organization, the psychological and physical effects on injured workers are real, but they vary widely in their severity. Victims may be forced to leave the workplace and may not be rehabilitated for viable work alternatives. In many instances, the symptoms can be lasting and may result in permanent disability. As one international professional noted, "deliberately breaking people's spirits is making the rounds in everyday work life" (Heine, 1995, p. 41). He also wrote, "Severe mental disturbances—psychiatric illnesses—of employees must be prevented before they occur and *supervisors* must take action to combat mobbing-related problems as early as possible" (p. 42). These concepts will be explored further.

BEHAVIORAL REACTIONS OF VICTIMS OF MOBBING

Heinz Leymann (1990) divided worker behavioral reactions and responses into four categories: (1) social responses, including social isolation, stigmatization, voluntary unemployment, and social maladjustment; (2) social psychological responses, including loss of coping skill and breakdown of coping systems; (3) psychological responses, including feeling desperate, helpless, full of rage, and anxious; and (4) psychosomatic/psychological responses, including depression, hyperactivity, compulsions, and suicidal ideation.

Leymann predicted dire outcomes for mobbed workers, including administrative action and expulsion from the workplace. These can occur via illness and disability, being fired, premature retirement, or simply quitting a job without having another one lined up. When any of these outcomes occur, the victim is portrayed as being at fault, and the removal of the victim from the workplace is represented as the victim's choice (Davenport et al., 2002).

Djurkovic, McCormack, and Casimir (2005) examined three categories of reactions by victims, including (in order of frequency) avoidance, assertiveness, and seeking formal help. In a study of 127 undergraduate employees who had experienced workplace bullying, offensive behaviors included threats to professional status, destabilization, isolation, overwork, verbal taunts, and even violence. An earlier study by Djurkovic, McCormack, and Casimir (2004) examined the physical and psychological effects of workplace bullying and its relationship to intention to leave the workplace. Undergraduate students at Australia's University of Melbourne who had been employed in the past 12 months were sent questionnaires about their histories of having been mobbed. A total of 150 (18 percent of 800 surveys sent) were returned. Using the five categories of mobbing presented by Rayner et al. (2002) in an earlier mobbing survey instrument, Djurkovic et al. (2004) determined that respondents categorized their experiences as five types of distress:

1. *threats* to professional status
2. *threats* to personal standing
3. *isolation*, including being prevented access to opportunities and physical and social isolation
4. *overwork*, including undue pressure to produce, impossible deadlines, and constant unnecessary interruptions
5. *destabilization*, including not being given credit when it was due, being assigned meaningless tasks, being repeatedly reminded of blunders, and being set up to fail

Rayner et al. (2002) used a large convenience sample of undergraduate students, who were also employed part-time, in the United Kingdom, to examine the relationship between being targeted for bullying and negative affect. Results suggest correlations between being bullied with negative mood (affect) and physical symptoms. In addition, data from this study also demonstrated a correlation between being bullied and an employee's intention to leave the job. In general, the greater the extent of bullying (amount, severity, and duration), the stronger the intention to leave.

In a 2006 study in the United States, Bamberger and Bacharach identified a relationship between abusive supervision and problem drinking in 1,473 blue-collar workers in 55 different work units. They examined whether problem drinking began or worsened as a result of workplace practices and conditions, including abusive supervision. Researchers hypothesized two possible explanations. First, employees in work units characterized by abusive supervision were more likely to seek retribution or find a means to voice their anger and frustration. The adoption of problem drinking could be one way of seeking such retribution or expressing such anger. The other explanation, and the one more prevalent among staff in work units headed by abusive supervisors, is that subordinates might see the supervisory style as a significant source of stress and adopt problematic use of alcohol use as a way to cope with stress. The findings were mixed, and clearly no simple cause-and-effect relationship could be substantiated. The authors also cited studies of medical students and interns by Richman (1996) suggesting that abusive supervision is associated with elevated levels of problem drinking (Bamberger & Bacharach, 2006). Although the data also addressed more complex issues, such as conscientiousness, stress, agreeableness, and neuroticism, findings supported the notion that a moderate but steady positive correlation exists between an increase in problem drinking in employees and the presence of abusive supervision (Bamberger & Bacharach, 2006). However, it may also be true that problem drinking in workers could be an "antecedent" of abusive supervision. It was not clear which came first.

Koonin and Green (cited in Geffner et al., 2004) lamented that all too often victims take on the responsibility for bullying behaviors and attempt to change themselves in an effort to "fix" things. Reactions such as these prevent the real aggressor(s) from being identified and disciplined in an appropriate and timely manner. In addition, because the bullying behavior itself is often subtle, the abuse may be hard to see or to prove. It may happen behind closed doors, so the victim may be afraid to tell anyone (Koonin & Green, cited in Geffner et al., 2004).

DATA ON PHYSICAL AND EMOTIONAL SYMPTOMS AND REACTIONS

Like intimate-partner violence data and child abuse data, the frequency and severity of workplace mobbing is difficult to determine because of underreporting. Fortunately, however, a considerable body of research has emphasized the negative effects of workplace emotional abuse on psychoemotional health, physical health, workers' performance, and effects on workplace relationship. These negative effects include reduced job satisfaction, embarrassment, guilt, shame, self-doubt, loneliness, powerlessness, poor concentration, obsessions, intrusive thoughts, distrust cynicism, burnout, and suicidal thoughts (Blase et al., 2008). Some of the more relevant studies are reported here.

A survey querying 172 teachers from the United States and Canada who had reported mistreatment by principals asked about the levels of harm respondents had experienced and how they had coped. Regarding level of harm, 78 percent of respondents reported at least moderate harm to themselves, and 49 percent rated the harm as "serious" or "extensive." Regarding harm to their families, 58 percent reported at least moderate harm to their families, and 31 percent rated the harm to their families as serious or extensive (Blase et al., 2008). Commonly reported coping strategies included such behaviors as confronting the bully, reporting the behavior to the bully's boss, getting help from occupational health professionals, consulting with a union representative, and making plans to leave the job.

Brennan (2003), citing Lenehan and Turner, described affected workers expressing symptoms that included crying spells, feeling worthless, lack of direction or motivation, fatigue, irritability, and disturbances in eating and sleeping. These symptoms, depending on their severity, corresponded with the diagnostic criteria for major depressive disorder. The most adaptive responses reported in the Brennan study included self-talk, putting the experience into perspective, cognitive restructuring, and the use of a soothing "mantra" to help with focus and symptom reduction. While these might be construed as therapeutic techniques for treating depression, they may also be self-help techniques that help workers cope with their situations.

University of Chicago researchers Rospenda, Richman, Ehmke, and Zlatoper (2005) studied workplace harassment within a stress framework, documenting the effects of generalized workplace harassment as having similar characteristics and consequences on mental health as sexual harassment (for example, anxiety, depression, PTSD, and effects on general well-being). An ongoing (longitudinal) study of current and former students, faculty, and other employees of a large university setting was conducted. Measures included sexual harassment, generalized workplace harassment, job stress, and illness/injury/assault. The researchers concluded that harassment may be hazardous not only to a target's health but also to the health and financial well-being of the organization (Rospenda et al., 2005).

A 2000 study published in *The Lancet* examined the health status of 1,100 workers in the National Health Service in England. Thirty-eight percent reported being bullied in the previous year, and 42 percent had witnessed someone else being bullied. Those who had been bullied reported significantly lower levels of job satisfaction and higher levels of work-related stress, depression, and anxiety. Those who were bullied were also more likely to leave their employment situations (Cusack, 2000). A similar study in two hospitals in Finland found that while only 5 percent reported having been bullied, victims had a 26 percent increase for medically certified absence, and a 16 percent had an increase for self-certified absence (Cusack, 2000).

A relatively new concept, that PTSD can be induced not only by a single traumatic incident but also by long-term exposure to less serious events, was introduced in the mid-1990s in Scandinavia and England (Scott & Stradline, cited in Rayner et al., 2002). Persistent symptoms of insomnia, migraine headaches, lower gastrointestinal distress, and tinnitus were all reported by long-term sufferers of workplace emotional abuse. In addition to depression, anxiety, aggression, hopelessness, and despair, suicide and suicidal ideation are high risks for bullied targets.

While by no means exhaustive, this brief summary of worker symptoms and reactions indicates that not all mobbing is experienced the same way, not all mobbing results in the same type of psychoemotional symptoms, and responses from targets vary depending on many factors. Resultant psychiatric conditions can range from mild to moderate adjustment disorders with depressed, anxious, or combined moods, to anxiety disorders and major depressive disorders requiring more aggressive interventions, including medication and hospitalization. In some victims, symptoms of PTSD will emerge and may become chronic if left untreated (APA, 2013).

OUTCOMES FOR EMOTIONALLY INJURED WORKERS

Outcomes for emotionally injured workers vary from worker to worker, culture to culture, and industry to industry. Keashly et al. (1994) studied 59 psychology students who voluntarily completed a four-part questionnaire on interpersonal relationships in the workplace. Four parts of the survey instrument queried respondents in four domains: job satisfaction, specific events in the workplace, maltreatment of women, and dealing with hostile situations. Designed to determine the extent to which emotional abuse occurred, the study identified the following types of abusive behavior:

- intellectual belittling
- public putdowns
- sarcastic tones when addressing the student
- swearing at or "glaring" at student workers
- being the target of temper tantrums
- being intimidated with unreasonable demands

Results from respondents indicated that 14 percent had been the target of multiple events of bullying. The impact on workers included lowered job satisfaction, low satisfaction with supervisors, and low satisfaction with coworkers. Although workers all had some previous work experience, one significant limitation included the fact that undergraduate students generally do not have extensive experience across a number of occupations. They are also likely to be relegated to lower-paying jobs, which may have fewer inherent constraints to prevent employee abuse. Another limitation was the survey method, often subject to bias related to memory and candor. The small sample size was another limitation.

Ashforth (1994, in Einarsen, 1999) suggested the following outcomes from the low job satisfaction reported by victims of emotional abuse at work:

- frustration, stress, and reactance
- helplessness and work alienation
- lowered self-esteem and productivity
- lowered work-group cohesiveness
- impacts on psychological health and well-being

As mentioned in the previous section, Rospenda et al. (2005) examined the outcomes of respondents surveyed at a Midwestern university over a period of several years. Respondents were surveyed four times during the study period to determine to what extent the effects of bullying were long-lasting. Conclusions were that exposure to workplace harassment increases the risk for illness, injury, or assault. Thus, harassment may be hazardous to an employee's health, but it also put the worker and the organization at risk for injury or work-related illness.

In a study of 172 American teachers in elementary, middle, and high schools, Blase et al. (2008) reported the following feelings in those teachers who had been bullied by their administrators:

- reduced satisfaction with work
- feeling desperate and incompetent
- guilt, shame, and embarrassment
- doubt about professional competence
- loneliness and isolation
- helplessness
- loss of concentration and other cognitive impairments
- emotional exhaustion
- general job burnout
- disorientation
- shock and fear
- anxiety symptoms such as social phobia and panic attacks
- severe depression

The authors identified that responses from the field of education focus primarily on those injured workers who chose to do nothing in response to bullying. Intensity of harm determined by raw scores of 38 mistreatment items suggested that female teachers experienced more harm than male teachers; teachers with union contracts had higher degrees of intensity of harm than nonunion teachers; divorced teachers had greater intensity of harm; and no discernible differences existed between different school grade levels, age groups, degree groups, and years of teaching experience (Blase et al., 2008). These findings suggest interesting questions. Why do union-represented teachers and divorced teachers experience a greater intensity of harm when bullied? Answers were not apparent in the study, nor were these specific findings replicated by other researchers. While findings did not address this issue, speculation could identify a number of possible influences.

Kivimäki et al. (2003) identified a correlation between bullying at work and risks for the onset of depression and cardiovascular disease. In two (sequential) surveys of a cohort of 5,432 hospital employees in Finland, researchers found a 5 percent prevalence rate for bullying at the time of the first survey and 6 percent at the time of the second survey. After adjusting scores for respondents who were overweight, bullying was correlated to the onset of depression and cardiovascular illness. Of those who had reported being bullied in the first survey, 64 percent did *not* report being bullied two years later. This fairly low continuity of bullying suggests that bullying may be sporadic rather than chronic. A high body mass index also did not correlate with bullying as a consequence of victimization (Kivimäki et al., 2003). Thus, a question about whether being bullied leads to overeating and obesity remains.

Does bullying always end in negative outcomes? The findings are mixed. For example, Vega and Comer (2005) suggested that the long-term effects of being bullied may lead targets to a need to protect their self-image by working harder and longer. They may also engage in efforts to strengthen their self-respect through any means available to them. In more serious cases, however, such as some cited in studies in the United Kingdom and Norway, bullying has been linked to suicides (Vega & Comer, 2005). Hubert (2003, in Vega & Comer, 2005) recommended beginning with informal interventions and proceedings and turning to more formal ones only later, if needed. A study in the Netherlands by Dehue, Bolman, and Pouweise (2011) identified active coping strategies that appeared to help mediate the effects of bullying. These included believing that the stressful condition could be changed, compensation, denial, adopting a positive attitude, and seeking social support.

In some cases, the bully may honestly not have awareness of his or her offenses. If the victim is not confident enough to approach the bully, engaging an impartial mediator might be appropriate. However, mediation is not without difficulties. If the victim "wins," the bully may have thoughts of revenge and may retaliate. When more formal interventions are used, the need for comprehensive training of supervisors and managers is needed (Vega & Comer, 2005). Glendinning (2001) emphasized the need for an anonymous reporting procedure. Victims may be more likely to speak out if they have a shield of anonymity. Exit interviews can also be helpful, but by the time a victim leaves the workplace, the damage to the victim and the organizational culture may already be severe, and opportunities for intervention may be limited (Glendinning, 2001). As the United States begins to pay greater attention to the phenomenon of workplace bullying, outcomes studies about physical and emotional harm, as well as those about preferred courses of action, will be an important research domain.

RESILIENCY, PROTECTIVE FACTORS, AND PROGNOSIS

Protection and protective factors are those that may predict future outcomes. They may be factors that modify or mediate risks. They may provide resistance to risk or buffer the effects of risk. A factor is not protective simply because it is the *opposite* of risk. It needs to contain some compensatory factors that actually help to directly *reduce* a problem or a disorder (Fraser, Richmond, & Galinsky, 1999). Finally, resilience is the capacity to learn from experience. The concept of resilience may be applied to families, groups, or organizations. Resilience can be understood from three frameworks:

- the ability to overcome adversity and being successful despite exposure to situations of high risk
- the ability to remain competent and successfully adapting to high-stress situations, even while under extreme pressure

- skills at recovering from trauma and successful life adjustment, despite very negative events

In all three, resilience is described as successful functioning in the context of high risk. Because people are malleable, it is important to distinguish resilience from mere survival (Wolin & Wolin, 1993, in Fraser et al., 1999). For a complete understanding of individual response to the trauma of workplace emotional abuse, it may be necessary to have a more complete and precise understanding of pre-mobbing personality functioning, coping skills used during the experience, and the ways in which people restructure their lives once they are no longer being bullied. Clearly, social work must concern itself with the exploration of these concepts if solutions are to be identified.

From a social work perspective, any review of social problems or life stressors must take into account the risk, protection, and resilience of the people who are exposed to the problem or condition. In both academic and popular media, the relationships of the concepts of risk, protection, and resilience have emerged as constructs for understanding both social and health problems (Fraser et al., 1999). Risk is the probability or likelihood of a future situation or event, given a condition or set of conditions. Risk is a concept central to the field of public health. Nonspecific risk factors might include individual, family, and outside family factors that can affect the development of various disorders. These risks might be genetic, or they may be environmental, but they are likely to be an intricate combination of the two (Fraser et al., 1999).

The responses to workplace mobbing are varied and may result in different outcomes. Survival strategies and recovery options are covered in a later section of this book, but some tactics can be briefly mentioned here. According to Davenport et al. (2002), the victims who had the best strategies for enduring their mobbing experiences were those who were able to understand what was happening to them and responded confidently to the attacks. Successful survivors avoided game-playing with the bully and refused to view themselves as victims. Survivors also tended to show both spiritual and psychological strength. They believed that things can change and diverted their attention to positive, pleasurable activities. Finally, those who were successful stopped investing their energy and creativity in the organization and diverted these elsewhere.

CASE HISTORIES

Elizabeth

Elizabeth was a 55-year-old middle manager working as a fiscal manager in a large public-sector agency. With an MBA and a specialty in accounting, Elizabeth had been hired six years earlier to manage income and expenses in one of the agency's several departments. Departments in the agency were decentralized and had a fair degree of autonomy in managing their finances. Most income streams were from public sources. Elizabeth had been an exemplary employee, with strong performance reviews and a solid track record of good work. Elizabeth had remarried later in life and had a loving relationship with her husband and adult children. She had a rich network of friends and no financial difficulties. Her health was good, with no ongoing medical conditions. Elizabeth had no history of psychiatric conditions, no history of job problems, and no notable earlier life stressors, although she and her previous husband had divorced after 20 years of marriage. The divorce occurred several years prior to Elizabeth's employment in the public sector and did not seem to have any aftereffects.

After Elizabeth had been functioning successfully in her position for six years, her immediate supervisor retired early due to a chronic health condition, and a new fiscal head of the agency was promoted from within the organization. Elizabeth had always had a cordial relationship with this new supervisor, having worked together cooperatively for six years. But without warning, Elizabeth's assignment changed. She was transferred back to central operations and placed in charge of HRM. Her "fiscal manager" position was eliminated, although there were no financial reasons for doing so, and she was demoted to a supervisory but nonmanagement status. While Elizabeth had completed some coursework and had some professional experience in HR, it was not her area of specific expertise or the area in which she had been hired to work. Nonetheless, Elizabeth oversaw the personnel functions for a 1,100-employee agency, including direct supervision of a team of seven clerical staff.

Elizabeth received constant criticism from her immediate supervisor, as well as curt treatment and innuendos from the agency director. She sought legal counsel to identify courses of action available to her and also had several short-term counseling sessions with a therapist at the employee assistance program for symptoms of mild anxiety and mild depression. Because Elizabeth had been in a managerial role at the time of her demotion, she was not a member of the union, which represented nonmanagement workers in that public agency. Elizabeth's goal was to survive until she had worked a total of 10 years for her employer, so she remained in her position for another four years after the difficulty had started. Daily work conditions were challenging and demoralizing.

Elizabeth ultimately met her 10-year employment goal and retired immediately. An energetic professional with an interest in continued professional involvement, she did some part-time operations and fiscal oversight work for a large nonprofit organization in the community and was eventually hired as a full-time contracts manager with that program. She remained in this contract-management capacity for several years before retiring permanently. She later served as a member of the board of directors for another private nonprofit entity in the community. She reports no ongoing symptoms of anxiety or depression but remains mildly unhappy about her treatment in the public sector.

Robert

Robert was a 48-year-old senior manager working as a research consultant in a midsize department of a large public-sector health-care delivery system. He had been a successful professional within the organization for almost 20 years and had a track record of very good performance with high productivity and increasingly demanding responsibilities. Although a change agent who creatively challenged others, Robert was respected and highly regarded by management and peers. From a psychosocial perspective, Robert was a single dad, raising a 14-year-old son, having undergone a divorce six years earlier. His lifestyle was stable, and he had a rich network of social supports, including other single parents, and adequate finances. Robert's health and that of his son were both excellent.

A change in administration resulted in significant changes in staffing patterns and management practices in Robert's organization. Several non-health-care professional managers were hired as administrators, and morale in the workplace began to decline. Robert was among the victims of the changeover in administration. The new director publicly harassed and ridiculed him, calling him "Bobby Boy." Robert was no longer allowed to participate in management team meetings, and his opinions, when he was allowed to express them, were disregarded or mocked. He began to be the subject of disciplinary action over petty infractions and misinterpretations. At one point, an unstable "consumer" (or patient) threatened Robert's life, but department heads did not make any efforts to warn or protect him. Robert's response was to feel intimated, anxious, fearful, and threatened.

Over a period of several months, he grew increasingly demoralized. After seeking medical attention, Robert was prescribed medication for depression and migraine headaches and was referred for brief psychotherapy. He attempted to obtain assistance from the agency's HR department, with little results. The agency HR manager was new and not yet well versed in the intricacies of a civil service work system.

Robert did not seek legal counsel, but although his position was classified as a management one, he voluntarily joined the union representing nonmanagement employees so that he might have the benefit of that union's protection. The president of the local union personally advised and represented Robert. When an alleged "disciplinary" meeting was botched by the new management team, Robert and the union president negotiated a transfer to another department as a conciliatory measure. Robert has remained in the new department, with a change in some of his responsibilities, for over 10 years and has done well. The leadership of Robert's former department has since been replaced.

Linda

Linda was a 49-year-old married woman working in an economically depressed region of the United States. She was married for 25 years to a caring and supportive husband. Both of Linda's parents and one younger sister were deceased. Linda enjoyed good friendships with peers and had a number of community interests. In spite of the poor economy, she and her husband had managed their finances well and had no financial problems. Both were in good health. Although Linda had a degree in art design from a local school of fine arts, she had spent most of her adult life working in outside sales and manufacturing.

Linda's employment at the time of her mobbing incident was at a manufacturing firm that made industrial supplies. She was assigned a position as a lead worker of a production line, where she oversaw but did not directly supervise younger workers. Linda was Caucasian, but most of the other workers were of an ethnic minority group. They openly criticized Linda when she was absent from the production line. Although she was absent only for official purposes, such as receiving management directives and attending required meetings, the other workers complained openly to her. Linda sought help from her immediate supervisor and from the HR department but was advised to "just ignore it."

Over several months, Linda's health began to suffer. She sought medical care for anxiety, depression, sleeplessness, and lack of appetite. The situation persisted for over 18 months, and Linda was ready to resign but decided one more attempt at getting assistance from HR was worth a try. She made her case convincingly, and while none of the perpetrators had any consequences for their actions, Linda was transferred to another work unit at another location. She remains on medication for depression but reports much improvement in work and social functioning.

Rosalie

Rosalie was a 49-year-old leader in a large public-sector health-care system. Her work history involved increasing professional responsibility and multiple promotions since her hiring by the public-sector system 14 years before. Rosalie had a post–master's-degree work history of almost 20 years of successful professional employment. The only remarkable outside stressor was that Rosalie had gone through a divorce in the preceding 18 months but was well past the acute crisis and had made peace with her former husband, with an amicable division of assets. In addition to her graduate degree, Rosalie had a strong track record in her field. She was known as a good team member and a good manager.

Due to recent political events in the community and much media attention, Rosalie's immediate supervisor, the department head, had been asked to resign. After another director's position was eliminated, Rosalie was the remaining leader of the department's workforce of over 400 employees. But at the hand of the agency director, Rosalie was being publicly admonished and humiliated in front of her peers and her subordinates. In private, the agency director made veiled threats to Rosalie about demoting her or eliminating her position, even though she had no history of any performance problems. Rosalie began to suffer from anxiety, sleep disturbance, and elevated blood pressure. Her private-care physician was supportive and tried to convince her to take a leave of absence to protect her health. Rosalie consulted with a labor attorney who advised her to do everything she could to save her job. Rosalie consulted with a deputy director of the HR department, who advised her that the agency director had no grounds to discipline or dismiss her and "not to worry."

After several weeks of mistreatment, Rosalie's blood pressure rose to 180/110, and her physician authorized a medical leave of absence. Rosalie was prescribed medication for sleep and for anxiety and was recommended dietary modifications, including an increase in B vitamins. She was encouraged to exercise regularly, and a consult was ordered with a cardiologist. Rosalie completed a full cardiology workup, including EKG and treadmill test. Although no heart disease was diagnosed, she was advised by the cardiologist that the leave of absence was appropriate and indicated, given her symptoms.

Rosalie immediately began a process of seeking alternative employment, although she did not want to leave the relatively high-paying, civil-service position she'd held for 14 years, as her retirement plan, health-care plan, deferred income plan, and longevity benefits were substantial. During the early days and weeks of the medical leave of absence, Rosalie's situation and health status were made public by the agency director, and accounts of her health status were published in the local newspapers. After 5 months of medical leave, Rosalie was able to secure another managerial position within another large public agency in the community and ultimately went back to work at a reduced salary, but with her retirement plan and benefits intact. After about 18 months in the new position, Rosalie retired from the public sector to pursue other career opportunities.

During the lengthy retirement application process, Rosalie learned that she could possibly be eligible for a service-connected disability retirement because she had become disabled within the context of her duties as a leader in a large department. Rosalie secured an attorney from a firm specializing in that type of claim and was forced by her employer to undergo a psychiatric evaluation. Fortunately, Rosalie had kept meticulous logs of events and conversations with the previous agency directors, all supporting the notion that she had been subjected to a highly hostile work environment. During a seven-hour legal hearing in which she was examined by her attorney and cross-examined by her employer's attorney, she gave clear testimony. Rosalie did prevail and was ultimately awarded the disability retirement, a lifetime benefit of half of her full-time salary payable as nontaxable income. Although Rosalie busied herself with other work, she remains bitter about her experiences and saddened that the career she had enjoyed had been shortened.

SUMMARY

In conclusion, this chapter has highlighted that targets respond to bullying with some characteristic behavioral, emotional, and cognitive reactions. These include disbelief, guilt, shame, inability to make things better, and premature job termination. This type of victimization occurs around the globe. Outcomes for injured workers vary with internal and external resources along with public policy about workplace abuse. While resiliency and protective features may help to mitigate the damage caused by workplace bullying, many workers are severely harmed.

Chapter 6 presents a closer look at a variety of clinical presentations, some recommended treatment interventions, the importance of the therapeutic relationship in helping the victim to recover, and a role for public policy in addressing this malady.

6

Interventions with Individuals

The WBI states that over 70 percent of bullied workers seek mental health treatment to help them cope, understand, and recover from their experiences (Namie, 2013). Namie suggested that as of 2013, only 30 percent of therapists were very aware of the effects of workplace bullying and were effective at treating injured workers. An additional 23 percent could be considered sympathetic but inexperienced at treating clients who had been bullied. In spite of their lack of experience, these 23 percent were able to provide their bullied clients with a safe therapeutic environment. The study suggested that 70 percent or more of mental health professionals could benefit from continuing education about workplace emotional abuse.

Because the issue of emotional abuse in the workplace is so new to clinical literature and practice, best practices have yet to be established. In spite of this limitation, some commonsense guidelines can help clinicians to be most effective in their treatment of targets of bullying. In addition, because of the severity of symptoms in extreme cases, clinicians cannot be overeducated or overtrained in responding to clients who have been exposed to workplace emotional abuse.

A basic principle is that clients cannot be well served by treatment professionals who do not understand the dynamics and the real trauma of workplace bullying. It is impossible for clinical interventions to be effective if a social worker or other clinician does not understand the overwhelming sense of hurt, betrayal, humiliation, and terror that victims may feel. To be effective, clinicians must set aside their judgments about client responsibility for what is happening and any sense that clients should just be tougher or more objective. For the worker in crisis, the experience is not *just* subjective—it is *all* subjective.

While discipline-specific treatment responses have not yet been identified in the helping professions, a thorough understanding of crisis-intervention techniques, trauma response, and response to victims of other abuses will help guide interventions.

CRISIS DEFINITIONS, INTERVENTION, AND RESPONSES

Crisis-intervention responses will vary depending on client needs. Definitions of crises vary as well. Caplan (1961, in James & Gilliland, 2005) identified a person being in crisis as one who faces an obstacle important to life goals, which leads to a period of disorganization. Caplan (1964, in James & Gilliland, 2005) refined the term *crisis* to be the result of impediments to life goals that people believe they cannot overcome through their usual behavioral choices. Carkhuff and Berenson (1964, in James & Gilliland, 2005) stated that a crisis is a crisis because the person has no response to deal with it. Belkin (1984, in James & Gilliland, 2005) defined a crisis as a personal difficulty or situation that immobilizes a person and prevents the person from effective action. Brammer (1985, in James & Gilliland, 2005) described crisis as a state of disorganization in which a person faces frustration of major life goals or profound life-cycle disruption. The term usually refers to the feelings of shock, fear, and distress about a life disruption. All suggested that crisis is a perception or experience of a situation as intolerable, exceeding the person's ability to effectively manage it (James & Gilliland, 2005). James and Gilliland further stated that crises must be assessed in terms of the client's response in affective, behavioral, and cognitive functioning (the ABC model).

Kanel (2007) defined crises as having three parts: a precipitating event, a perception of the event that causes subjective distress, and the failure of a person's customary coping skills. Since mobbing is *not* a crisis event but rather a *process of injury*, the onset of the crisis is likely to be more insidious than a single crisis-triggering action or event. A crisis is, by definition, time limited, because a person cannot physically and emotionally withstand the extreme stress and psychological disequilibrium for long periods of time. A crisis state will eventually stop, usually within four to six weeks. According to crisis theory (Caplan, 1964, in Kanel, 2007), if one has been effective in coping with a crisis, that person's coping skills will have been strengthened. If the person is not successful, he or she will be reduced to a less effective level of psychosocial functioning. In cases of mobbing, because victims are likely to have been trying to cope with emotional abuse for an extended period of time, usual coping skills are not just deficient—they may have been eroded.

For clinicians treating clients who are the victims of emotional abuse in the workplace, interventions will likely include crisis intervention, risk assessment, medical evaluation or referral for medical evaluation, appropriate diagnosis, creating and sustaining a therapeutic alliance, or providing direct clinical interventions to address anxiety, depression, panic, and other disorders created by the abuse. Finally, it will be important for a treating clinician to assist the client in developing an exit plan from the organization. James and Gilliland (2005) identified the six-step model of crisis intervention: define the problem, ensure client safety, provide support, examine alternatives, make a plan, and get client commitment (buy-in).

An interesting contrast can be found in accounts by the American Red Cross working with victims of another type of crisis, the 1991 East Bay Hills Fire in Oakland, California. Researching that event and effective crisis response, Armstrong et al. (1995) evaluated the use of stress debriefing of people who had been affected. They found it helpful for people to use limited venting about the experiences and to avoid viewing themselves as "ill" when troubled with stress responses to disaster. It is not known, however, if the MSD approaches advocated for disaster response could be effective for workers in crises due to emotional abuse at work.

The Crisis Associated with Job Loss

The crisis of job loss should not be underestimated. Doka (2002) described job loss as a type of *disenfranchised grief*. Job loss is often a type of loss that is overlooked. In many instances, the loss of a job by decision or by forced termination can significantly affect self-esteem. In addition to creating financial strain, it can involve other losses, such as the loss of relationships at work, the loss of work-related activities, the loss of meaning and purpose, and in some instances the loss of faith. Because work is so much a part of identity in the Western world, especially the United States, job loss can also have significant impacts on spouses and children and the overall social functioning of the entire family (Doka, 2002). Clinicians working with displaced workers, especially those who experienced emotional abuse at work, would be wise to be mindful of the meaning of the job loss to the person and the degree to which grieving is occurring or is needed. Job loss represents a loss of a part of the self. People have been bullied and who no longer work for the organization where the bullying occurred will likely experience symptoms of bereavement when they leave a job, either voluntarily and involuntarily.

An injured worker's response to bullying is likely to be strongly influenced by that person's individual attitude toward work. Sperry (2009) differentiated between job orientation and career orientation. Employees with a job orientation view their work as just a job, a means to income. By contrast, employees with a career orientation value pay, opportunities for promotion, and the status afforded them by their career choice. All these contribute to the self-esteem and sense of personal power of worker and are tied to personal identity (Bellah, 1985, in Sperry, 2009). Clinicians working with bullied workers will be wise to understand clients' orientations to work to assist with process and meaning.

Families will experience stress over financial concerns and also over the mood state of the displaced worker. One could conclude that both individual support and family support will be important in the recovery process. Individuals will need to come to terms with the meaning of work and the meaning of the job loss for themselves. Such people will also need help to become proactive in identifying areas of strength and coping that have been helpful to them in the past. In addition, families can benefit from psychoeducation about both the mobbing syndrome and recovery from it.

Brammer (1985, in James & Gilliland, 2005) described a crisis as a state of disorganization in which a person faces having life goals and the life cycle disrupted. Crisis is a term that usually refers to the feelings of shock, fear, and distress about the disruption. Gerald Caplan, often referred to as the father of modern crisis intervention, describes crisis as an obstacle that, for the moment, is insurmountable and an event for which one's customary coping skills are not effective (Caplan, 1964, in Kanel, 2007). In Chinese, "crisis" can mean both danger and opportunity (Janosik, 1986, in Kanel, 2007), suggesting the potential for either responding adaptively or failing to do so. Kanel (2007) suggested that outcomes to crises will depend on the person's material resources, personal resources, and social resources. All suggest that the most important feature of a crisis is the subjective perception or experience of a situation as intolerable, exceeding the person's ability to effectively manage it (James & Gilliland, 2005).

Clinicians who treat victims of emotional abuse in the workplace will likely use crisis intervention, risk assessment, medical evaluation or referral for medical evaluation, and appropriate diagnosis. They will also need to work to create and sustain a therapeutic alliance and provide direct clinical interventions to address anxiety, depression, panic, and other disorders resulting from the abuse. Finally, a treating clinician will need to assess and, if needed, assist the client in developing an exit plan from the organization.

Risk Assessment and Crisis Intervention

Initial steps of crisis response include risk assessment. A person who has undergone a mobbing experience at work may be suicidal. According to data from Leymann (1987, in Leymann, 1990) about 10 to 15 percent of the suicides in Sweden each year are people with a recent history of workplace emotional abuse. Clinicians can respond to this danger and assess it the way they would assess any other person in crisis. Kanel (2007) suggested getting responses to the following questions:

- Does the person have thoughts of killing himself or herself? How often? How badly does the person want to die? Does the person see suicide as weak or strong?
- When the person has thoughts of self-harm, what sort of method would be used? Does the person have the means to do this?
- Has the person given away any possessions or said goodbye to people, or both?
- Who else knows that the patient is thinking of self-harm? What have family members and friends said about the threats? Is the person being taken seriously? Does the person have a history of suicidal ideation or attempts?
- To what degree does the person feel he or she has control over events in life?
- Does the person have symptoms of mental illness? Does the person need hospitalization to prevent self-harm?
- If not, ask the person for a commitment to talk with you, to do no self-harm today, and to see you again tomorrow.

Many clinicians advise getting a written "no suicide" contract drafted, with alternative coping behaviors clearly identified, that the client can sign and date.

Admittedly, a signed contract is not real protection in any legal or objective sense, but clients are sometimes able to honor a commitment to someone else that they might not honor for themselves or for any other reason.

Davenport et al. (2002) pointed to the serious condition that sometimes injured workers take revenge by using violence. Kanel (2007) identified questions that can be used to manage a client who may be a danger to others:

- Is the client actively or passively engaged in dangerous behavior, especially violent behavior?
- Does the client think she or he is "going crazy"?
- Does the person have a plan to follow through?
- Does the person have the means to follow through?
- Does the person have a background of violence?
- Has the person acted on plans for violence in the past?

Medical Evaluation

Medical evaluation is often an important step in the crisis-intervention response. The first professional with whom an injured worker comes in contact may be a family physician or emergency room physician rather than a mental health professional. For medical doctors, Manning (2001) advised physicians to know (or get to know) their patients well and to listen to their version of the experience. By listening carefully, primary care physicians can make accurate assessments of patients' physical and psychological functioning. Listening empathically and responding to both the factual content and the emotional content of a patient's communication will help a physician to begin to develop a prudent treatment plan. Since estimates are that anywhere from 30 to 40 percent of absence from work is due to some type of emotional stress, primary care physicians will serve their patients well by understanding the various types of harm that can occur in the workplace. Often pain, including grief and loss, is expressed through physical symptoms. When patients present any of the following symptoms, treating physicians would be wise to inquire about any emotional upsets in the person's life, including job stress and losses:

- frequent illness
- colds
- cystitis
- thrush
- cold sores
- appetite changes
- decreased libido
- ejaculatory problems
- weight gain or loss
- bowel upsets
- heart palpitations
- skin problems
- eczema

- psoriasis
- aches and pains
- ulcers

A general practitioner may be a significant source of advocacy for an injured worker, so medical professionals are wise to be mindful of the notion that "perception is reality" (Manning, 2001). In other words, if the patient is distressed over work-related emotional concerns, the threat is real from that patient's point of view. Applegate and Shapiro (2005) identified the stress response as an important coping mechanism that includes emotional, cognitive, and behavioral elements. Neurobiology acknowledges that adults exposed to trauma can develop a number of symptoms that can produce states of chronic arousal, intrusion, and even avoidance, as would be found with chronic reactions to acute stress (Applegate & Shapiro, 2005). Are there any assessment tools for MDs? A short screening instrument called the Job Induced Stress Scale (House & Rizzo, 1972, in Bilgel et al., 2006) could be used by physicians for initial screening. Three brief screening scales by Aaron Beck could be administered with minimal time or disruption. These include the Beck Hopelessness Scale (Beck, 1986), the Beck Depression Inventory (Beck & Alford, 2009), and the Beck Anxiety Scale (Beck, Epstein, Brown, & Steer, 1988).

Ewing (1984) developed a quick screening instrument for primary care physicians to use for alcohol problems. The following questions have come to be known as the CAGE questions:

- C: Have you ever felt a need to *cut* down on the amount you drink?
- A: Have you ever felt *angry* at someone's criticism of your drinking?
- G: Have you ever felt *guilty* at behavior you engaged in while drinking?
- E: Have you ever taken an early morning *eye-opener* to get started the day following a drinking episode?

As of this writing, no quick screening tool for workplace bullying similar to the CAGE questions has appeared in the literature, but this writer suggests a few screening questions that could be helpful for primary care physicians, as well as mental health clinicians (letters from the italicized words form the word "ABUSED"):

- A: Do you feel *afraid* of anyone at your workplace?
- B: Have you ever felt publicly *belittled* by someone in your work environment?
- U: Does anyone at your job try to *undermine* your efforts?
- S: Do you ever feel severely high levels of *stress* at your job?
- E: Do you ever feel that you are being *excluded* from activities or decisions that would normally be a part of your job functions?
- D: Does your work ever get *devalued* by your supervisor or colleagues?

These questions can be asked and answered in less than one minute. Those answered in the affirmative could be further explored in another few minutes. Screenings such as these take some time but can provide a thorough practitioner valuable information about either etiology or exacerbating conditions in a patient's life that could assist with diagnosis and treatment planning processes.

While few physicians routinely use the MMPI-2 or similar instruments, complex measurements such as formal assessment tools can provide useful information. Clients who are prone to utilize such mechanisms as *somatization* (the tendency to experience emotional distress with physical health symptoms) are likely to experience health challenges requiring medical attention.

Stress effects of bullying on endocrine markers are apparent in workers who incur high levels of stress in their jobs (Ohlson, Soderfeldt, Soderfeldt, Jones, & Theorell, 2001). Perceived job strain was studied in 103 employees who had elevated levels of cortisol, prolactin, thyroid-stimulating hormone, testosterone, and immunoglobulins. Patients with elevated endocrine panels completed surveys designed to address demand-control issues—that is, the degree to which patients felt their jobs were demanding and the degree to which they felt powerless or lacking in control to mediate these demands. Such issues as quantitative demands of jobs, workload changes, mandatory overtime, emotional demands of jobs, and burdens of overresponsibility were explored, along with the qualitative demands of emotional expenditure required by the job. Job demands correlated with endocrine markers of stress were correlated only with increases in cortisol; the models for the other four stress markers were not significant. Emotional job strain showed a stronger association with prolactin than job strain involving quantitative demands. Results were inconclusive, partly because of the small sample size and partly because of inability to control for exercise and alcohol consumption the night before lab work. Both exercise and alcohol consumption can alter results of endocrine function tests (Ohlson et al., 2001). Kivimäki et al. (2003) identified a correlation between bullying at work and risks for the onset of depression and cardiovascular disease.

When Immediate Escape Is Not Possible

When immediate escape is not possible, finding ways to feel safe and secure about survival correlate with a good outcome. Proctor and Tehrani (2001) identified several potential supports for targets of workplace bullying:

- telephone helpline services provided by unions or internal workplace counselors
- information and advice via employer-generated materials addressing policies and procedures for dealing with bullies
- identifying a "confidential supporter" with whom the injured employee can talk
- formal support processes related to a formal complaints procedure
- mediators or conciliators as a nonformal approach to resolving interpersonal problems
- counselors the person can approach to help them to deal with bullying

Bibliotherapy, or the practice of assigning reading homework for clients, has shown promise. Clinicians who provide treatment to targets can provide information about recent written works addressing workplace emotional abuse. Such books can provide victims with information to normalize their experiences and even to begin to identify strategies for coping with emotional abuse at work. Reading assignments can help targets to begin to actively involve themselves in a recovery process (Lewis, Coursol, & Wahl, 2002). The authors cautioned that bibliotherapy should never take the place of competent clinical work—that is, individual psychotherapy or counseling.

As an alternative to responses that will ultimately harm the victim and others, Lewis et al. (2002) suggested specific steps that targets of bullying can and should take. Specifically, victims are urged to be proactive in their response to bullying and get help immediately. Davenport et al. (2002) suggested a number of options for targets of abuse. Targets can analyze what is happening to them and try to understand it. They can take steps to try to work out differences with the bully or bullies. Targets can decide to either stay but protect themselves or make plans for escape, with or without another job lined up. Injured workers may elect to fight legally whether they are still at the job or not. (Finding knowledgeable legal counsel will be necessary.) Finally, targets can learn from their experiences and use them to prevent future bullying.

Some injured workers will benefit from contacting EAPs within their organizations, but those who do so need to be mindful of some of the realities of the role, function, and scope of services provided by EAPs. EAPs who work within the organization are employees (or contractors) of the organization. Referrals from supervisors are generally given the highest priority, so self-referrals may take longer to get an appointment. Protection from privacy invasions may *not* be guaranteed. Peer counselors may not be truly qualified clinicians (Namie & Namie, 2003). Unions can be another source of assistance, as can local chambers of commerce.

Family therapy authors Sperry and Duffy (2009) suggested that a therapist's role includes working with the victim to understand how organizational dynamics affect them, to examine options, to collaboratively support the client's decision to leave (or to stay), and to help with implementing the decision. The role can be expanded to help with returning to work or assisting with issues when attorneys are providing representation. Because an injured worker is already feeling powerless and humiliated, it will be important for the treating clinician to avoid inadvertently joining with the critics or bullies in contributing to the client's sense of feeling damaged, weak, or flawed.

Importance of the Therapeutic Alliance

A sound therapeutic alliance is imperative for a mental health professional to be effective in helping targets of bullying. According to Lewis et al. (2002), the clinician's knowledge of workplace harassment is critical to treating targets of workplace emotional abuse. Because harassment is so insidious that clients often do not understand they are targets, clinicians' awareness is paramount—otherwise a risk emerges of holding the target responsible for the abuse and the symptoms they develop. Self-blame, shame, inadequacy, and lack of self-confidence can all result from mobbing, but the victim may not link them to the mobbing itself.

When mental health professionals identify these feelings in clients who have been abused, they must be able to help clients understand their source and assist them in regaining a sense of professional competence (Lewis et al., 2002). Most abused workers find comfort in knowing that what they have experienced has a name, along with identifiable causes and symptoms.

Social work educator Hollis (1972) suggests that all therapeutic relationships begin with the professional asking himself or herself three questions: What is the problem? What contributes to the problem? What can be changed or modified?

As simplistic as these may sound, a professional needs to grasp that the client is in distress not only because of the failure of his or her unique coping strategies but also because the client has experienced a grave social injustice in one of his or her most significant institutions—the workplace.

Bordin (1979, in Cooper & Lesser, 2002) agreed with Freud that the alliance between the client and the clinician is one of the factors, if not the most important aspect, of the change process. The effectiveness of the therapeutic process depends largely on the sturdiness of the therapeutic alliance. Clients grow, change, and heal as a result of the understanding and contributions of the therapist.

Rogers (1977, in James & Gilliland, 2005) described the most effective helper as one who can provide three necessary conditions for client healing: empathy, genuineness, and acceptance. Creating a climate of empathy means that the clinician accurately reads the feelings and meanings of the client and communicates understanding. Genuineness means that the professional is open in the relationship. Finally, acceptance can be understood as *unconditional positive regard*. A reasonable approach to creating a working therapeutic alliance with an emotionally injured worker would be to attend to the basic assumptions highlighted above.

Finally, sound treatment for any type of trauma involves three primary functions: helping the client to soothe himself or herself, helping the client develop language to describe the experience, and encouraging the client to weave the experience into some sort of life narrative to create meaning. Balducci et al. (2009) and Lewis et al. (2002) cautioned clinicians to be aware of workplace bullying as a growing workplace problem and its effects of targets. Lewis et al. (2002) emphasized the importance of clinicians' knowledge of workplace bullying:

> Critical to the diagnosis and treatment of targets is the counselor's knowledge and awareness of workplace harassment. Counselor awareness is paramount because harassment is so insidious that clients often do not recognize that they are targets. A lack of awareness about workplace harassment can lead counselors to hold targets responsible for their condition or diagnose them inaccurately with a pre-existing condition. The effect of inaccurate diagnosis often intensifies the suffering of targets. (p. 114)

Targets commonly fear that no one believes them and worry that they are powerless. It is imperative that clinicians treating targets of emotional abuse at work communicate an understanding of the client's experience. Understanding can be communicated by helping the targeted clients name and describe their experiences. The process of naming an experience and identifying symptoms and stages can help the client to begin to recover self-esteem and empowerment (Namie, 2000). Material about mobbing is becoming more and more available, so targets can be given assignments to complete reading as an adjunct to therapy (Namie, 2000). Again, having a name and identifiable symptoms helps to reduce the general sense of shame and victimization that targets are likely to experience and helps them begin to move toward recovery and life planning.

Because of the trauma associated with being the target of workplace bullying, some broad clinical recommendations can be helpful. Wurmser (Kilburg, 2009) identified the need to (a) help clients clarify what is happening to them, (b) remain mindful that helping clients create time and space for reflection is always part of the goal of therapeutic work, (c) help clients with reality testing, and (d) help them to "bear witness" to their experiences while protecting themselves.

Understanding the issues created by work problems and the role that inequity and injustice can play in a client's life is important for professionals treating injured workers. It may help if the therapist has worked for a living in an organization and thus better understands organizational and workplace pressures. Clinical language should focus on concepts of PTSD. A therapist qualified to address mobbing will have a clinical style that is interactive, directive, and solution focused. Although authors Namie and Namie (2003) have suggested that victims garner initial support from family and friends, they also offered suggestions for selecting professional services. A good therapist for targets of bullying will need to tell the client exactly what information in a clinical record is protected from both employer and courts and what is not protected. In addition to safety and trust, therapists who are not psychiatrists should have the ability to refer a bullied client to a medical doctor who could prescribe medications if warranted. Therapists also need to consider seeking resources about mobbing from organizations such as the WBI.

Diagnosis and Treatment of Disorders Identified in Targets of Bullying

Diagnosis and treatment of disorders will involve the typical knowledge and skills sets used by clinicians. By definition, the referral of someone who has been mobbed may be one of the best examples of social work's historical emphasis on *the person in environment*, or PIE. The concept is central to clinical social work and refers to three constructs: the person, the person's situation, and the interface between the person and the situation (Hamilton, 1939, in Woods & Hollis, 2000). The concept of a *situation* frequently implies a human situation, such as family, friends, classroom, and employment. Woods and Hollis (2000) further suggested that a person's situation or context is at least as complex as the person. One of the primary purposes of social work casework includes helping the person to resolve the problems that arise from a dynamic when a problem exists between the person and that person's environment. However, sometimes individuals and their families are "pathological." Problems may be found in the interplay between an individual and his or her situation. As in other areas of human functioning, problems that develop between a person and the workplace are greater than the sum of the problem's individual parts.

The diagnostic interview can resemble any other clinical assessment process. It should include information about the presenting problem, the duration of that problem, an understanding of client goals and expectations, and a comprehensive psychosocial history. As in other treatment cases, good psychosocial assessments would include family history, educational background, employment history, military history, legal history, psychosexual history, substance-use history, psychosexual history, current living situation, and level of social activity. For people in grave clinical risk or those being treated for a medical condition in inpatient medical/surgical facilities, a recent requirement is that a spiritual assessment be conducted. While this is not yet uniformly required in outpatient setting, knowledge of a client's spiritual belief system can be part of assessing both current types of support, as well as existential issues. Woods and Hollis (2000) recommended assessing the specific ego functions of the client in such domains as reality testing; regulation and control of drives, affects, and impulses; object relations; thought processes; autonomous functioning; and mastery competence—that is, how competent the person feels. A mental status exam to assess affect, mood, perceptual processes, orientation, thought processes, judgment, insight, memory, speech, abstract thinking, and general intellectual functioning should always be included in initial assessment processes. Kaplan and Sadock (1996) suggested assessing the client for tendencies toward violence, delusional systems, and suicidal potential.

Professionals should be current on the topic of workplace emotional abuse. They should avoid criticism, remain positive and hopeful, avoid asking questions about "why" the target did what he or she did, and let the story unfold at the client's own pace. Professionals should assume the client's position and avoid trying to present another perspective. It may be helpful to validate the client's description of the experience.

Proctor and Tehrani (2001) addressed the importance of listening, helping clients to understand their rights, providing support, clarifying, and assisting the client with immediate decision making. Clients will need reassurance about confidentiality, rules for the negotiated clinical relationship, and issues of informed consent. Clients may also need assistance in identifying previously unutilized or underutilized resources, general information, options about action plans, and clues on how best to proceed. If the clinical professional is part of the injured worker's organization, boundary issues must be addressed and clarified.

Another way to enhance clinical understanding of an emotionally injured worker is from crisis-intervention literature. According to James and Gilliland (2005), one type or domain of a human crisis can be one known as an *existential crisis*. Existential crises include but are not limited to inner conflicts and anxieties that tend to accompany important human concerns, such as purpose, choice, autonomy, freedom, and commitment (James & Gilliland, 2005). Certainly the crisis that emerges for a worker caught in a mobbing scenario can be defined as existential, as well as one of survival, and should be treated as such.

D. W. Johnson and Johnson (2003) defined the process of treatment and the severity of symptoms based on the following continuum of needs that is very relevant to recovery from workplace emotional victimization:

- the need to protect the client
- the need to help stabilize the client
- the need to help the client access life skills
- the need to have client use life skills in a directed way
- the need to educate the client about the recovery process
- the need to assist the client in reintegration

Depression

Depression is one of the most common emotional experiences of victims of workplace mobbing. Professionals need to be alert to indications that the target of abuse intends to harm themselves or others (Lewis et al., 2002).

Major depressive disorder, the most common type of mood disorder, frequently appears in the general population, with a lifetime prevalence of about 15 percent and possibly as high as 25 percent for women (Kaplan & Sadock, 1996). A long-standing clinical perception indicates that stressful life events often precede the first episode of mood disorders such as depression. Beck and Alford (2009) addressed some of the unresolved questions about depression. One is whether depression is an exaggeration of a mood experienced by most normal or "well" people and whether the difference between what relatively well people experience and what disordered people experience is actually measurable. Other issues to understand are what causes and defines depression and what are the most effective treatments. A third question is whether the depression is a reaction to life events or a condition resulting from internal processes. Finally, regarding the onset of depression, was it created by some identifiable stress or conflict in the person's life?

The DSM-5 (APA, 2013) defines a major depressive episode as having five or more of the following symptoms during the same two-week period and being different from the individual's previous functioning:

- depressed mood (in children and adolescents, the mood can be irritability) most of the day nearly every day, as suggested by either self-report of the person or via clinical observation
- significantly diminished interest or pleasure in all, or almost all, activities most of the day
- substantial weight loss or gain
- insomnia or hypersomnia (sleeping too much)
- psychomotor agitation or retardation
- fatigue or loss of energy
- feeling worthless or excessively guilty
- compromised ability to think and concentrate
- indecisiveness
- recurrent thoughts of death not limited to fears of dying

In addition, the symptoms do not meet the criteria for mixed-episode depression, do not cause significant distress or impaired functioning, are not due to substance use, and are not better accounted for by bereavement after the death of a loved one (APA, 2013).

After the client's safety and clinical risk have been assured, treatment can included a variety of interventions, including, but not limited to, individual psychotherapy (especially that involving cognitive–behavioral approaches), bibliotherapy, and the possible use of medication to alleviate depressed mood. Depending on their education and professional disciplines, professionals may include a variety of testing procedures to gather objective data. In particular, brief screening instruments such as the Beck Depression Inventory (Beck, Steer, & Brown, 1996) and the Beck Hopelessness Scale (Beck, Weissman, Lester, & Trexler, 1974) can be helpful in validating assessment data gathered in the interviewing process. In addition, clinicians may want to include some sort of personality profile measurement, such as the MMPI-2. While no guarantee of premobbing personality functioning is possible to obtain for most victims, the MMPI-2 can provided helpful and objective insight into the personality motivations of clients and may help to separate personality styles form symptoms of distress.

Segal and Hersen (2010) advised using additional guidelines when working with clients with depressed mood, suggesting that clinicians should assess the clients' biopsychosocial needs, educate them about assessment and treatment, involve other family members if appropriate, use valid and standardized assessment tools in addition to self-report, and avoid excessively "pathologizing" the clients.

Anxiety

A common symptom experienced by mobbing targets, anxiety can also be used to refer to a variety of disorders. In many ways, anxiety may be considered to be part of an adaptation system that allows people to plan for the future. If anxiety were only beneficial, however, people would not spend billions of dollars annually to rid themselves of anxious feelings (Barlow, 2002). Early psychologist Liddell stated,

> The planning function of the nervous system, in the course of evolution, has culminated in the appearance of ideas, values, and pleasures, the unique manifestations of man's social living. Man alone can plan for the future, man alone can be happy, but man alone can be worried and anxious. (Liddell, 1949, in Barlow, 2002, p. 1)

Beck and Emery (1985) distinguish anxiety from fear and panic. Anxiety can be thought of as an intense emotional state, generally involving future dangers. Fear comes from Old English, meaning something presenting a sudden calamity or danger.

The two concepts of anxiety and fear may be further distinguished by understanding anxiety as an emotional process, while fear is a cognitive process (Beck & Emery, 1985). Another distinction can be found in a temporal concept. Fear involves a present danger, while anxiety usually refers to something dreaded in the future. Normal anxiety is experienced by almost all humans. It is characterized by a vague sense of apprehension and may be accompanied by somatic complaints (Kaplan & Sadock, 1996). The role of anxiety in survival is well documented. It warns us of threat. But a question arises about how one copes with human experience when the threat is both internal and external, as in the case of workplace emotional abuse. The external threat of a hostile workplace gives subtle and overt cues about the dangers. Anxiety, then, can be an appropriate and adaptive response. But if anxiety becomes debilitating, it can prevent a person from making informed decisions, identifying coping strategies, or developing an exit plan for long-term survival.

The DSM-5 (APA, 2013) defines generalized anxiety as excessive worry occurring in most days for at least six months. These worries focus on various events or activities in the person's life. The person suffering from anxiety finds it difficult to control worry. Anxiety and worry are associated with three or more of the following symptoms:

- restlessness or feeling edgy
- tiring easily
- problems with concentration or "blank mind"
- increased irritability
- tense muscles
- sleep problems (early or middle insomnia)

In addition, anxiety, worry, and physical symptoms cause significant distress or impairment in social or occupational functioning or other important areas of functioning (APA, 2013).

How does one account for the origins and causes of anxiety? According to Kaplan and Sadock (1996), traditional psychoanalytical theories explained anxiety as falling into four primary categories:

- Id, or impulse-control, anxieties are related to primitive discomforts such as those felt by infants when they have needs or feel overwhelmed.
- Separation anxiety occurs when a person is a bit older and involves the loss or potential abandonment by important people in one's life.
- Castration anxiety occurs in relation to a child's fears in response to sexual development.
- Superego anxiety is the result of the final development of the moral, governing aspect of the personality.

This psychoanalytical orientation to understanding anxiety can have applicability in helping to understand, assess, and organize diagnoses and interventions for employees who have been emotionally harmed at work. In some ways, mobbing can produce all four types of anxiety. People who are being mobbed or bullied can feel very disarmed and overwhelmed. They may be surprised that their customary coping mechanisms are so compromised. Separation anxiety can occur as an injured worker contemplates the imagined or real loss of workplace relationships and structure, as well as the loss to income and well-being. Males or females can feel that they have lost a part of themselves as autonomously functioning people. Finally, the person can experience large degrees of guilt over the inability to prevent or stop the abuse, as well as shame over not being strong enough to withstand it. Very primitive anxiety about needs and safety, anxiety involved in fearing loss of the significant functions of work, fears about autonomy and harm as one asserts self-control, and fears of being blamed and shamed are all common subjective experiences of bullying targets that are well explained from a psychoanalytical perspective.

Behavioral theories explain anxiety in terms of conditioned responses to environmental stimuli. People can be sensitized to feel fearfulness and anxiety about real or neutral stimuli depending on the environment cues and consequences (Kaplan & Sadock, 1996). More recent cognitive–behavioral approaches interpret anxiety as the culmination of negative outcomes of irrational belief systems and maladaptive thinking habits. People who have been mobbed can become anxious while at work. Fearfulness and anxiety about work-related environmental cues, such as contact with work colleagues, work-related topics, and physical proximity to the workplace, can also develop. In this way, neutral cues (conditioned stimuli) can become as threatening as the original feared stimulus, and the fear response (conditioned response) becomes generalized.

A cognitive–behavioral perspective would suggest that realistic *self-talk* (such as "I can survive this," "This is unfortunate, but it does not have to be a disaster," and "I don't want to have to find another job, but I can do so if I need to") becomes replaced with irrational beliefs (such as "I can't stand this," "This is terrible," and "I'll never find another job, and I'll lose everything"). Cognitive–behavioral theory encourages a person to carefully examine and challenge the exaggerations and distortions in thinking that contribute to and even worsen feelings of distress.

Existential theorists suggest that anxiety is created by the profound sense of "aloneness" and nothingness that people may experience in life (Kaplan & Sadock, 1996). A bullied worker almost certainly feels alone in the misery created by the mobbing. Observers may be afraid to provide support to the target because of their own fears of the bully's retaliation, or they may simply not understand the severity of the distress caused by the bullying. If the organization is highly dysfunctional, the bullied person may be isolated by organizational structure and practices. Finally, biological theories have emerged in conjunction with neuroscience, explaining anxiety as a result of complex biopsychoneurological processes among all humans, produced in some combination of experience and biological vulnerability. This biopsychoneurological process, together with cognitive–behavioral habits, may be the best explanation for what combines to create severe anxiety in the face of emotional abuse at work.

An emotionally hostile workplace may contribute to profound anxiety and distress in targeted workers. While the experience may be adaptive and give the employee cues that he or she must make changes for emotional and physical survival, unchecked it can cause debilitating health and even death from stroke, heart attack, accidents, or malignancies.

Treatment for anxiety depends on the theoretical framework of the clinician.

Social work practice advocates the importance of collaborative planning with the client in defining goals and objectives. It may be argued that cognitive–behavioral treatments are generally effective for treating symptoms of anxiety (Barlow, 2002), yet it may also be acknowledged that numerous biopsychosocial treatments can be effective. Many anxiety disorders have symptom overlap with mood disorders; thus, many treatments of anxiety conditions are similar to those for treating depressive conditions, including the use of certain medications such as selective serotonin reuptake inhibitors (SSRIs).

Clark and Beck (2012) proposed various therapeutic techniques and styles typically used by cognitive–behavioral therapists, including education, collaboration, Socratic questioning, guided discovery, and collaborative empiricism. They also emphasized the tendency for anxious people to overestimate the danger in situations and to underestimate personal abilities to coping with those dangers. In *The Anxiety and Worry Workbook,* Clark and Beck (2012) advocated helping clients to search for safety that is both behavioral and cognitive and to rigorously apply mental self-help exercises. Cooper and Lesser (2002) advocated additional behavioral approaches, including goal setting, reinforcing positive coping behaviors, social skills training, assertiveness training, and relaxation training. All of these behavioral interventions could be effective in treating bullying-related anxiety symptoms.

A postmodern approach suggested by Cooper and Lesser (2002) is called "narrative therapy." In the use of language narrative, the clinician listens to the client's story and attempts to make a new story (called meaning making or narrative creation). Using narrative as a response to workplace-induced anxiety symptoms may not seem immediately beneficial; however, it can be used to chronicle progress in therapy as a client works toward resolution of a painful situation (Cooper & Lesser, 2002). Poulin (2005) recommended using strengths-based practice when working with distressed clients. Such methods would include support and assistance with problem solving for targets of bullying (Clark & Beck, 2012).

Segal and Hersen (2010) recommended obtaining context-specific information from the client and behaviorally specific, open-ended questions during assessment interviews. They also strongly cautioned against dismissing the client's input and perceptions and against overreliance on objective assessment procedures at the expense of developing and maintaining rapport.

Panic Disorder

Panic disorder involves a discrete period of intense fear or discomfort, also known as panic attacks, in which at least four of the following symptoms are present (APA, 2013):

- heart palpitations or rapid heart rate
- profuse sweating
- shakiness or trembling
- shortness of breath or the sensation of being smothered
- sensations of choking

- pain or discomfort in the chest
- gastrointestinal distress or nausea
- dizziness or lightheadedness
- feelings of unreality (derealization) or feeling detached from oneself (depersonalization)
- intense fear of losing control
- fear of dying
- paresthesia (numbness or tingling sensations)
- chills or hot flashes

From a diagnostic perspective, panic disorder is generally not coded alone but in conjunction with another category of anxiety disorder. Emotional abuse commonly results in symptoms of panic disorder in conjunction with or in the absence of other diagnoses in targets.

Clark and Beck (2012) described panic attacks as the tsunami of anxiety and emphasized that a person with panic attacks quickly identifies the situations that trigger them and soon learns to avoid these situations. Preoccupation with the physical symptoms of autonomic system hyperarousal is a typical feature. Along with this preoccupation is a tendency to exaggerate the danger of situations and overreact. To begin to remedy these cognitive habits, Clark and Beck (2012) recommended helping clients to develop coping strategies, including modifying anxious thinking, developing awareness and understanding of physical symptoms, searching and finding evidence of safety, practicing breath control, initiating relaxation responses, creatively visualizing effective coping, and increasing physical exercise. All of these can be helpful, along with exposure training and awareness strategies. Although many "hard-line" cognitive–behavioral therapists do not advocate the use of medications for treating anxiety, medications can have a place in the treatment of panic conditions, especially when they are used for short periods of time. Many short-acting antianxiety medications are contraindicated for people with histories of substance-use disorders; however, short-term rather than open-ended use of medications can be a powerful adjunct to cognitive–behavioral treatment approaches.

Beck, Emery, and Greenberg (1990) have outlined strategies and techniques for cognitive restructuring for clients with anxiety. Emphasizing that anxious clients often seem free from anxiety while in the therapist's office (which requires greater creativity in the clinician), they suggested specific questions to use in assisting clients with increased awareness and countering automatic thoughts. In cognitive restructuring, clients are queried about the evidence and logic for their cognitive distortions. They are encouraged to consider whether a causal relationship actually exists between events and conditions. Anxious clients in cognitive therapy are challenged to consider the difference between habits and facts. Perceptions of reality and interpretations of events are examined. Clients undergoing treatment with cognitive restructuring are questioned about all-or-nothing thinking while analyzing exaggerations. Details are checked to ensure their interpretation within the context of events. Information sources are clarified for their reliability. Possibilities not previously considered are generated. Probabilities of feared events are evaluated. Feelings are distinguished from thoughts, and relevant facts are separated from irrelevant ones.

In using this method of query, the clinician should be direct and specific while avoiding a tendency to answer questions for the client in distress. In addition to these guidelines, questions should be timed to help with the development of rapport and collaboration. To shorten the cognitive challenge process, Beck et al. (1990) suggested limiting questions to three basic ones: What's the evidence for what you believe? What's another way of looking at it? So, what if it does happen? Note, in applying these approaches to panic disorders correlated with workplace bullying, these questions should be used to provide basic symptom relief. They should not be utilized to minimize the importance or the severity of the workplace emotional abuse.

ASD

ASD occurs when a person has been exposed to a traumatic event or process (such as bullying), with symptoms lasting from three days to one month. Examples of ASD symptoms in the DSM-5 (APA, 2013) include intense distress, hypervigilance, and disturbed concentration. It is a short-duration type of PTSD. In these disorders, symptoms are *not evident prior* to the onslaught of the stressor or trauma. Preclinically, the person generally functioned quite well, and symptoms only emerged in the wake of the acute life stress condition (Segal & Hersen, 2010). Conditions needed for ASD involve an experience in which the person witnessed, experienced, or was presented with events that involved actual threat to life or serious injury or threat to the physical integrity of self or others, in which the person's response involved intense fear, helplessness, or horror (APA, 2013). Barlow (2002) included *psychological vulnerability* in the definition surrounding the experience of trauma. This can certainly include the psychological vulnerability experienced by targets of mobbing. Beck and Emery (1985) discussed the phenomenon of a traumatic psychosocial event. The problem can start with an identifiable "cause," such as a threatened breakup of a relationship, a sudden and unexpected increase in demands placed on a person at work or home, or an increase in the most threatening components of a situation. The effect of the event is that it places in danger or jeopardizes certain valued functions for the person, such as performing adequately at work. The person fears what might happen, has images of being fired, and has continuous anticipatory anxiety. In addition to the anxiety, the person may develop a range of physical symptoms, including headache, gastrointestinal problems, sleep disturbances, chest pain, and heart palpitations. These symptoms can, in turn, trigger more and increasing fears.

ASD symptoms also include re-experiencing the traumatic event, marked avoidance of stimuli that arouse recollections of the trauma, marked symptoms of anxiety or increased arousal, and disturbances causing clinically significant distress or impairment in occupational or social functioning. Finally, the disturbance cannot be due to the direct physiological effects of substance use and cannot be better accounted for by the definition of brief psychotic disorder (APA, 2013).

Treatment of ASD often occurs first in the emergency room or in the office of a treating physician. A wise practitioner will query the patient about recent changes and stressors. Segal and Hersen (2010) suggested that for most people with ASD, psychological approaches may be the best alternative. Antianxiety medications, however, can be an important adjunctive treatment, especially if the client has severe agitation or severe insomnia. Medications used to treat daytime anxiety include those in the benzodiazepine category. For sleep, sedative-hypnotic medications may occasionally be prescribed. Both of these classifications of medications have high potential for habituation (dependency) and should only be used for very short periods—generally one to four weeks—and in combination with other psychological treatments, especially cognitive–behavioral ones (Segal & Hersen, 2010). Longer acting antianxiety medications and even medications originally used to treat depression, such as SSRIs, can be considered but may have limited usefulness because of the time (up to 6 weeks) it can take before full therapeutic levels are reached in the bloodstream.

PTSD

PTSD for the target can be perhaps one of the most debilitating outcomes of the bullying process. PTSD requires exposure to an extreme stressor and a set of symptoms that have lasted one month or longer. A number of severe life experiences can cause PTSD, including natural disasters, accidents, sexual assault, combat, severe abuse and neglect in childhood, hostage situations (with or without torture), and the unexpected death of a close loved one (Foa, Davidson, Frances, & Ross, 1999).

According to Foa et al. (1999), a person with PTSD has three primary types of symptoms. The first set involves re-experiencing the traumatic event or events, as evidenced by intrusive and distressing memories of the event(s), flashbacks (feeling as if the event is occurring again while the person is in a waking state), night terrors, and exaggerated emotional and physical reactions to triggering events that are similar to the trauma or that remind the person of the trauma. The second group of symptoms involves emotional numbing and avoidance. These include avoiding activities and places, lack of interest in life, detachment from others, and a restricted range of emotional expression. Finally, the third category of symptoms involves increased autonomic nervous system arousal. Included in this set of symptoms are disturbed sleep, angry outbursts, increased irritability, impaired concentration, a hyperstartle response, and extreme alertness about environmental dangers (Foa et al., 1999).

Reactions to mobbing can be so severe as to mimic the symptoms of PTSD but not meet the full diagnostic criteria. While clinical literature generally defines the nature of the stressor or trauma as a severe threat to life or physical safety, Leymann (1990, in Davenport et al., 2002) suggested that the excessive threat and danger caused in the mobbing situation manifest in symptoms that mirror PTSD. The risk of PTSD is also high when the stress is severe, prolonged, repetitive, humiliates the victim, or destroys the victim's community and support system (Namie & Namie, 2003). Von Bergen, Zavaletta, and Sober (2006) identified physical, mental, and psychosomatic health symptoms in mobbing targets. These can include stress, depression, reduced self-esteem, self-blame, phobias, sleep disturbances, digestive and muscular-skeletal problems, and PTSD.

Some people recover from trauma, and others do not. While it generally is not known why some affected workers have more difficulty than others, some variables may affect the likelihood of recovery, such as

- the severity and duration of the trauma;
- the physical and emotional proximity of a person to the traumatic event;
- the degree of danger, both real and perceived;
- the number of previous times the person has experienced trauma;
- who inflicted the trauma; and
- the type of reaction a victim received from family and friends (Foa et al., 1999).

The trauma created by a bullying situation may not seem as severe as a natural disaster or a crime of physical violence, but the duration of the bullying, according to literature cited earlier, can be a year or more. In addition, the perpetrator may be a person or group of people with whom the target has had previously positive relationships, so the bullying can represent a severe betrayal. Finally, others in the organization and friends and family outside the organization may not understand the degree to which the abuse is vicious, targeted, and demeaning, so they may fail to provide appropriate support responses.

Treating symptoms of PTSD always depends on the severity of the symptoms. Psychotherapy alone may be sufficient when symptoms are milder or the person is pregnant or breast-feeding, has strong resistance to taking medications, or has a medical condition that might be complicated by the use of medications (Foa et al., 1999). Others may need medications, especially if symptoms are severe or of long duration, they have another psychiatric disorder, they are suicidal or homicidal, they have a high level of stress, or they are having difficulty functioning. A recommendation for medication may be of particular importance if treatment with psychotherapy alone does not reduce the severity of symptoms (Foa et al., 1999).

Foa et al. (1999) also suggested that treatment should focus on anxiety management, with such cognitive–behavioral interventions as training in relaxation and breathing, assertiveness training to improve communication skills, examining and reframing self-talk, practicing a technique called "thought stopping" for intrusive thoughts, and undergoing supportive therapy and various other forms of cognitive therapy, such as systematic desensitization and in vivo exposure.

Medication treatment can vary from the use of antidepressants such as SSRIs, including sertraline, paroxetine, fluoxetine, fluvoxamine, and citalopram. Some newer SSRIs have shown promise, including nefazodone and venlafaxine (Foa et al., 1999). Older antidepressants in the tricyclic category, including imipramine and amitriptyline, can be helpful but may have more side effects than newer medications, including weight gain, craving for sugary foods, sleepiness, and impaired sexual functioning. Mood stabilizers such as divalproex (Depakote) are sometimes added if symptoms do not respond well to other medications. They can be of particular value for people suffering from PTSD.

Antianxiety medications can also be used to reduce symptoms and provide some immediate relief. They include diazepam, alprazolam, clonazepam, and lorazepam (Foa et al., 1999). However, these medicines are indicated for short-term use only and need careful monitoring due to their high habituating potential. Most practitioners recommend their use only in conjunction with other therapies. If medication is needed, it is usually needed for only six to twelve months. Clients and patients may need extra support to cope with such medications' side effects if they are problematic.

Treatment for PTSD also includes ensuring that the client learn about the disorder, and it might be necessary for the client to gradually expose himself or herself to situations that remind him or her of the trauma (desensitization). Like any medical treatment, if medication is prescribed it must be taken as directed to ensure maximum benefits. Clients who are victims of emotional abuse will also be wise to refrain from the use of alcohol or other drugs, to continue to find reasons for hope, and to join support groups so that they may share experiences with others (Foa et al., 1999).

Substance Abuse

Substance abuse in subordinates targeted by abusive supervisors was identified by Bamberger and Bacharach (2006). The explanations providing a substance-abuse response were twofold. First, Skarlicki et al. (1999, in Bamberger & Bacharach, 2006) suggested that employees in units characterized by abusive supervisors may seek retribution and voice their anger in hope of change. The adoption of problem drinking as passive resistance may be a means for accomplishing this. Alternatively, according to the stress paradigm, problem drinking may develop as a means of coping with stress (Bamberger & Bacharach, 2006). Whether substance abuse is a means of demonstrating passive resistance or a coping mechanism, once a person comes to rely on the use of alcohol or other drugs, a risk of abuse and dependency arise. The need for intervention will likely relate to the degree to which the substance use has become problematic. The DSM-5 (APA, 2013) distinguishes between substance use and substance-induced disorders. *Substance-use disorders* involve problematic patterns of substance use that leads to significant distress or impairment in the person's life. *Substance-induced disorders* are those conditions created by the use of substances, such as various types of psychosis, anxiety, mood conditions, and withdrawal conditions. Substance-use disorders can involve increased use, unsuccessful efforts to quit or cut down, craving, continued use despite adverse outcomes, reducing or discontinuing social or personal responsibilities, hazardous use, and increased tolerance. Many people with substance-use problems can cease use or use in moderation once a problem has been identified. Not all people with substance-abuse diagnoses will go on to develop full substance dependence, but many will do so if the abuse if not addressed and corrected.

The DSM-5 defines, and distinguishes between, substance-use disorders differently than previous versions of the manual. Specifically, tolerance can now be defined as both a marked increase in the amounts needed to achieve intoxication or by marked diminished effects with continued use. Withdrawal can be defined as becoming ill when one stops using, then using again for symptom relief.

Treatment for substance dependence depends on the severity and duration of the addiction, the age and health of the person who has the disorder, the substance to which the person has become dependent, and the resources available. Basic principles include establishing abstinence and then preventing relapse. Establishing abstinence may require medical intervention and treatment to prevent withdrawal-related health complications, such as delirium tremens and seizures. Once detoxification is completed, a program of psychoeducation about addiction disorders, treatment of co-occurring psychiatric disorders, stress management, communication skills, relapse-risk identification, and help in resolving legal, family, and financial problems may all be included in the treatment approach. Treatment can be inpatient, outpatient, residential, day treatment, partial day treatment, or any combination of these. Treatment choice is often determined by individual resources and what the community offers. It may be advisable for people with histories of sexual trauma or physical trauma to wait until some abstinence has been established before dealing with traumatic histories.

It may not be possible or realistic for someone with a recent history of workplace emotional abuse to wait to begin to address these issues. In fact, working on a recovery plan to recover from work-related mobbing may be imperative for ensuring maximum benefit and overall good treatment outcomes.

Other Disorders

Other disorders can also develop in response to mobbing. Milder diagnoses, such as adjustment disorders with depressed, anxious, or mixed features, are a common occurrence. The DSM-5 (APA, 2013) defines these conditions as the emotional or behavioral symptoms in response to identifiable stressor(s) occurring within three months of the stressor(s). Symptoms or behaviors are clinically significant as shown by distress or impairment. In addition, the condition does not meet the criteria for other specific disorders and does not represent bereavement. Conditions are identified as acute (if less than six months) or chronic (if longer than six months or if the stressor itself has long-term consequences). Such could certainly be the case for many who suffer from workplace emotional abuse.

Family Life and Intimate Relationships

Family life and intimate relationships do not escape the trauma of workplace mobbing. Sperry and Duffy (2009) used the term *vicious irony* to describe the how spouses, partners, family members, and close friends who are called upon for support by the victim of workplace mobbing are themselves affected by the effects of the mobbing on their family member or friend. In many instances, because of the trauma of the mobbing relationship and the injuries suffered by the mobbing victim, qualities such as intimacy, spontaneity, and closeness are all negatively affected. In referring to the effects of PTSD among mobbing victims, Hartig and

Frosch (2006) emphasized that both social networks and marriages can suffer and break down. Bullying targets are in the difficult bind of needing support from others but without the internal resources to be able to provide reciprocal caring. The support needed by spouses and friends can put mobbing victims and their families in an ongoing struggle for survival. With this in mind, clinicians who work with couples, families, and spouses or partners of targeted workers would be wise to understand the dynamics of workplace bullying and its systems impacts.

CROSS-CULTURAL CONSIDERATIONS

Clinicians must be mindful of the need to ensure cultural competency with bullied clients. Included in these areas of cultural competency are such dimensions as culture-bound values, verbal and emotional expressiveness, insight, distinctions between mental and physical functioning, communication patterns, class-bound values, and language barriers. Of particular importance are differences in communication style, factors such as nonverbal communication, proxemics (perception and use of personal space), and paralanguage, those vocal cues other than spoken language that are commonly used in communication (Sue & Sue, 1990). Treatment professionals should take care to understand the nuances of their clients' cultures. While no one text can provide all that clinicians need to know about cultural diversity issues, of special importance to the bullied worker in crisis is how the client interprets the bullying and how this interpretation fits with cultural expectations and role functioning within their culture.

DEVELOPING AN EXIT PLAN

Treatment will depend on the symptom severity, the needs of the client, the stage in the intervention or recovery process that a client is experiencing, and other factors. Clinical risk management is always a primary consideration, as it can include the issues of suicidal intent, psychosis, homicidal intent, child abuse and neglect, elder abuse and neglect, and grave disability (that is, being unable to care for one's own basic needs). Assessing a client's suicidal intention, homicidal intention, and degree of hopelessness or despair are always important considerations. While any qualified mental health professional may be the primary treating clinician, the clinician's familiarity with the mobbing syndrome and its effects on targets is of very high importance if treatment is to be effective.

Delayed stress disorder can also occur, but it takes a somewhat different course. Although the symptoms of PTSD usually begin immediately after or within weeks of a trauma, with delayed stress disorder, symptoms do not occur until months or years later. The onset of delayed symptoms most often occur on the anniversary of the traumatic event or if another trauma is experienced, particularly one that may remind the person of the original event (Foa et al., 1999).

Another syndrome, discussed by Namie and Namie, is a condition called prolonged duress stress disorder, or PDSD. Its symptoms do not result from a single traumatic event but rather from the latest in a serious of cumulative bullying events (Scott & Strandling, 1994, in Namie & Namie, 2003). ASD, PTSD, and PDSD can all result in serious debilitation and destabilization for targets of mobbing.

Treatment for anxiety disorders can vary but generally involve a combination of insight-oriented treatment; cognitive–behavioral therapy; psychoeducation; behavioral interventions such as systematic desensitization, relaxation training, and guided imagery; and, if necessary, short-term use of appropriately prescribed medications. Primary care physicians may want to ensure that behavioral interventions such as systematic desensitization, relaxation training, and guided imagery (and, if necessary, short-term use of appropriately prescribed medications) are all considered. Primary care physicians will also want to ensure that the symptoms are the result of stress only and not evidence of an even more serious threat, such as heart attack or cerebral vascular accident. If the client is suffering from severe hypertension, management and control of blood pressure will be important. Physicians may do a cursory review of client's diet and health habits to ensure that nutrition is sufficient and health habits such as diet, exercise, and avoiding overuse of caffeine, sugar, and alcohol have all been addressed. In some cases, nutritional supplements may be advised or prescribed, especially those replacing nutrients easily depleted by severe stress.

Exclusions

This discussion excludes diagnoses related to personality characteristics that may cause subjective distress, mood instability, impairment in social or occupational functioning, or impulse-control problems that may be considered character traits in nature and long-standing in duration. Although the presence of a personality disorder could be a risk factor in being targeted for mobbing, no evidence was identified in the literature that points to a necessary or predictive condition of personality disorders in mobbing targets.

Personality disorders fall into three categories: those that create personal distress for the person who has the condition, those that create problems for others who relate to the person in some way, and those that create impaired functioning. Problems can emerge in people who have been emotionally abused at work, so the symptoms alone are not sufficient to warrant a personality-disorder diagnosis. Any or all of these types of symptoms—subjective distress, mood instability, impaired social functioning, or poor judgment—can result from the experience of being mobbed. Clinicians need to be mindful of the variety of atypical behaviors presented by a person in extreme distress. These behaviors may be situational only and not indicative of a personality disorder.

What about Those Who Don't Receive Treatment?

Unfortunately, not everyone who needs treatment to recover from workplace bullying receives it. The reasons for this are many and varied. The target may already feel too much guilt, embarrassment, and shame so that he or she may be reluctant to encounter the additional stigma of professional mental health treatment. An injured worker already feels stigmatized. He or she may have real fears about what mental health treatment means. If the person has a strong belief system about being strong and not letting others know of personal problems, the prospect of telling a therapist, psychologist, social worker, or physician can be humiliating.

The victim also may not have resources or insurance. Part of the dilemma of being a targeted worker is that financial limitations may be very real and severe. The target may have already exhausted financial resources or may fear using available resources that might be needed for living expenses. Some injured workers have no health benefits or access to treatment. Since, from a workers' compensation perspective, emotional injury is more difficult to prove than physical injury, it is not certain whether the employer would ever be held liable for psychiatric care. The target may fear that entering treatment would complicate or jeopardize a legal claim that is in progress. The likelihood that mental health treatment records could become part of the evidence in litigation is threatening both to the client and to the treatment professional. No client wants his or her mental health history subjected to court scrutiny, and most clinicians dread and avoid the prospect of going to court or having case records subpoenaed.

The victim's family and friends may also be advising the person to "just get over it" and get on with life. Family members and spouses may fear that the victim will lose his or her job and create added financial burden on, and risk to, family resources. The risk for this is greater if the target's support system does not understand the dynamics of workplace mobbing. Finally, the person may not recognize and understand the symptoms well enough to comprehend the potential value of professional help.

Prognosis and Outcomes

Prognosis and outcomes vary with the severity of the symptoms, the duration of the stressor, the client response to treatment, and the client's motivation to recover. Outcomes will most certainly be affected by the organization's response to the situation and whether conditions are remedied. Davenport et al. (2002), as mentioned earlier in this chapter, suggested that the best outcomes occurred when targets demonstrated a number of healthy survival behaviors. First, they understood what was going on and responded to the situation confidently. Second, they refused to participate in the bullying process and avoided victimization. Third, they demonstrated a number of emotional, physical, and mental coping strengths. Finally, they focused their attention outside of work and the bullying situation while making specific plans to leave the job.

Namie and Namie (2003) suggested some general guidelines for the recovery process once a person gets help, including

- assess the bully's impact,
- establish and protect personal and professional boundaries,
- avoid unattainable standards,

- control destructive mind games, and
- address feelings of anger and shame.

Davenport et al. (2002) emphasized the importance of targets avoiding the temptation to become isolated. They need to build (or rebuild) their self-esteem and deal with feelings of loss and betrayal. Techniques such as journaling, meditation, and exercise are all suggested as adjuncts to the recovery process. A number of survival behaviors that may be helpful exist, such as conscious grieving, believing that change can produce good outcomes, getting support from friends and family, having a pet, and involving oneself in strengthening activities such as exercise and art. Those with survival skills will limit their social contacts to people who build rather than degrade self-esteem, learn some new skills that are work related or not, attitudinally "detach" from work, and take inventory of the many areas of life the person does control (Davenport et al., 2002).

Finally, Davenport et al. (2002) emphasized that the healing process for mobbing targets will depend on a number of variables, such as the seriousness of the injury, the rate at which the target understood the situation, the availability of social supports, the degree to which the target's health was damaged, the effectiveness of any therapy the person received, and the degree to which the target felt successful and appreciated at an alternative employment situation.

Tehrani (2001) provided examples of "morals to stories" about workers who had been harmed by workplace harassment. These morals reflected themes of hope and reframing. Examples included the following:

- Despite hardship, a person has the strength to stand up for what is right.
- The truth about a situation will eventually be known.
- Bullies can prevail when others fail to take action to prevent their behavior.
- Dysfunctional organizations tend to protect bullies.
- When a person has a mental illness, dealing rationally with the person is impossible.
- No one needs to tolerate bullying, but bullying cultures are very hard to change.
- Being injured in the search for justice is preferable to participating in injustice.
- Recovery doesn't happen overnight, it takes time, but it is possible for a victim to become a survivor.

Ochberg (1993, in Tehrani, 2001, p. 57) proposed "The Survivor's Psalm":

I have been victimized. I was in a fight that was not a fair fight. I did not ask for the fight. I lost. There is no shame in losing such fights, only in winning. I have reached the stage of survivor and am no longer a slave of victim status. I look back with sadness rather than hate. I look forward with hope rather than despair. I may never forget, but I need not constantly remember. I *was* a victim. I *am* a survivor.

Developing an Exit Plan, Career Changes, and Redefining the Self

Developing an exit plan and redefining the self will be important for survival. A person who is anxious or depressed because of emotional abuse at work is not in a good frame of mind to garner the energy required for job-search activities. Nonetheless, seeking alternative employment and professional engagement will be important for most targets and will have a significant impact on the recovery process and outcomes.

Physician Spencer Johnson (1998) created a whimsical allegory about change in his best-selling self-help book *Who Moved My Cheese?* Johnson tells a fable of two mice, Sniff and Skippy, and two small people, Hem and Haw. They have parallel lives and each day race into a maze looking for workplace rewards, characterized as cheese.

In this daily quest for cheese, some profound principles were uncovered by the characters. First, having cheese makes one happy. Second, the more important cheese is to you, the more you want to hold on to it. When the location of the cheese is changed, adaptation becomes necessary, so the third principle the characters learn is that if one is not able to change when the rules of cheese-gathering change, one may become extinct. The fourth principle challenges the characters by asking them to think about what they would do if they were not feeling afraid. The fifth principle reminds the characters to smell the cheese often so they will know when it is getting old! Next, they learn that moving in a new direction helps them to find new cheese and that when they move beyond their fear, they feel better! The little characters are advised to imagine themselves enjoying new cheese even before they are able to find it. This visioning actually helps to lead them to new sources of cheese! They learn painful lessons about the importance of letting go of old cheese to find new cheese sooner, that it is safer to search in the maze for new cheese than to remain in a cheese-less situation, and that, unfortunately, old beliefs do not lead one to the new cheese. The characters begin to triumph when they can see that in finding and enjoying new cheese, they can change courses in life. In retrospect, the mice and tiny people come to appreciate that noticing small changes in the location and supply of cheese will help one to adapt to bigger changes as they occur. Finally, all characters learn to "move with the cheese" and enjoy it.

The tale concludes with clearly outlining the handwriting on the wall, truths that can help with survival:

> Change happens: They keep moving the cheese. Anticipate change: Get ready for the cheese to move. Monitor change: Smell the cheese often so you know when it's getting old. Adapt to change quickly: The quicker you learn to let go of old cheese, the sooner you can enjoy new cheese. Change: Move with the cheese. Enjoy the change!: Savor the adventure and enjoy the taste of new cheese! Be ready to change quickly and enjoy it again and again: They keep moving the cheese. (S. Johnson, 1998, p. 72)

While employees who are trying to escape from a serious bullying situation may not immediately appreciate the wisdom in the parable of *Who Moved My*

Cheese?, the principles can be valuable for assisting one in the painful process of negotiating career and, perhaps, lifestyle changes. The book, a small volume with a foreword by Kenneth Blanchard, can be read in less than an hour. It offers a profound message of hope. Clinicians may want to obtain and loan the little publication in their work with people who are being or have been mobbed. While bibliotherapy is never a substitute for symptoms-oriented psychotherapy, reading assignments such as *Who Moved My Cheese?* can offer a broader perspective and a more realistic appraisal of the change process.

Edwards and Edwards (2001) offered some steps that a person must take in the career-change process. Their concrete and usable series of recommendations are designed to help one with midlife career adjustments. First, the person must come to terms with the need to make a change, by attending to both internal and external indications of the need for change. Victimized people may experience disbelief, fear of the unknown, shock, disequilibrium, and feeling overwhelmed and helpless before becoming ready to move on. These are symptoms similar to those one experiences with other types of losses, such as death, divorce, separation, and loss of status. Their suggestions for getting ready to change involve

- careful introspection and self-evaluation;
- a mourning process;
- evaluation of the readiness to let go and move on;
- depression, anger, and resentment; and
- regret about past failures, both real and imagined.

When a breakthrough occurs, the person can become willing and able to begin the exciting, although perhaps daunting, process of reinventing the professional self.

Work to enhance the imagination's capacity for envisioning something new can be an exciting and creative endeavor. Clients can be encouraged to explore their favorite work experiences and their favorite non-work-related life experiences, paying attention to patterns, themes, and images they have used for life planning in the past. Clients in the midst of change may find it helpful to reconnect with childhood experiences and dreams, uncovering the themes and feelings that may tend to pervade in these memories. Finally, a new, revised version of professional self can begin to emerge. Edwards and Edwards (2001) suggested that job- or career-changing adults define themselves using a system of questions involving the "four Cs of creative change": *comfort* (for example, what is one's personal style?), *clarity* (for example, what is the situation?), *creativity* (for example, what are the available options?), and *commitment* (for example, what's been done and what are the next steps?).

Clients in the process of job or career change may find it helpful to write descriptions of the qualities they want, need, or require in a new job. Although these may need to be modified during the search process, having a vision can be a powerful starting point. Using the process of creating a "vision board" or treasure map can be a fun way for clients to get a visual picture of what their next job might look like. These can be done by cutting and pasting pictures from various sources onto a piece of poster board or construction paper to make a "job vision" collage. Once the new employment situation has been secured, clients can refer back to their collage to see how well the new position meets the vision. While the exercise may seem silly to the more cerebral, the visual and tactile process can be helpful in both integrating the recovery process and stimulating the imagination for thinking of future possibilities.

Like the ending of other types of relationships, the end of a job will eventually involve some rigorous self-honesty on the part of the target. There may be things that the person did or could have done differently that might have affected the way in which events unfolded. Facing these with both self-honesty and self-compassion will be an important part of the healing and recovery process. Even the highest-functioning, hardest-working person with the most integrity and greatest degree of professional commitment can uncover insights about what they wish they had done differently. As in a marital dissolution, mature people will eventually be willing to face their errors of commission and omission if they are to move forward into a new "relationship" in the future.

From a clinical perspective, solution-oriented therapy involves defining and clarifying the problem, assessing strengths and vulnerabilities, collaborative goal setting, and solution-focused strategies (Cooper & Lesser, 2002). *Constructivism* is a framework useful in a narrative approach to psychotherapy. Constructivism emphasizes a person's subjective perception and experience of a problem. From a philosophical perspective, constructivism concerns itself with the nature of reality and being (and metaphysics and ontology) and the nature of human knowledge and how it is acquired. According to Cooper and Lesser (2002), narratives or stories of life events are a reformulation of constructs or memories. A person who has had an experience will go through a series of steps that include reformulating memories of the event, changing the narratives about the event from time to time, and, finally, recounting the events to a professional who can be present as a participant observer. Narratives involve the client views of the problem or event. At some time in the recovery process, it may become important for a person to begin to deconstruct the narrative to understand his or her role in it.

In this way, the person can begin to take responsibility for behaviors and begin to fight the effects of the problem. Both personality traits and behavioral traits may place the victim at risk. It is generally agreed that wise and emotionally healthy people are those who are honest with themselves about what they might have done differently. Developing this inventory can also help the person avoid repeating the behaviors that might have been problematic. Admitting errors and thinking of alternative ways of handling situations in the future can be an empowering part of the recovery process.

A competent clinician should encourage a client to understand the effects that the client's own perceptions and interpretations have had on his or her life and how they have influenced relationships with others (Cooper & Lesser, 2002). This would not mean that the victim is encouraged to engage in self-blame; rather, he or she can reach an understanding of levels of personal power for recovery. Using this approach, which tends to be a somewhat brief form of therapy, clients may experience various stances in the treatment-and-recovery process. The eliciting stance occurs where the client who has been harmed shares ideas about the problem. In the probing stance, the clinician may offer alternative descriptions to those offered by the client. For a contextualizing stance, the therapist moves the client to understand and verbalize about others in the client's life. The matching or mirroring stance involves the clinician reflecting back what the client has said. Finally, in the amplifying stance, the therapist pays attends to specific emotions and behaviors (Cooper & Lesser, 2002).

Clients can also be encouraged to examine the *landscape of action questions*, in which the professional tries to help connect the client with past experiences, and the *landscape of consciousness questions*, in which the client verbalizes and tries out alternative courses of action and points of view. Finally, there is the *landscape of experience questions*, in which the client may reflect on another's experience of himself or herself (Cooper & Lesser, 2002).

The process of redefining the self involves knowing who one is, knowing how one derives joy in life, knowing what is important, and being clear about what one wants and does not want. Edwards and Edwards (2001) defined these as part of a person's internal compass that can be relied upon to determine whether one is on track. A person in recovery from emotional abuse at work and its aftermath will need to wrestle with tendencies to feel overwhelmed, deenergized, and rejected.

After a client is stable, has identified life skills, knows how to use them, is knowledgeable about the recovery process, and has begun reintegration, the practical issues of creating a new path for life's work can begin. A number of assessments can help with client's redefinition of self. If the client has a well-established professional identify, another position or venue for using existing knowledge and skills may be a good choice. For some clients, a complete mid-career change may be in order, including job retraining or higher education. Two widely used career development instruments can help facilitate the change process.

One of the most helpful tools can be a Personal Career Development Profile, or PCDP (Walter, 1995, in Zunker & Osborn, 2002). Founded on over 30 years of research, the PCDP is designed to identify a number of areas of behavior that can have an effect on career satisfaction and work performance.

Problem-solving resources describe a person's overall strengths for solving most problems and usual approach to resolving problems encountered. Patterns for coping include those efforts someone uses to react to emotionally charged events and likely actions when conflict or opposition occurs. Interpersonal interaction styles examine preferences for relating and communicating with others. Organizational role- and work-setting preferences describe a person's unique style in leadership and subordinate roles in organizational settings, along with work-setting preferences.

Finally, career activity interests are those characteristics inherent in one's personal strengths and general personality orientation. These can then be synthesized or distilled so the person has a better understanding of who they are, how they behave, and what types of work environments work best for them. Self-awareness about personal style and preferences can help to prevent a mobbing situation in the future. After all areas have been assessed, a *personal career lifestyle effectiveness plan* can be created that both summarizes the individual's typical responses and preferences and provides some guidance about career path and organizational infrastructure, which can help in career selection and redevelopment (Walter, cited in Zunker & Osborn, 2002). Career and lifestyle planning can be an excellent tool for people who are trying to recreate their professional selves.

MYERS-BRIGGS TYPE INDICATOR

Another helpful tool for career-choice assessment and personal reflections about strengths and preferences for career-change planning is the Myers-Briggs Type Indicator (MBTI). The MBTI is a measure of psychological types based on the early work of C. G. Jung. Jung suggested that the basic differences in behavior are the ways that people customarily choose to use their perceptions, judgments, and decision-making skills (Jung, 1921, in Zunker & Osborn, 2002). The four-letter "profile" comprises the results of the MBTI two-choice inventory format that requires a person to make a selection between responses that measure preferred modes of interacting with others (Myers & Briggs, 1985, in Zunker & Osborn, 2002), as shown below. The outcome results in 16 type categories:

Extroversion (E) vs. Introversion (I)
Sensing (S) vs. Intuition (N)
Thinking (F) vs. Feeling (F)
Judging (J) vs. Perceiving (P)

How valuable is the MBTI? As with any measure, one should never rely on it alone. Any clinician hoping to use the MBTI should also have formal training in its use before administering and interpreting it. Historically, employers have sometimes administered the MBTI prior to extending offers of employment to candidates and used them for training and job-matching purposes.

Some limited work shows a correlation between MBTI scores and career obstacles. For example, Healey and Woodward (1998, in Zunker & Osborn, 2002) found that high scores in a combination of either judging or perceiving in women were found to be related to some lack of surety in decision-making processes. For men, higher scores on either thinking or feeling can be related to methods for dealing with the stress of obstructions caused by external demands (Healey & Woodward, 1998, in Zunker & Osborn, 2002). Using MBTI scores in career planning can have difficulties, however. Some career-planning counselors have objected that some of the scales do not represent Jung's original definitions. Others have argued that knowledge of one's mode may not improve career decision making at all (Zunker & Osborn, 2002).

Nonetheless, a MBTI profile can be helpful in identifying those career choices that the midlife career changer might find the most rewarding and for which he or she might be the best suited. A goal in the recovery process and the process of reinventing one's professional self is to find work that closely resembles the type of work the person would find most fulfilling and what the person might do best.

An employee who has been subjected to emotional abuse at work who decides to create a new career path (either by design or by default) is usually extremely vulnerable. Clinicians and career-development professionals alike must be very cautious about purporting that any tests or screening instruments are the sole basis on which major life decisions should be made. Generally, a more comprehensive examination of self that includes examining values, vision, areas of expertise, and areas of vulnerability will need to be part of the career-change process. In addition, Zunker and Osborn (2002) offered some valuable suggestions for adult career development. Adults can be asked about how their personal characteristics and traits influenced their career choices in the past. They can be encouraged to describe the match or lack of match between their personal characteristics and their past work experiences. Adults might be well served if they can examine how their personal characteristics, traits, and values have influenced their interactions with coworkers and supervisors. They may also benefit from identifying what led them to career decisions at any particular moment in time. Examining how well one's values and needs might be fulfilled in any given role or work setting can also be an important part of career change and planning.

Career-change planning and oversight does not substitute for competent psychotherapy or medical treatment. But career-change exploration can be an adjunct to other therapies offered, including risk management and bereavement work for a displaced worker. Clinicians and HR professionals who work with clients who have been mobbed will often find career exploration to be a helpful aspect of treatment and recovery. In addition, injured clients can begin to reclaim their strength and internal locus of control when they participate in career redefining.

EVIDENCE-BASED PRACTICE

The role of evidence-based practice is a major new focus for social work education. In the wake of social workers using novel and not yet empirically supported treatment interventions, social work researchers Pignotti and Thyer (2009) examined interventions used by licensed clinical social workers in 34 states. More than half of respondents admitted to using one or more not-yet-supported treatment interventions in the preceding year. While most practitioners support the notion of evidence-based practices, a trend toward limited and prudent use of not-yet-tested interventions seems fairly common. A new specialty in treating workplace emotional abuse is an obvious future trend, but social work has been largely silent on the issue of mobbing, bullying, and emotional abuse at work.

Liefooghe and Davey (Geffner et al., 2004) concluded that bullying becomes part of institutional life when organizations value compliance over personal identity and reinforce it with threats against workers. Sheehan, Barker, and Rayner (1999) stated the following:

> In the rush to globalization and increased competition, many organizations are restructuring and downsizing as part of a perceived need to change. Frequently there is a failure to account for the wider implications of the change process because change is looked at from a narrow perspective and short term solutions are sought for what are often complex problems. (p. 52)

Koonin and Green (Geffner et al., 2004) admonish organizations to take stock of their corporate cultures and make changes. Changing organizational practices and policies can be a major step toward reducing the likelihood of workplace bullying.

LEGAL CONSULTATION

Legal consultation is a step that anyone who has been emotionally harmed at work will want to investigate. This will be particularly true if diagnosable illness or temporary or permanent disability has resulted, or if a job change is necessary. Injured workers should select their legal representatives carefully. If an injured employee seeks legal consultation, it is important to screen attorneys to ensure that the professional selected for legal representation be "proemployee," as well as knowledgeable about workplace emotional abuse. Many good attorneys, even those who specialize in workers' compensation and employment law, are not yet knowledgeable about the liabilities created by emotional injury in the workplace. Identifying an employment-law specialist who is sensitive to the needs of emotionally injured workers will be critical. Namie (2008) suggested selecting an advocate who has a fighting spirit, has empathy, has both wisdom and court experience, can be realistic about what outcomes might be expected, and can explain the law clearly to a layperson. They also caution injured workers against expecting a legal representative to serve as a therapist. Finally, even excellent attorneys cannot manufacture a law. Any attorney will be limited by what legislators have written and how courts have interpreted these laws. The degree of accurate and detailed documentation, as well as the credibility of a potential plaintiff, will have a large impact on the willingness of an attorney to take a case involving workplace emotional abuse (Namie & Namie, 2003).

The degree of accurate and detailed documentation, as well as the credibility of a potential plaintiff, will have a large impact on the willingness of an attorney to take a case involving workplace emotional abuse. For attorneys, the ability to assess whether the client can be a good witness on his or her own behalf is often a factor in whether an attorney takes on a case. When a client has been severely damaged as a result of the workplace's impact on the client's psychosocial functioning, he or she may not appear to be able to express himself or herself well. The attorney must be able to discern if the client can be helped to heal enough to present well. This will involve finding every form of assistance possible to bring the client to sufficient stability to deal with the rigors of litigation. When one prevails on a client's behalf, the client feels vindicated. The vindication itself can be very healing. For some clients, however, it may be better to settle the case and avoid a trial. This would be particularly true if the client is extremely fragile.

Redress for Victims

Redress for victims in the United States and internationally can vary significantly. There is currently no legislation to address workplace bullying at the national level. Although in 2004 Sen. Tom Harkin (D-IA) introduced an omnibus bill called the

HELP (Healthy Lifestyle and Prevention) America Act (S2558) (Von Bergen et al., 2006), it did not specifically address workplace mobbing and did not pass. A question exists about whether the "sexual harassment cause of action" of the 1964 Civil Rights Act's Title VII might be extended to include emotional abuse at work. The response to this question is that although workplace bullying is not yet protected by Title VII, there may be a trend toward awarding judgments in favor of plaintiffs if the workplace emotional distress is inflicted intentionally, if the behavior was extreme, if the defendant's actions caused the plaintiff emotional distress, and if the resulting emotional distress was severe (Von Bergen et al., 2006). However, for now, treatment providers should be aware that clear prohibitions are often not in place for harmed workers.

Proposed Solutions

Solutions may lie in workplace bullying legislation. Gary and Ruth Namie of the WBI have helped to coordinate efforts at state levels for passing the HWB, authored by attorney and law professor David Yamada. (This bill will be discussed at length in chapter 8.) Important features include definitions of an abusive work environment, including acts or omissions that are made with malice, that are abusive, and that cause tangible physical or emotional harm. Redress for victims may include expenses for work time lost, medical expenses, punitive damages, attorney fees, and disability compensation (Bible, 2012). Real solutions for prevention and redress may result from passing of the HWB. Many of its advocates claim that current laws do not adequately address true victim damages nor do they prevent workplace bullying.

Current thinking suggests that bullying will more likely occur in situations of power imbalance for workers, low perceived costs for perpetrators, lack of clear policies for prevention, and lack of punishments for bullies. These factors, along with the fact that few claims actually result in damages to victims, make litigation an unlikely and inadequate alternative. Even some advocates of the bill suggest that the HWB would not be sufficient to address all the nuances of workplace bullying. Opponents, on the other hand, fear that such legislation would create additional layers of government oversight and open the door for frivolous lawsuits that are complex and costly. David Yamada offered a response to the concern about frivolity of claims, recognizing that although some risks would exist with the passage of the HWB, these would be offset by the low possibility of success with lawsuits (D. Yamada, cited in Bible, 2012). In addition, most attorneys understand that lawsuits have nuisance value, even if the likelihood of a favorable outcome is not high. The HWB would also not prevent injured workers from pursuing other avenues of recovery, including those for "maligned intentional infliction of emotional distress" (Bible, 2012, p. 38).

Experts in the field recognize that current legal tools are limited in their ability to address workplace bullying, and, to date, no states have enacted legislation to prevent bullying. Short of individual state laws, employers would be wise to be proactive and develop their own policies to prevent and address workplace emotional abuse (Bible, 2012).

Protection for Victims

Legal options for victims seem less than adequate. A well-known case, cited by Texas law professor Jon Bible, concerned bullying perpetuated by Indiana surgeon Daniel Raess. According to allegations, Raess repeatedly threatened and harassed a surgical team member, Joseph Doescher, during and after surgeries.

Indiana's Supreme Court eventually upheld an earlier verdict awarding the plaintiff, Doescher, a $325,000 award for "assault" after allegations that Raess screamed and swore at him. As of 2012, *Raess v. Doescher* is the only reported appellate court decision addressing workplace bullying (Bible, 2012). Although Doescher did win the case on the theory of assault, in most cases involving workplace bullying, targets have not been able to withstand the high levels of proof of harm that most state laws require.

David Yamada has identified five reasons why the American workplace is at such high risk for bullying and emotional abuses: the growth of service-sector work, pressures from the global market system requiring workers to produce more for less cost, declines in union membership, an increasingly diverse work environment, and the shift to reliance on work that is contracted and provided by temporary employees. Yamada outlined the existing tools for combating workplace bullying as prevention, with guidelines for healthy work environments that can minimize the risk of bullying; self-help protections for workers who use self-help measures for remediation, coupled with incentives for responsive employers; relief, compensation, and restoration for victims when self-help approaches are not helpful, including ensuring that the perpetrator is either removed or has undergone behavioral change; and, finally, punishment for bullies and enabling work environments. Unfortunately, most state laws fall short of meeting these goals. Because there are no legal grounds for addressing bullying itself, injured workers generally must rely on producing evidence of actual harm to health caused from "intentional infliction of emotional distress," which is a legal theory that has obtained relief for targets. Unfortunately, plaintiffs must prove that extreme or outrageous behavior from the defendant caused severe emotional reactions or distress (Bible, 2012). This is a very high standard and may not be realistic for many victims to meet.

Some victims may claim that the bullying behavior resulted in interference with the business relationship between the plaintiff and the employer. This would be true if the victim resigns from his or her position. Court decisions when this allegation is used have been mixed.

Another avenue for victims and their counsels has been to claim ongoing abuse from a *hostile work environment*. Such action is barred by the Civil Rights Act. According to its Title VII, if a workplace involves severe intimidation, ridicule, or insult that occurs with frequency and severity, it may be considered illegal but *only* if it involves a trait that is protected by the Civil Rights Act: race, color, sex, religion, or national origin. Unfortunately then, most (75 percent or more) of bullying occurs *outside of these definitions.* Even more ironically, recent laws, including protections from sexual harassment at work, further limit rights for targets of bullying if the bullying is by an "equal opportunity harasser"—someone who mistreats both sexes (Bible, 2012). The Americans with Disabilities Act (ADA) provides protection for those people who have one or more disabling physical or mental conditions that result in occupational impairment. These standards are very strict, however, so the ADA has not been effective in helping to address workplace bullying. Additional statutes that may apply in bullying cases include the following:

- The Age Discrimination in Employment Act
- Fair Labor Standards Act
- Occupational Safety and Health Act
- National Labor Relations Act (NLRA)
- Employee Retirement Income Security Act
- FMLA
- Fair Credit Reporting Act
- False Claims Act

According to Bible (2012), in the public sector (federal, state, and local), claimants may rely on the First, Fourth, and Fourteenth Amendments in the U.S. Constitution. According to Bible, few cases have proceeded under these theories.

Preexisting Conditions

Preexisting conditions can complicate an already complex and difficult situation. Courts have applied an "eggshell plaintiff" concept as one whose injuries are much worse than those of a typical person because of a preexisting factor or condition. Unfortunately, an increasing number of plaintiffs are asserting that because of their background of prior victimization or prior psychiatric condition, they are even more susceptible to injury from mobbing at work and that an employer should pay for the inordinate damage that allegedly resulted. Although legal issues and precedents will be examined later in this chapter, it is true that not all courts will hold a defendant liable for all of a plaintiff's emotional damage—that is, not all of the emotional harm from mobbing. This can be particularly true if a preexisting condition can be verified. According to McDonald (2006), courts have applied an "eggshell plaintiff" rule to mental and emotional injuries and may make award decisions based on the existence of a preinjury condition that was made worse by workplace emotional abuse. Some caution that if a plaintiff is using the "eggshell plaintiff" concept to establish liability, she or he is likely to fail (McDonald, 2006). While courts might be sensitive to the issue of an exacerbation of a preexisting condition, an injured employee should be aware that attempting to establish employer liability on the basis of this preexisting condition would not likely be successful.

SUMMARY

Lewis (1999, in Geffner et al., 2004) stated, "Unfortunately, some of the recent trends in business to focus on excellence and quality have put pressure on workers, line managers, and supervisors, creating an environment ripe for bullying" (p. 76). Liefooghe and Davey (Geffner et al., 2004) concluded that bullying becomes part of institutional life when organizations value compliance over personal identity and reinforce it with threats against workers. Koonin and Green (cited in Geffner et al., 2004) admonished organizations to take stock of their corporate cultures and make changes. Changing organizational practices and policies can be a major step toward reducing the likelihood of workplace bullying.

This chapter has examined clinical features of injured workers in crisis, risk management, clinical evaluations (including medical evaluations), and the importance of the therapeutic alliance. It has also identified clinical syndromes of targets of workplace bullying and treatment interventions. Exit planning and career-change guidance were offered to help in client in job transitions. The United States, unlike the European Union, has not been proactive in passing legislation to protect workers or to remediate workplace problems. Social workers should be advocates for ensuring worker safety. This suggestion is supported by the NASW (2008) *Code of Ethics*, section 6.04, "Social and Political Action," standard (a), which reads in part: "Social workers should be aware of the impact of the political arena on practice and should advocate for changes in policy and legislation to improve social conditions in order to meet basic human needs and promote social justice." Standard (b) states that "social workers should act to expand choice and opportunity for all people, with special regard for vulnerable, disadvantaged, oppressed, and exploited people and groups."

The next chapter examines high-risk organizations and some workplace interventions that can help to reduce the incidence and severity of workplace bullying.

7

Workplace Interventions

This chapter begins with a description of typical organizational responses to bullying. It then provides specific recommendations for organizational interventions for prevention and remediation of workplace emotional abuses. A variety of U.S. and international experts are cited. These references include information about policy development and implementation, training, and intervention from a variety of theoretical perspectives.

This chapter also presents a broad array of proactive workplace prevention strategies designed to help to minimize both the risk and the effects of workplace emotional abuse. Rather than merely providing a cookbook recipe for preventing and responding to bullying, it examines a variety of preventative leadership practices, organizational cultures, and leadership styles. Utilizing organizational structures, policies, and behaviors to reduce risk, this material will provide readers with a number of approaches for effectively managing change, understanding conflict, and increasing the likelihood of healthy organizational functioning. Upon completion of this chapter, readers will understand the role that healthy organizational functioning can play in reducing risk exposure for workplace bullying and for quickly addressing bullying when it occurs.

TYPICAL ORGANIZATIONAL RESPONSES

Gary and Ruth Namie of the WBI lament that the most common organizational response to allegations of bullying is *inertia* (2009). A WBI 2007 study (cited in Namie & Namie, 2009) garnering data from more than 1,500 respondents indicated that 44 percent of the time, organizational leaders did nothing in response to allegations of bullying, while they addressed and partially or completely resolved matters in a helpful manner 32 percent of the time. More than 18 percent indicated that interventions from top management worsened the plight of injured employees, exacerbating the already hostile environment. A 2004 study by NIOSH suggested some startling trends: When queried, 76 percent of employers said that bullying never happens in their worksites, and another 17 percent suggested bullying occurs only rarely. Clearly there has been a disconnection between administrative assessment and known prevalence trends (NIOSH, 2004, in Namie & Namie, 2009).

Risk management is defined as the processes, planning, responding, understanding, and monitoring of controlling risk in an organization. It is an ongoing process that focuses on recognizing various types of workplace infractions that could occur and identifying ways to avoid or minimize the effects on both the individual and the organization (Project Management Institute, 2008, in Carden & Boyd, 2013). The following sections will address workplace protections and interventions from the United States and a variety of other nations.

BULLY-PROOFING THE ORGANIZATION: PREVENTION VIA ASSESSMENT, POLICY, AND TRAINING

Loyola University Chicago researchers Fox and Stallworth (2009) identified the key role of consultants in organizational programs. They suggested the following steps for organizations to take in addressing bullying:

- Develop clear definitions of bullying
- Raise awareness within the organization.
- Clearly define consequences for offenders.
- Implement specific processes for remediation.
- Ensure that all personnel who may be involved in response to bullying are guided in prevention and response, including managers, HR leadership, union representatives, attorneys, and any mental health professionals involved in employee assistance.

The first recommended step is to conduct a comprehensive needs assessment. Such an assessment should be designed to provide clarity about the prevalence and severity of the problem. To humanize the issue, needs assessments should also include narratives from those who have been harmed, thus attaching real-life examples. Finally, needs assessments should identify previously implemented action steps to avoid duplication.

The second step is to provide mandatory training. The specifics of training should include scripted videos and interactive exercises that focus on questions such as, Is this bullying? Are the actions legal? In what ways is emotional abuse at work similar and different from harassment and discrimination? Are there differences in gender, race, and status roles in the organization? What is the target's role in bullying behavior? Is the target in any way responsible for what happened? What are the consequences to the person, the organization, and the industry? What can bystanders do? What should the response be from management and HR? What should the organization do to prevent or repair the situation? What organizational resources should be deployed in the examples discussed?

According to Fox and Stallworth (2009), training materials should include the following:

- definitions of workplace bullying and clarification of various types of bullying behavior
- clear, outlined information about the potential consequences and costs of unchecked bullying, along with explanations of the effects of bullying on the target, the work group, and the organization
- distinctions between those types of abuses that are specifically covered and not covered by current laws
- clear action steps for individuals and for the organization
- clear guidelines for response to bullying, including information about what targets can do, what bystanders can do, and how managers should respond to allegations
- demonstrations of how the bullying policies relate to knowledge of organizational policies
- identification of data-collection systems for outcomes once trainings are developed and delivered

Although creating a one-size-fits-all antibullying policy is not advisable or possible, such policies can include written statements of policy, commitment of leadership, clear definitions of bullying, a confidentiality statement, protections against retaliation, open communication channels, procedures for reporting bullying, and designated officers to whom reports can be made (Fox & Stallworth, 2009).

Einarsen, Hoel, Zapf, and Cooper (2011) were among the first researchers to examine the broad policy issues of workplace bullying, emphasizing the importance of policies in preventing and responding to bullying. In creating and sustaining effective policies, a number of assurances must be in place. First, ownership of the policy must be by a department having sufficient formal authority and influence to ensure compliance. The policy should be unique enough to specifically address bullying. Policymakers should be prepared to include feedback from organizational members and make revisions as necessary. Next, once policies are adapted, they should be made clear in a writing style that communicates the importance of the policy to the organization's functioning. When breaches occur, organizations can choose from both informal and formal responses, depending on the type of complaint and the health urgency created by it. Finally, compliance with antibullying policies should be monitored and revised to ensure current language, content, and law.

Gary and Ruth Namie (2011) cautioned that one person should never write a policy alone. Instead, group and multidisciplinary collaboration will produce a better product. Inclusion in policy development will also help with buy-in and compliance once the policy is established. Key components of a typical policy can include

- a clear statement that the organization opposes bullying;
- clear rationale for the need for a policy;

- clearly naming appropriate and desired workplace behavior, such as respectful, civil, etc.;
- clear definitions of bullying;
- examples of unacceptable behavior;
- guarantees of rights of managers as long as not exercised abusively; and
- a clause ensuring freedom from retaliation and appropriate response if it occurs.

In preparation for the antibullying initiative, organizational leaders should prepare themselves by recognizing the existence of bullying; trusting reports they are receiving that allege incidents of bullying; acknowledging their behaviors and changing, if leaders themselves are the problem; and supporting antibullying as a workplace value and process and recognizing the importance of workplace and employee health (Namie & Namie, 2011).

UK researchers Rayner and Lewis (Einarsen et al., 2011) recommended policies that are short and clear enough for all employees to understand. To ensure systemwide buy-in, the policy development team should include wide and diverse representation from within the organization. Team members should draft antibullying statements for the organization that include examples and state the relevance of the antibullying policy to other organizational practices. These concepts can then be included in recruitment materials and other organizational literature. Employers should also distinguish between informal and formal handling of bullying complaints. Informal handling can generally be done by line managers, but only if they have skills and confidence and only if they are not involved in the bullying incidents (Einarsen et al., 2011). Big organizations may have a team of specialists to provide investigation and interventions. Sadly, many bullying scenarios cannot be resolved informally, so more formal interventions become necessary. Some words of caution: There is a need for high levels of sensitivity on the part of investigators (perhaps requiring specialists), so that the investigative process does not create additional trauma. External investigation for difficult or high-profile cases may have to be considered.

Unfortunately, some policies fail. The causes for failures are many and varied, including an organization's failure to promote the policy effectively, the failure to embed the antibullying message into other workplace guidelines so it is regarded seriously, and poor sequencing practices, such as policy implementation without training (Rayner & Lewis, cited in Einarsen et al., 2011).

U.S. DEPARTMENT OF LABOR, OSHA

In 2011, OSHA adopted an antibullying policy for its own field services and workers. This policy is important because it emphasizes the need to provide employees with an environment free from recognized hazards that can harm health. The original 1970 Occupational Safety and Health Act did not include workplace bullying as harmful to physical and emotional health because it predated most of the research in this domain. The 2011 *OSHA Safety and Health Manual* states in chapter 10 that a workplace needs to be free from violence, harassment, and intimidation. The policy defines *intimidating behavior* as threats or behaviors that create a hostile work environment, impair operations, or frighten others. Included in the definition is a specific reference to verbal intimidation, including malicious rumors, disparaging and disrespectful comments, and rudeness. The definition includes communications that are verbal or written or that involve physical aggression and places burden on management to ensure workplace safety (U.S. Department of Labor, 2011).

One of the best outlines for workplace intervention can be found in the OSHA Guidelines for Preventing Workplace Violence for Health Care and Social Service Workers (U.S. Department of Labor, 2015). Although developed for prevention of workplace violence, these guidelines can be adapted to provide a template for organizations wanting to reduce risk and prevalence of workplace bullying. An adapted list of requirements for a bullying prevention program would include the following:

- Recognize the value of a workplace free from emotional abuse.
- Allocate authority and resources to assure implementation of the policy.
- Assign responsibility and authority for workplace bullying prevention program.
- Maintain a system of accountability.
- Support and implement appropriate recommendations from all staff members.
- Establish a comprehensive program of support services including, but not limited to, medical and psychological care.
- Ensure that reporting, recording, and monitoring of bullying allegations is established and that reprisals do not occur.
- Clearly communicate management's commitment to a workplace that is supportive of employees.

ORGANIZATIONAL STRUCTURES, RESPONSES, AND INTERVENTIONS

A number of theorists offer recommendations for organizations and consultants in responding to incidents of workplace emotional abuse, including mediation. Namie and Namie (2009) categorized strategic practice interventions as *moderation/mediation, coaching,* and *organizational development*. Moderation is a process designed to clarify issues for parties to allow them to move beyond misunderstandings. Mediation is a conflict-resolution process. They cautioned that moderation and mediation should be used only if they can prevent escalation of a difficulty. These processes can help employees to feel heard and go far beyond a "work it out yourselves" response to conflict. Mediation and moderation are generally best when conducted by paid professional or trained peer mediators for the processes.

Coaching, or the development of solutions case by case, can include a variety of supports, including tactical advice, emotional support, and career planning.

Coaching may be directed toward an employee with bullying behaviors and can clarify expectations. It may be indicated when a leader must confront a peer or a colleague and teach the impact of bullying on the organization. Coaching can also help to prepare leaders for organizational changes. Namie and Namie (2009) cautioned that coaching not be utilized too early in the bullying resolution process, as it can reduce the importance of organizational bullying to an employee problem rather than an organizational problem, thus not resolving or addressing organizational precipitators or workplace culture influences.

Finally, organizational development is a strategy that creates new standards for process and behavioral changes. The organizational development path sees difficulties as organizational problems, not just employee problems (Namie & Namie, 2009). It includes the development and implementation of policies to prevent bullying.

Gardner and Johnson (2001) suggested strategies for handling workplace bullies when they are identified. Some of these include

- training managers and employees about bullying at work and setting a zero-tolerance policy;
- helping targets cope with what has happened to them;
- refocusing the way the issue is addressed so that prevention is preferred to remediation;
- adopting progressive selection tools, such as written tests, interviews, performance tests, and psychological testing, for hiring and promotions;
- treating workers fairly;
- developing antibullying policies; and
- understanding that targets may seek legal redress if the workplace cannot address, contain, and prevent bullying.

These strategies would require that managers and supervisors understand that, if they choose to avoid addressing and preventing bullying, they can be held responsible for the negligence and the harm created.

Rayner (1999) recommended similar approaches to prevention and redress. Her approaches include the following:

- Identify the bully.
- Identify if there are sufficient deterrents in place to prevent bullying. This means eliminating any benefits or rewards to bullies. It may be possible that there is a belief among employees that bullying is acceptable. Make sure that it is understood that it is *never acceptable* to emotionally abuse others.
- Deal with each case individually, and take complaints seriously.
- Send a message within the organization that emotional abuse and bullying are taken very seriously by the organization.

Rayner's suggestions would be an indication that a leader or an organization take seriously the role and responsibility of managing and preventing risk.

Labor and industry literature provides interview themes from an exploratory study of workplace bullying. Questions that should be asked when investigating allegations of bullying and analyzing the organization are as follows:

- What was the climate of the organization at the time of the bullying?
- Does bullying often occur in this type of industry?
- Has the target been bullied in the past at this job? At a previous job?
- How can the relationships between supervisors, staff, and management be characterized?
- What is the organization's size?
- What are the demographics of the organization?
- How does the target view the bullying?
- Who is the bully?
- How does the target define the bully?
- What's the victim's definition of what happened?
- At what stage did the target realize the behavior was bullying?
- How long did it occur? Start? Stop?
- Does the organization have an antibullying policy?
- If yes, what are the procedures are in place for reporting, investigating, and resolving complaints? (Buttigieg et al., 2011)

Einarsen et al. (2011) proposed that interventions need to occur at a variety of levels in an organization. The primary stage of these should be at the prevention level. The secondary stage should be interventions designed to reverse, slow down, or reverse the progression from bullying to ill health. The third (tertiary) stage should include interventions that are rehabilitative for the person and for the organization. The organization needs to communicate clearly that there is no room for bullying within the organizational culture, and it must then create and implement policies and procedures that prevent problems or respond quickly when problems occur. Organizational interventions should include antibullying policies and clear guidelines for how bullying will be addressed should it occur. Organizational interventions for reducing or preventing bullying should also include risk assessment and identifying workplace conditions that contribute to bullying. When bullying does occur, procedural justice and support for the victim are imperative.

Key steps to be taken and a key role for HR professionals in addressing workplace bullying include gathering evidence of history of complaints; identifying tangible losses to the organization via consulting with risk management; creating a report from an outside employee-assistance person/organization, ensuring anonymity for bullied targets; organizing policies to reduce redundancy and overlap; selecting a work group for policy writing; creating an educational plan for new policies and procedures; finalizing the policy implementation plan; creating a training team to be given extensive training about bullying; securing the services of an outside investigator for instances when a high-ranking person in the organization is the perpetrator; and training managers in both identifying signs of bullying and effective intervention methods (Namie & Namie, 2011)

Our society can be overinvested in looking at individual causes of abusive behavior. If the main cause of workplace emotional abuse is not the individual person but rather group and organizational dynamics, then intervening with either the bully or the target or both is likely to be unproductive. Instead, organizations would be wise to consider work-group dynamics, group cohesiveness, formal and informal group dynamics, and organizational structure, culture, and leadership, along with the external environment, such as the presence or absence of laws or legal recourse when attempting to address emotional abuses at work (Sperry, 2009).

Cross-Cultural Workplace Interventions

Landmark decisions about the need for workplace changes in Australia and awards to people harmed by bullying have garnered the attention of legislators and labor leaders (Sheehan et al., 1999). Similarly, in the United Kingdom, personal-injury case decisions about emotional injuries incurred at work have provided economic evidence of the need for protections for workers (Sheehan et al., 1999).

Australia reached landmark decisions by 1999 (Sheehan et al., 1999), awarding damages to those injured by emotional abuse at work. In addition, the International Labour Organization, the arm of the United Nations (UN) that develops international labor standards via conventions and recommendations, has set minimum standards of basic labor rights for all member nations. These were adopted in a UN resolution titled "Collective Agreements on the Prevention and Resolution of Harassment-Related Grievances" (International Labour Organization, 2001). For UN member nations, *workplace harassment* is defined as

- Measures to exclude or isolate a worker
- Persistent negative attacks
- Manipulation of a person's professional reputation
- Abusing power by undermining someone's work
- Unreasonable monitoring
- Unreasonable refusal of leave (Von Bergen et al., 2006).

Clearly, a relationship exists between bullying and the psychosocial environment of the workplace. Australian researchers proposed an interaction of the work environment, the work-pressure demands of the job, and the level of social support for workers. According to the DCS model (Karasek et al., 1990, in Tuckey et al., 2009), a job can be defined in at least two dimensions: (1) job demands and (2) the control that workers have to make decisions and control when and how job functions are accomplished during the work shift. Jobs that are high on demand and control are considered "active," while jobs that are low on both are "passive." Jobs with low demand but high control are not taxing, but those with high demand and low control are considered more stressful. This theory posits that if a person's job demands are high and his or her ability to control his or her own work processes are low, poor health outcomes may result. All of these conditions are mediated by the presence or absence of social supports. This theory also links high job demands and low job control to bullying. The DCS model suggests that dealing with demanding work tasks without the ability to exercise autonomy in the performance of these tasks and the absence of adequate social supports creates tension and, over time, will result in disease and ill health. These conditions can make a workplace very high risk for bullying (Tuckey et al., 2009). Social work could have an active role in helping organizational leaders, managers, and supervisors understand the relationship between DCS and help with job redesign or social-support improvement to decrease risk. A good role for social workers would be to assess the psychosocial work climate of the organization.

Poland has had workplace prohibitions in place for almost four decades, but the rules have changed since the collapse of the Soviet Union and the shift from socialism to a capitalistic economy. According to Ryan (2006), Poland's recent poor economy has worsened conditions for its workers. Although Polish labor laws are very favorable to employees, evidence exists that there are increased pressures on Polish workers. In addition, he cited ethical issues in recruitment, hiring, performance appraisals, and promotions, and abuse of authority.

Einarsen et al. (2011) reported a model used by the Finnish Occupational Safety and Health Act for preventing harassment and inappropriate behavior at work. This model focuses on four recommended target domains: the structure of the working community, the person (target and perpetrator), corrective measures, and preventative measures. Such a multifaceted approach would be wise for American organizations to use.

In South Australia, new laws refer workplace bullying disputes to the special South Australian Industrial Relations Commission for mediation. South Australia's legislation may also punish private and public employers for failure to manage bullying behavior in the workplace. In the United Kingdom, recent findings have addressed redress for victims based on whether the mobbing behaviors constitute a breach of contract, on the nature and quality of the evidence, on the weight of the evidence (one victim versus several alleged perpetrators), and on whether the employer holds vicarious liability for the perpetrators (Ramage, 1996).

One commentary could be that those UN member nations that have histories of one of the worst human rights abuses—the slave trade—have been slow to address workplace emotional abuse. They would include the United States. The international landscape indeed looks somewhat more favorable than in the United States. According to Von Bergen et al. (2006), many European and Scandinavian countries, including France, Germany, Italy, Spain, the Netherlands, and Norway, have introduced legal responses to workplace mobbing. As of 1999, several countries have initiated efforts to legislate against workplace emotional abuse.

In the United States, since 2003, an initiative called the HWB (Healthy Workplace Bill) has been introduced in 26 states plus two territories (Puerto Rico and the Virgin Islands). In each state, the bill tends to get stalled in committees, or, as in the case of New York, it gets passed but the governor refuses to sign it. This is an unfortunate statement about the value of workers in the United States at the dawn of the 21st century. Until recently, no states have passed or enacted this bill in its original format; however, in 2014, some legislative activity in California and Tennessee has provided a good first start. These new developments will be discussed later in this chapter.

THE ORGANIZATIONAL CLIMATE AND RELATED VARIABLES

Calls to "drain the swamp" when one is being attacked by alligators is a solution that is "too little, too late." Bullying, like alligator problems, needs to be dealt with firmly, swiftly, and consistently. With bullying, that means via policy, prevention, training, intervention, and remediation. However, what about the swamp itself? What about the larger context of the organization and how it functions? It would seem almost naive to attend to workplace bullying in isolation, apart from larger organizational practices. The remainder of this chapter addresses leadership strategies, conflict resolution approaches, and larger organizational functioning issues.

Work–Life Programs

Work–life programs began to emerge in the American workplace more than two decades ago. George Washington University researchers Chalofsky and Griffin (2005) explained that in preindustrial society, work was done in the same communities where people lived. Everyone knew the person (and that person's family) who made shoes, repaired wagons, made cheese, made clothes, or crafted furniture. People socialized with the same people with whom they had daily commerce. As agriculture declined and mechanical production work emerged, people became wage earners working for others, and the sense of "community" began to decline. The early Industrial Revolution was very dehumanizing, breaking these bonds.

Since then, many changes and studies of changes at work have evolved. Goodman (2001, in Chalofsky & Griffin, 2005) found that within work-group culture, the values of the work group are correlated with higher degrees of work satisfaction. Berg et al. (2003, in Chalofsky & Griffin, 2005) found that when the work organization helped employees to achieve work–life balance, they achieved the highest degree of work commitment. Today, the best employers are committed to helping people develop through support for career development and education, a genuine commitment to diversity, and a spirit of service to workers (Chalofsky & Griffin, 2005).

Levering (cited in Chalofsky & Griffin, 2005) talked with hundreds of employees and then revisited 20 especially good workplaces for further interviews with low-level employees, top officers, and founders. Distilling his data to five phrases that describe the best organizations, these themes emerged: friendly, no politics, fair, like family, and more than a job. It appears that employees need to feel that their work is more than a paycheck and that needs beyond economics are met at work. Organizations wanting to prevent or alleviate high rates of mobbing should examine some of these values and variables.

Diagnosing Organizational Culture

Organizational theorists, practitioners, and consultants need a broad-based method to diagnose organizational culture and identify embedded areas of difficulty within a workplace. One approach, the Organizational Culture Inventory (OCI) developed

Table 7.1. Three Distinct Types of Organizational Cultures Measured by the Organizational Culture Inventory

Constructive Cultures	Passive/Defensive Cultures	Aggressive/Defensive Cultures
Members are encouraged to interact with others and approach tasks in ways that will help others to meet their own satisfaction needs. Constructive cultures are characterized by the following norms:	Members believe they must interact with people in ways that will not threaten their own security. Passive/Defensive cultures are characterized by the following norms:	Members are expected to approach their work tasks in forceful ways to protect status and security. Aggressive/Defensive cultures are characterized by the following norms:
• Achievement • Self-Actualizing • Humanistic-Encouraging • Affiliative	• Approval • Conventional • Dependent • Avoidance	• Oppositional • Power • Competitive • Perfectionistic

Source: Research and development by Robert A. Cooke, PhD. Style names, descriptions, and items are copyrighted © and used with permission. From *Organizational Culture Inventory: Strengthening Organizations Through Individual Effectiveness* by Robert A. Cooke and J. Clayton Lafferty (1987), Plymouth, MI: Human Synergistics International. Copyright © 1987 and 2014 by Human Synergistics, Inc. Used by permission.

by Robert A. Cooke and J. Clayton Lafferty and implemented by Human Synergistics, Inc., is an organizational survey offering a method for everyone in the organization to provide feedback about their organizational climate experience.* When using instruments like these, employee safety and confidentiality are critical. Often it is best to use an outside consultant who can administer and interpret the instrument without appearing to be intimidating.

The instrument asks participants to review 120 statements that describe the cultural styles that typically exist in their workplace. These include styles and behavioral choices that members of the organization might be expected to conform to in carrying out their daily duties. The instrument can be administered in group or individual sessions and measures cultural styles in the organization.

The OCI measures 12 interrelated norms and expectations that can significantly affect how people think and behave in the workplace. It sorts organizational cultures into three primary categories, with variations included in the categories (Cooke & Lafferty, 1987). These distinctions are indicated in Table 7.1.

Cooke and Lafferty (1987) further suggested that in the OCI theoretical model, environmental and organizational factors can be understood in terms of

*Research and development by Robert A. Cooke, PhD. Style names, descriptions, and items are copyrighted © and used with permission. From *Organizational Culture Inventory: Strengthening Organizations Through Individual Effectiveness* by Robert A. Cooke and J. Clayton Lafferty (1987), Plymouth, MI: Human Synergistics International. Copyright © 1987 and 2014 by Human Synergistics, Inc. Used by permission.

external environmental influences and constraints such as the economy, technology advances, social pressures, legal climate, and competition. Organizational factors can be understood in terms of the foundations of the organization, including the philosophy of leadership in top administrators, assumptions about power, the presence or lack of a sense of continuity, and the organization's history. Emergent factors in the organization include concepts such as mission, vision, goals, strategies, policies, organizational size, organizational structures, and systems.

The OCI model emphasizes that the outcomes at the organizational level or subunit level are important to consider. These outcomes are the results of aggregate effects of the norms and practices of the organization. For example, the quality of work life is higher in organizations that have constructive cultures than in those with defensive cultures. Leaders in constructive cultures are rated as higher than in other types of cultures. The authors note that when organizations adopt more constructive styles, workers' sense of well-being, as well as their sense of personal accomplishment and effectiveness, improves. Workers who report cultural styles such as Self-Actualizing and Affiliative tend to have fewer stress-related symptoms than those with styles such as Approval, Avoidance, and Perfectionistic (Cooke & Lafferty, 1989). It would seem that those workplaces have styles that are both more relaxed and possibly easier in which employees can connect.

Most organizational scholars understand that organizational culture has a powerful effect on both the performance and long-term effectiveness of the organization. Research in organizational culture supports its importance to the functioning and well-being of corporate life. Cameron and Quinn (1999) suggested that a number of recent factors have affected traditional organizations. Some of these include the fact that most work environments have implemented measures to improve quality, reduce labor forces through downsizing, and redesign work processes. Unfortunately, these changes and others cannot be successful if the organization's culture is not effectively managed and sustained. In many instances, organizational cultures will need to change to be successful at 21st century solutions.

Given the manner in which corporations have done business of late, such as hiring only contractual workers, shipping jobs overseas, disarming unions, lobbying for more permissive corporate practices with fewer safeguards (BP's 2010 oil spill in the Gulf of Mexico, for example), and less protective workers' compensation laws, many practices will need to be reversed or revamped if organizations want to effectively manage risk.

These issues of style can be important in understanding the context or backdrop where mobbing may occur. It seems reasonable that emotional abuse would be much more prevalent and pervasive in organizations typified by either passive-dependent or aggressive-defensive styles than in those that are more "constructivistic."

Leadership Strategies and Practices

Distinctions about leadership styles are very central to discussions about preventing bullying at work. Although there does not yet appear to be empirical evidence, it is much less likely for mobbing to exist and persist in organizations with principle-centered leadership. Principled leaders are more likely to create and foster positive self-esteem and cooperation among workers in the organizations they serve. Some theorists, such as Stephen R. Covey (1991), suggest that one approach organizations can take to ensure healthy workplace practices is to encourage principle-centered people to become principle-centered leaders. Organizations would be wise to screen carefully for sound leadership qualities when hiring new managers or promoting managers from within the ranks. The questions should always be asked: Is this person emotionally intelligent? Can this person use power wisely, with empathy and grace? Does this person have the temperament, the integrity, the emotional sturdiness, and the principles to be a good leader in addition to knowing the work that needs to be done? Unless the answers are unreservedly "yes," organizations will be at risk for bullying from the top, for these are usually not qualities that can be taught via management training.

Organizational leader and author Max DePree emphatically stated that the first responsibility of a leader is to define reality for members of the organization. The last responsibility of a leader is to say "thank you." In between these two actions, a leader must be a servant and a debtor (DePree, 1989). DePree suggested that "true leaders don't inflict pain, they bear pain" (p. 11) and further defined outstanding leaders by outcomes in the organization, including the following:

- Employees reach their potential.
- Employees are learning.
- Employees are serving.
- Employees achieve the required results established for them.
- Employees manage change and conflict well.

Defining a leader's role as a debtor, DePree (1989) asserted that leaders *owe* their institutions a value system; preparation of future leaders; momentum; responsibility for effectiveness; and the ability to develop, express, and defend civility and values. This can be accomplished by respecting people, agreeing on the rights of workers, understanding the contractual relationships between staff and management, and understanding that relationships are more important than structures in organizations.

Mature management functions in organizations include

- successfully managing long-range issues, such as public policy and legislation;
- tolerating frustration and delaying gratification;
- being achievement-oriented, working toward both concrete and symbolic rewards;
- setting standards by "external demand," or those imposed from outside the organization;
- recognizing that employees have rights and being mindful of ensuring the protection of these rights; and
- ensuring both affirmative action and employee security (Etzioni, 1964, in Ginsberg & Keys, 1995).

A note of caution about an organization's key values. Values must be constantly communicated. Author and consultant Kenneth Blanchard (1999) reflected that real communication occurs when people "feel safe" at work.

Prevention via effective leadership strategies cannot be emphasized too strongly. Covey (1991) described effective leadership in terms of four dimensions: *security, guidance, wisdom,* and *power*. Security symbolizes a human need for self-worth, identity, and emotional stability. Guidance refers to the sense of direction that one has in life, especially direction provided by someone who ascribes to a set of standards or ethics for decision making. The concept of wisdom means to have understanding of how principles of life combine to make sense or how various component parts can be gathered to create a unified whole. Finally, power is the capacity to act and the strength and confidence to accomplish something with purpose.

Covey's model places these dimensions on a compass described as *alternative life centers*. In alternative life centers, whatever is most important to a person becomes the primary source of that person's life-support system. These include such things as family, home, church, relationships, money and assets, friendships, leisure activities, and those with whom one may have conflicts. The primary source is surrounded by other life-support centers. Covey's model suggests that organizations can have principles at their centers as well.

These are those qualities or values that are more important to that organization. Covey asserts that real empowerment in a workforce comes from having the principles and the practices clearly understood by all people at all levels of the organization. Covey describes principle-centered leaders as men and women with character who build natural principles into others, leading by being a light not a judge, by being a model instead of a critic.

While Covey's ideals may sound somewhat too lofty to have practical value in today's lean, mean, competitive, and fast-paced organizations, his conceptualization of the types of power found in organizations is worth understanding. The first type of leader, according to Covey (1991), is the one whom others follow because of fear. Followers of fear-based leaders follow because they're afraid of what will happen to them if they don't. This type of power is known as *coercive power*. A second type of leader is one who encourages others to follow because of the rewards or benefits that may be earned by following. This type of power is called *power of utility*. The third and most noble form of power is *principle-centered power*, based on the power some people have with others because they believe in others and in what others are trying to accomplish. Principle-centered leaders are trusted, respected, and honored. The esteem in which they are held is not because they demand it but because they evoke it naturally, by genuinely caring about the success of others:

- Coercive power places an emotional burden on both leaders and those they lead. It can foster deceit, suspicion, and dishonestly and can ruin organizations.
- Power based on utility is the type of power that holds most organizations together. People will do as they are asked if they believe they are being treated fairly—that is, if the rewards are sufficient for the effort expended.

- Principle-centered power, although rare, marks quality in an organization and can ensure respect in all relationships.

According to Covey (1991), "the hallmark of principle-centered power is sustained, proactive influence" (p. 104).

Author and consultant Peter Drucker (2008) suggested that the most important questions to ask about one's organization are the following:

- What is the business of the organization? What does it do and for whom?
- Who are the customers for this organization? Are they consumers of products, services, or information?
- What does the customer want? What is important to the customer, and how does the organization know this?
- What are the outcomes or results of the organization? Are customers satisfied? Are workers and leaders satisfied?
- What are the plans for this organization in the next year, the next five years, and the next 10 years?

Such clarification of who, what, when, where, and how should be the foundation of any plan for intervention and change in organizational life.

Modifications and reframing of typical leadership practices to provide increased emphasis on principle-based management were suggested by Boyett and Boyett (1998). Leaders must shift to *walking the talk:* doing as one says one will do, setting a good example, and living by the rules that others are required to live by. Leaders must shift from systems architect to change agent and servant. Bartlett and Ghoshal (Boyett & Boyett, 1998) state that, too often, the very systems that exercise control and advocate conformity actually inhibited creativity and initiative:

> Stripped of individuality people often engage in the very behaviors that the system had been designed to control. At best, the resulting organizational culture grew passive; with amused resignation, employees implemented corporate led initiatives that they knew would fail. At worst, the tightly controlled environment triggered antagonism and even subversion; people deep in the organization found ways to undermine the system that constrained them. (p. 34)

Change agents were defined by Boyett and Boyett (1998) as focusing less on directing and controlling employees and more on developing employee initiative and supporting employee ideas. For servant leader, Boyett and Boyett drew from the work of Robert Greenleaf, former director of research and management of AT&T. Greenleaf elaborated on the concept of servant leader in his writings, saying that the greatest leader is the one who is seen as servant first, deep down inside. According to Greenleaf (Boyett & Boyett, 1998), the gift of leadership is granted to the person who is, by nature, a true servant.

Church and Waclawski (1998) discussed the relationship between personality orientation and executive leadership abilities. The authors suggested that the

MBTI provides an approach to understanding personality differences. It has been extensively used and shown to be effective in examining managerial performance, team-building skills, and the ability to give feedback to employees.

As an example, the combination of ENTP (extroverted, intuitive, thinking, perceiving) could be particularly well suited to leadership. An ENTP manager would focus more on external interactions with people as opposed to being overly introspective or thoughtful; he or she would prefer more to rely on intuition of ideas and hunches rather than on "sensing" information via the five human sensory systems; the manager would use reason, logic, and critical thinking skills in decision making rather than going by feelings alone; and, finally, the person would promote an open and flexible workplace with respect for orientation to the rest of the world (Church & Waclawski, 1998). Traits such as these could also be considered to be among those who could help to create a high-functioning organization where the risks of employee emotional abuse and mobbing are minimal.

Emotional Intelligence

Another method of examining traits can be found in the fairly recent study of what is known as EI. Discussed in an earlier chapter, EI comes from the work of Daniel Goleman (Goleman, 1995, in Blank, 2008). EI is the ability to recognize one's own feelings and the feelings of others. This can be helpful in motivating oneself and others and for effective management of one's own internal emotional states. A number of personal competencies for managing ourselves are included in the concept of EI, including

- *self-awareness*, or the ability to recognize and understand the impact of one's personal emotions, which includes qualities such as accurate self-assessment and self-confidence;
- *self-management*, which includes the ability to exercise emotional self-control, the willingness to operate with honesty and integrity, and adaptability or flexibility; and
- *social competence*, including qualities of social awareness, empathy, organizational awareness, relationship management, inspirational leadership skills, abilities at influencing others, good conflict-resolution skills, and abilities in giving feedback.

Blank (2008) posited that while no one has strong skills in all of these competencies, those who perform in an outstanding manner generally have many of them. This would be particularly true for effective leaders, given the nature of leadership functions and their relationship to human interactions. It might be that selecting and promoting people with high levels of EI could help to foster positive workplace relationships, minimize conflict, and set a tone for cooperation and respect. This would help significantly in reducing the risk of emotional abuses in organizations.

Unfortunately, if mean-spirited or sociopathic bullies are allowed to persist in their abusive behaviors, even emotionally intelligent leaders can have high-risk environments. Some suggest that they may even become the victims themselves, depending on organizational practices.

Creating a Learning Organization

Creating a learning organization to revitalize and strengthen organizational functioning is recommended by Peter Senge, former director of the Systems Thinking and Organizational Learning Program at MIT's Sloan School of Management.
Learning organizations are organizations that build continuous learning into the
workplace culture so that learning becomes generative rather than merely adaptive. In learning organizations, leaders are actually designers, and leadership is
the social architecture behind the scenes. In learning organizations, leaders are
teachers, leaders are stewards, and leaders are responsible for creating and communicating a vision that can be shared (Senge, 1990b). In outlining some problem
thinking in today's organizations, Senge (1990b) cited the ways that people confuse
their jobs with their identity, a belief in external controls or blame, an illusion that
aggressive responses to situations are productive, fixations on events not processes,
and the delusion that one always learns from experience. Senge's illusion of aggressive responses also refers to a maladaptive manner of ignoring increases in threats
to survival as organizations become toxic.

Senge (1994) proposed that the essence of a learning organization is that it
involves a deep learning cycle or a "domain of enduring change." This learning
cycle is one of new attitudes and beliefs, new awareness and sensibilities, along
with new skills and capabilities. Skills and capabilities involve such groupings as
aspirations, reflection and conversation, and conceptualization. New awareness and
sensibilities include shifts in the way one sees, experiences, and interprets events
and people. Finally, attitudes and beliefs begin to shift when one allows new awareness to be absorbed.

Creating learning organizations that foster learning and innovation through
involvement and engagement of employees may be a key factor in stanching the flow
of emotional abuse in the 21st century workplace. In learning organizations, emphasis
is placed on the process of learning to improve all areas of operations and taking away
the shame and blame typically associated with errors. By encouraging participation
and reducing fear of blame for mistakes, all members of an organization can focus on
participatory management and feel they have a real stake in the organization.

Choice Theory

Choice theory is psychiatrist William Glasser's most recent contribution to his
already significant body of writings on the psychology of reality and responsibility.
Glasser, best known for his practical approach to life via a method termed reality
therapy decades ago, has defined choice theory as a psychology of internal control.
Glasser (1998) suggested that people ask themselves whether their current behavior
is bringing them closer to others or moving them farther apart and whether their
internal thought behavior is helping or hurting their own well-being. Applied to
the workplace, choice concerns itself with how one interprets and responds to the

experiences of everyday work life. Glasser describes his wife's story told to her by an old man who had owned a paint factory during the Great Depression:

> In 1932, jobs were scarce; there were ten people ready to step up immediately if there was an opening. Six days a week—they regularly worked Saturday morning—forty employees saw the manager hard at work when they came in. A few came earlier and then a few more. They were afraid to say anything to her, and of course, she said nothing. Fearing for their jobs, they began to come in earlier and earlier until, in a few months, they were all coming in at eight and going right to work. When he told my wife the story, the old man laughed and slapped his leg saying, "A half hour free work, twenty hours a day, six days a week out of forty people for nine years." Then the war started, jobs were plentiful and the scam was over. (Glasser, 1998, pp. 283–284)

Glasser (1998) proposed the concept of *lead management* rather than *boss management*. By boss management, he meant that the practice of blatant bossing (or bossing via intimidation) usually does not occur at the very top level of an organization but, rather, often occurs by lead workers and those with greater seniority. Lead management, Glasser posited, includes four elements that are designed to create healthy, functional work environment:

1. Lead managers engage all employees in honest conversations about both the costs and the quality of work needed for organizational success.
2. Lead managers, or their designees, model jobs for employees so that workers know exactly what the manager expects of them.
3. Workers are made responsible for ensuring quality in their own work and how to be most cost-effective in their productivity.
4. Lead managers use all opportunities to teach continual quality improvement.

Glasser (1998) suggested that lead management creates greater productivity, leads to higher quality of work, and ultimately saves money for the organization. When one considers the organizational features that often create a climate where the risks of emotional abuse are high, Glasser's theory, applied to the workplace, makes good sense. It is humanizing, respectful, and empowering and could increase well-being and positive work relationships and greatly reduce the risk of bullying.

Leadership Practices Profiles

Leadership practices profiles are based on the Leadership Practices Inventory (LPI), which is among the most valid and reliable behavioral style measurements of any objective testing used in the workplace today. From a research and measurement perspective, an instrument is considered reliable when it consistently measures what is was created to measure. *Validity* refers to an instrument measuring what it is designed to measure. Three types of validity inherent in the LPI are *concurrent validity, face validity,* and *predictive validity*. Concurrent validity in the LPI means that high scores are correlated with positive outcomes in a leadership domain. Face validity means that the results make sense and are understandable to people. Predictive validity refers to results that can be used, beyond randomly, to predict high or low performance in various areas of leadership functioning (Kouzes & Posner, 2001). In addition, the five scales are independent from each other. They measure five separate and unique practices. Tested and normed on over 4,000 cases and over 200,000 surveys, the LPI can differentiate between low- and high-performing organizational leaders.

By examining and testing the process of surveys, Kouzes and Posner (2001) uncovered the five best practices of leadership:

- *Challenging the process* is being willing to assume risk by stepping into the unknown of innovation and experimenting to find better ways of doing things. The leader who challenges the process is one who recognizes good ideas, provides support for them, and is willing to challenge the status quo in service of discovering better ways of doing things.
- *Inspiring a shared vision* means having the ability to make things happen, to change the way things work, or to create something that may not have been created before. To do this successfully, inspiring leaders need to know the hearts and languages of those they lead.
- *Enabling others to act*, a good leader enlists the support of all whose cooperation is needed to make something work. In both an organizational sense and a community-organizing sense, it is to engage all stakeholders in a process and outcome. In government, it means obtaining support from elected and appointed officials. Leaders who are skilled at enabling others to act understand that people cannot do their best if they feel weak, incompetent, or alienated. People need to have a sense of ownership if they are expected to participate in results.
- *Modeling the way* means quite simply that good leaders do not expect anyone to do things they themselves would not do. Leading through modeling is to show the way by personal example and commitment to execution.
- *Encouraging the heart* involves genuine acts of caring that can provide support and encouragement. A leader who encourages the heart actually encourages and fosters self-esteem.

Kouzes and Posner have coined the term "The Ten Commitments of Leadership." Their LPI created an opportunity for participants to understand their particular leadership strengths and vulnerabilities and to identify ways to improve in all of them (Kouzes & Posner, 2001). The best applications of the LPI involve what has come to be known as 360-degree feedback. Participants complete the survey via self-report and also request that managers, peers, and subordinates complete one to provide feedback to participants. In doing the process and in undergoing LPI training, leaders can learn the "Five Practices of Exemplary Leadership" themselves and receive relevant feedback about their own uses of the five practices. Results for participants are generally shown in a summary plus several pages of tables and graphs that represent self-evaluation and observations of others. These results show both raw scores and percentile rankings so that participants can understand how their scores compare to others (see Table 7.2).

Table 7.2. Kouzes and Posner's Five Best Leadership Practices and 10 Commitments of Leadership

Practices	Commitments
Challenging the Process	*Search out* and challenge opportunities to change, grow, innovate, and improve.
	Experiment, take risks, and learn from the accompanying mistakes.
Inspiring a Shared Vision	*Envision* an uplifting and enabling future.
	Enlist others in a common vision by appealing to their values, interests, hopes, and dreams.
Enabling Others to Act	*Foster* collaboration by promoting cooperative goals and building trust.
	Strengthen people by giving power away, providing choice, developing competence, assigning critical tasks, and offering visible support.
Modeling the Way	*Set* the example by behaving in ways that are consistent with shared values.
	Achieve small wins that promote consistent progress and build commitment.
Encouraging the Heart	*Recognize* individual contributions to the success of every project.
	Celebrate team accomplishments regularly.

Source: From *The Leadership Challenge* by James M. Kouzes and Barry Z. Posner (1995), San Francisco: Jossey-Bass. Copyright 1993. Used with permission.

The value of LPIs and LPI trainings include the fact that training materials help participants to recognize the specific behaviors they regularly do and identify which exemplary practice those helpful behaviors address. Training and assessment processes also help participants to identify specific behaviors in which they can engage to foster improvements and build skills in their areas of vulnerability.

The relevance of creating a low-risk environment for mobbing seems fairly obvious. When leaders practice skills that foster vision, self-esteem, innovation, and achievement while honoring the rights and dignity of workers and offering recognition for work well done and goals met, they lead healthy organizations. A simple yet practical approach to building resilient, low-risk environments would be for all in leadership positions to participate in LPI assessment and training. A wise organization would go a step further, not limiting the LPI training to those in formal leadership positions but including all levels of employees in all job classifications and at all wage levels. Such fearless behavioral analysis would help to create healthy workplace functioning and would send a strong message about the climate that is valued in the organization.

Strategic Planning

Strategic planning is imperative for healthy organizational functioning. A number of models exist that can be incorporated into managerial functions. San Francisco's Support Center (2002) highlighted five tasks that must be accomplished to prepare an organization for strategic planning. These include identifying issues around which planning needs to occur, communicating participants' roles clearly, creating a planning team or committee, conducting an organizational profile analysis, and clarifying the information that will be important for good decision making. After completion of the tasks, the next steps include articulating a mission and vision; assessing the current situation; developing strategies, goals, and objectives; and, finally, completing a written plan. A mission statement shows that the planners know how the plan will be laid out and communicates the essential feature of the organization, including the organization's purpose, business, and values. A vision statement communicates what the image of success will look like for the organization. Once these have been identified, an assessment of the organization's strengths, weaknesses, and performance record can be conducted. When the organization's mission and central needs have been clarified, the plan for how to address these will include both the macro approaches and the specific goals and objectives to be accomplished. Finally, all this is committed to writing and becomes the organization's strategic plan. These steps, especially the last one, will take time and involves communication and flexibility (Support Center, 2002).

Another model for strategic planning dates back to the 1950s. While the origins of this model, SWOT, are not known, its early uses appeared at Harvard Business School in the 1950s and 1960s (Friesner, 2014). The SWOT model identifies the *strengths, weaknesses, opportunities*, and *threats* to an organization and allows for organizations to clarify the positive and negative influences that may have an impact on any proposed action or policy. Organizations attempting to address bullying would be wise to conduct such an analysis. Various templates are available, but implementing them is relatively easy. What is right about the organization? What is wrong, or what specific problems exist? What are the internal and external resources that will help the organization with implementing antibullying policies? What are the potential barriers for successful accomplishment?

SWOT analysis allows organizations to identify the positive and negative influencing factors inside and outside of a company or organization. In addition to corporations and businesses, other organizations, including some in health care and education, have found much use in this type of tool. The purpose of SWOT is to help develop a full awareness of all influences that may affect successful implementation of strategic plans and help guide decision making (Goodrich, 2013).

Teamwork

Not only an absence of abuse but also actual excellence in the workplace can be accomplished via well-functioning teams. Boyett and Boyett (1998) asserted that team development is a process that should be planned and managed. Initially, the team will need to help shape its own purposes and goals, gain confidence in each other, commit to the work at hand, and gain skills at working together. Fostering team development will include managing external relationships, removing obstacles that could impede group functioning, and creating opportunities for team members to excel. As the team takes on more and more responsibility, the leader's role can change to more coordination than supervision. Finally, a seasoned team can often function almost autonomously, leaving the leader to coordinate occasionally. If teams are to perform well, they will need technical skills, administrative skills, interpersonal skills, and decision-making skills (Boyett & Boyett, 1998). If only it were this easy!

Some predictable stages of team development will occur, including *forming, storming, norming,* and *performing.* Forming involves some insecurity and anxiety of the part of group members because no one is sure what will happen. During this stage, productivity is likely to be low. The second stage, storming, generally shows team functioning worsening. Members are impatient with their lack of process but are also trying to resolve issues such as power and authority, how decisions are to be made, and how to take on more responsibilities. The third stage, norming, involves the establishment of formal and informal rules for how team will conduct its business. In this stage, team members' knowledge, skills, and abilities are being utilized. Members are beginning to have respect for each other's expertise, and they begin to work collaboratively. Finally, stage four, performing, involves the team's confidence in its abilities to get the work done and consensus on who is who and who does what, at which point the team becomes representative of its members and their function (Boyett & Boyett, 1998). Some suggestions for ensuring team success include work redesign, changing performance criteria to emphasize teamwork, involving team members in appraising their progress, setting specific team-oriented performance goals, keeping the team small, and having a trusted person intervene when the team gets stuck.

High-performing organizations will support risk taking, emphasize learning new skills, design jobs to require many skills, provide regular feedback to employees, promote flexibility and team cooperation, share information about how the organization is doing, and have facilitators and coaches perform leadership functions. Finally, high-performing organizations pay for performance (Boyett & Boyett, 1998). If the absence of bullying and the presence of respectful communication and practices are the qualities that are rewarded, the likelihood of bullying will, by necessity, decrease.

Another feature of effective leadership that can enhance an organization's resiliency was proposed by Senge, Lichtenstein, Kaeufer, Bradbury, and Carroll (2007). These authors suggested that for major, systemic change, cross-sector collaboration will generally be needed. Unfortunately, no precedents for such collaboration have been established yet, so it must be created or cocreated by the major stakeholders who will be affected by the changes. This requires progressive thought and action on the part of leaders and workers alike (Senge et al., 2007).

While no specific examples are included in the article by Senge et al. (2007), anecdotal information about the success of multidisciplinary or interagency/interorganizational planning efforts have been highly successful. An example could be the introduction of the Temporary Aid to Needy Families legislation enacted during the Bill Clinton administration. Planning groups at the local level included job-development specialists, mental health specialists, addictions specialists, educators, vocational trainers, law enforcements, and elected officials.

Effectively managing change takes time and effort. Because organizations often have the need to change quickly, taking time for effective change management seems paradoxical. In the 21st century, however, because the work environment, along with the rest of the world, is in rapid transition, the wise leader in a highly resilient organization would do well to learn change-management principles and skills and be prepared to use them frequently. Effectively managing workplace changes could have a significant role in alleviating and preventing emotional abuse by supervisors, peers, and subordinates in an organization.

Work Processes

A variety of psychosocial factors can have large effects on organizational functioning. Namie and Namie (2011) posited that good leaders will be responsible for ensuring control of psychosocial factors. Task issues include workload and distribution, required work pace, inconsistency about breaks, interesting versus monotonous tasks, and the use of employees' skills. Standards concerning employee social interaction should also be monitored and ensured, as these can affect workplace performance, communication, and outcomes. Some of these can include

- the perception of fairness,
- inclusion in decision making,
- cooperation and interdependency among workers,
- performance reviews and feedback,
- opportunities to learn new tasks (or expand one's education),
- job security,
- emotional safety,
- respectful workplace treatment, and
- positive social interaction.

Managing Change Processes

Since times of rapid change tend to be high-risk ones for mobbing in organizations, it is imperative that organizations inoculate themselves by effectively managing change. Resistance to change can create unrest and uncertainty. Studies examined in both chapters 1 and 3 identified times of organizational change to be among the highest-risk times for emotional abuse. O'Toole (1996, in Boyett & Boyett, 1998) identified a number of reasons that employees tend to *resist* organizational change:

- Employees think the change will produce negative outcomes.
- Employees are afraid that the change will mean more work for them.
- Employees, like most people, do not generally like to have their customary habits broken.

- Leaders in the organization may not have done a sufficient job in communicating the nature of the change, the reasons for the changes, and the expected outcomes and benefits of the change.
- The organization and its leaders have not adequately aligned the organization, and employees themselves do not feel alignment with the organization's purposes.
- Employees fear that the change will force them to give up control of their own lives.

John Kotter (1996) identified seven necessary principles to understand when managing an organizational change process:

1. Establish the need for the change.
2. Create a clear and compelling vision that provides hope to employees that their lives will be better with the change.
3. Create some early wins, or early successes, in the change process.
4. Communicate clearly and constantly.
5. Create a strong, committed guiding team or coalition that includes top management and others from the workforce.
6. Keep the change process as simple as possible to minimize confusion.
7. Involve employees in identifying solutions in the change process, since people generally do not resist their own ideas!

Former Mills College professor William Bridges (1997) suggested the following actions to promote successful change: Describe the change clearly; identify additional (secondary) changes needed; identify who will need to "let go" of what; identify what is "over for everyone" (that is, the changes and losses everyone will experience); accept and empathize with the reality of employees' subjective losses; be prepared for (and not be surprised by) overreaction; accept grieving processes; if possible, compensate folks for their losses; and give information over and over to ensure that it is heard and applied with consistency.

Conflict Resolution

The distress created by workplace conflict is a part of organizational functioning that cannot be too heavily emphasized. Two excellent sources address conflict-resolution issues: the Thomas–Kilmann Conflict Mode Instrument (TKI) and the work of Canadian professor Allan Barsky.

Like other measurement instruments of human functioning, the TKI (K. W. Thomas & Kilmann, 2007) assesses one's preferred mode of conflict resolution. Preferred conflict modes are identified based on two dimensions: the degree of assertiveness displayed on a vertical axis and the degree of cooperation one typically uses when conflicts arise, displayed on a horizontal axis. An easy-to-score, 30-item instrument can be tallied to determine which of five conflict-resolution styles one typically uses when issues arise. Knowing one's style can be helpful, not only to effectively manage conflict but also to better understand the needs of others when conflicts occur. Knowing conflict modes and being able to use them selectively as situations arise can be invaluable:

- The *competing* mode is assertive and uncooperative—a power-oriented style. Competing might be standing up for one's rights or defending one's position. It might also be needed in emergencies when someone needs to take charge.
- *Collaborating* is both assertive and cooperative, offering an individual the opportunity to find solutions that can be fully appropriate to all concerned. The collaborating mode is challenging because it encourages people to continue in dialogue until consensus is reached and all parties have solutions that are not just acceptable but also satisfying.
- The *compromising* mode is an intermediate position between assertiveness and cooperation. When using the compromising mode, the objective is to find an expedient solution that is mutually acceptable to all involved parties. It means splitting the difference or making concessions in order to reach an agreement. Compromising is the mode typically used in mediation proceedings in which a mediator is trying to settle a dispute by helping parties to come to an agreement with which everyone can live.
- *Avoiding* is both unassertive and uncooperative. A person who is avoiding is not immediately pursuing his or her own needs and goals or those of others. Avoiding can have its place, however, such as in using diplomacy to sidestep issues until a more appropriate time can be found for resolution.
- Finally, *accommodating* is cooperative but unassertive. When accommodating, one ignores personal concerns in favor of the needs of others. It may have a place when is making a conscious concession for the well-being of others.

The need for skills enhancement in any of these conflict modes can be identified by the life problems created when skills are lacking. People scoring either too high or too low in a conflict mode might find that their overuse or underuse causes problems in primary relationships, both at home and at work. Helping organizations and employees who work in them to understand their conflict modes could help to decrease and minimize the impact that unresolved conflict has in the workplace. It might also lower the organization's risk for emotional abuse or mobbing.

Noted for significant experience in conflict resolution and mediation, Barsky has worked extensively in the areas of divorce, child welfare, and community mediation. His model examines the various roles played by people who are in conflict and by those who try to help mediate conflict and outlines the various functions those people serve. Barsky (2007) defined an *interested party* as someone who has direct stake in the outcome of a conflict. *Negotiation* is the manner in which people attempt to resolve a conflict. *Advocates* are those who act in support of one party or the other but generally not both. *Evaluators* have different types of expertise that social workers and others may assume. They assess the abilities of parties to fulfill the roles and typically help with child custody issues. *Experts* or *consultants* provide information and expertise, and *facilitators* assist parties with communication issues. *Mediators* are usually third parties who help with negotiating a conflict. *Healers* facilitate but also help parties to resolve underlying issues and are typically clinically trained professionals. An *arbitrator* is an independent third party who hears evidence from conflicting parties and makes decisions about resolution. *Administrators* help with implementation of the results of the resolved conflict once a decision has been made. Finally, *buffers* are those who separate parties during a conflict, especially if a dispute is in a very destructive phase.

Barsky (2007) proposed that the several principles of mediation are

- participating voluntarily,
- ensuring confidentiality,
- maintaining a nonadversarial tone,
- ensuring that any third party involved is truly neutral, and
- assuming that all parties involved in a negotiation have equal power in the mediation process.

Barsky clarified the basic skills for assisting with conflict resolution as listening skills, questioning skills or skills at eliciting information, skills at reframing and making statements, and skills in written communication.

A process called *transformative negotiation* would be a thoughtful approach to resolving workplace bullying if the problem resides at the individual, interpersonal level. Originated by Bush and Folger (Barsky, 2007), this type of negotiation involves a third-party facilitator whose role is to encourage empowerment and recognition between two parties. It involves getting to a result of an agreement but reaches that goal with techniques that provide respect, modeling, skills-building education, and empathy to hear the real issues that warring parties are expressing. The process becomes the goal rather than problem resolution. A mediator assesses the following areas of functioning prior to beginning the conflict mediation process:

- communication abilities of all parties
- conflict intensity
- nature and extent of any history of violence between parties
- levels of trust and mistrust
- degrees of flexibility
- interaction patterns
- dependency and attachment issues
- level of interest in resuming or terminating a relationship
- future focus of parties
- cognitive and social functioning of parties
- resources of parties, including financial, social, and emotional
- ethnocentric issues, if present
- critical incidents that led to the conflict
- potential conflicts with others that may impede the mediation process

An important note is that not all are in agreement with the practice of mediation in bullying situations. Outcomes on mediation's effectiveness have not been clear, and the practice may be highly unsuitable if the victim has been harmed considerably by the bully. Nonetheless, mediation can be considered as a viable alternative in some, if not many, situations.

MACRO APPROACHES TO PREVENTION AND REMEDIATION

In mid-September 2014, Gov. Jerry Brown of California signed legislation that required employers with 50 or more employees to have training and education about bullying for supervisors. Assembly Bill 2053 amended a California law that required training to prevent sexual harassment. Employers must now include "prevention of abusive conduct" in their education and training programs for supervisors. The definition of "abusive conduct" comes from the HWB, which is yet to be enacted by any state in its complete version despite over a decade of attempts.

Assembly Bill 2053 defines abusive conduct as:

> conduct of an employer or employee in the workplace, with malice, that a reasonable person would find hostile, offensive, and unrelated to an employer's legitimate business interests. Abusive conduct may include repeated infliction of verbal abuse, such as the use of derogatory remarks, insults, and epithets, verbal or physical conduct that a reasonable person would find threatening, intimidating, or humiliating, or the gratuitous sabotage or undermining of a person's work performance. A single act shall not constitute abusive conduct, unless especially severe and egregious. (p. 97)

Unfortunately, the new California law does not create a legal claim for bullying at work, but it was important step in recognizing the need to respond and prevent bullying. The other state to have recently enacted legislation is Tennessee, which directed the creation of a model antibullying policy for public employees. These measures are both significant, although not complete, efforts at creating public policy for workplace bullying prevention.

SUMMARY

Work environments where mobbing and emotional abuse are present can benefit greatly if professionals skillful at helping to resolve conflicts are engaged as well as those who can teach others conflict-resolution skills for future use. These professionals might include social workers with administrative or community-organizing skills, professional mediators, organizational consultants, EAPs, and even family therapists.

8

Social Perspective, Social Work, and Implications for Social Policy

This chapter addresses emotional bullying at work from a social work perspective, including policy, treatment, intervention, and advocacy. It examines, by state, the recent history and current status of the healthy workplace initiative in the United States. Upon completion of this chapter, readers will understand how workplace emotional abuse fits into the broader issues of social justice. Finally, successes and failures of state legislation to prevent workplace emotional abuse are highlighted. Answers to the following questions are addressed:

- To what degree are bullying and mobbing societal problems rather than social problems?
- Considering section 6 of the NASW (2008) *Code of Ethics*, with its emphasis on social responsibility, is it within social work's domain to respond to this workplace malady? If so, what might these interventions include at the micro, mezzo, and macro levels?
- What are the broader public policy implications?
- What can social work do to influence public policy?

POLICY IMPLICATIONS

Social work has been all but silent on the issue of workplace emotional abuse, which is surprising given its long history of advocacy on a number of social problems and public policy. Social work has been a pioneer in addressing child abuse and neglect, elder abuse and neglect, poverty, mental health, substance abuse, homelessness, immigration, and welfare reform, so the relative silence about workplace bullying is atypical. This author advocates for a more active role by social work and social workers in identifying, preventing, treating, and remediating this massive arena of human misery.

Policy Needs

David Yamada is one of the leading legal analysts in the emerging specialty of redress for emotionally injured workers. Author of the HWB, Yamada has identified the goals of public policy development and implementation, highlighting prevention as the first step. Prevention activities should include policy development and implementation, staff education, and supporting a respectful workplace culture. Next, the legal system should make redress and compensation available to targets, including punitive-damage awards, mental health treatment, and, where appropriate, return-to-work opportunities (D. Yamada, cited in Einarsen et al., 2011). Yamada has also outlined the categories of policy initiatives as

- amending and supplementing existing laws for workplace health and safety,
- recognizing bullying at the judicial and administrative levels for laws,
- voluntary employer acceptance of antibullying policies and labor agreements,
- enacting laws within current laws for torts and harassment, and
- recognition by policymakers of the needs for workplace bullying prevention and remediation.

Unfortunately, the United States has been among the most resistant to adopting such practices. The following discussion concerns the role or proposed role for social work in addressing these issues.

NASW *Code of Ethics* and Its Relationship to Workplace Bullying

A reminder of social work's code of ethics and core values is important at this juncture. The literature about mobbing and emotional abuse in the workplace can be found in journals of business ethics, HR, organizational psychology, victims studies, and various professional journals serving such domains as education, nursing, and medicine. The problem is that the issues of bullying or mobbing have rarely been addressed in social work literature.

The preamble to the NASW (2008) *Code of Ethics* states,

> The primary mission of the social work profession is to enhance human well-being and help meet the basic human needs of all people, with particular attention to the needs and empowerment of people who are vulnerable, oppressed, and living in poverty. A historic and defining feature of social work is the profession's focus on individual well-being in a social context

and the well-being of society. Fundamental to social work is attention to environmental forces that create, contribute to, and address problems in living.

Social workers promote social justice and social change with and on behalf of clients. "Clients" is used inclusively to refer to individuals, families, groups, organizations, and communities. Social workers are sensitive to cultural and ethnic diversity and strive to end discrimination, oppression, poverty, and other forms of social injustice. These activities may be in the form of direct practice, community organizing, supervision, consultation administration, advocacy, social and political action, policy development and implementation, education, and research and evaluation. Social workers seek to enhance the capacity of people to address their own needs. Social workers also seek to promote the responsiveness of organizations, communities, and other social institutions to individuals' needs and social problems.

The mission of the social work profession is rooted in a set of core values. These core values, embraced by social workers throughout the profession's history, are the foundation of social work's unique purpose and perspective:

- Service
- social justice
- dignity and worth of the person
- the importance of human relationships
- integrity
- competence

This constellation of core values reflects what is unique to the social work profession. Core values, and the principles that flow from them, must be balanced within the context and complexity of the human experience.

Of particular relevance to workplace bullying are the following core values, with their corresponding ethical principles here:

Value: Social justice.
Ethical Principle: Social workers challenge social injustice.

Value: Dignity and worth of the person.
Ethical Principle: Social workers respect the inherent dignity and worth of the person.

Value: Importance of human relationships.
Ethical principle: Social workers recognize the central importance of human relationships.

While a number of other principles in the NASW (2008) *Code of Ethics* are relevant, clearly social work has a role and a rationale for helping to ensure the safety and dignity of all workers based on these core values and ethical principles.

The Role of Social Work

As just noted, as of early 2015 the social work profession has done little to address workplace bullying. With the exception of a few articles in NASW journals, the profession has been tardy in addressing workplace bullying as a human rights and social justice issue. This is puzzling, since at least four of the eight core values in social work practice can be identified within the problems and issues of workplace bullying: social justice, dignity and worth of the person, the importance of human relationships, and integrity. Social work has a direct service role in addressing the needs of emotionally injured workers. It also has a role in consulting, supervision, training and education, advocacy, community organizing, administration, research and evaluation, and public policy.

At a microsystems level, social work is already involved with treating injured workers, yet the clinical literature about treatment has come from domains other than social work. At the mezzo level, families, work groups, and whole communities are affected by emotional abuses in organizations. For decades EAPs, many of whom are clinical social workers, have been treating individual and family cases for the effects of bullying. Independent social work clinicians and those employed by public and private institutions have provided clinical services for decades to those affected by workplace emotional abuse. In spite of this history, no specific technologies have appeared in social work literature to examine and test treatment guidelines or best practices. At a macro level, social workers should engage in initiatives to promote healthy and respectful workplaces and to encourage lawmakers to pass the dozens of bills that have been created to protect workers but that have faltered and died in the legislative process. The NASW (2008) *Code of Ethics* admits that

> instances may arise when social workers' ethical obligations conflict with agency policies or relevant laws or regulations. When such conflicts occur, social workers must make a responsible effort to resolve the conflict in a manner that is consistent with the values, principles and standards expressed in this Code. (p. 2)

Social workers have a much broader professional obligation than to engage in competent and ethical direct service. Their code *requires* them to be advocates for social justice and agents of change when needed. Preventing emotional abuse in the workplace, especially since it has become so rampant, should be of primary importance both to individual social work practitioners and to the profession as a whole. Poverty, racism, immigration, child abuse and neglect, adoption, education, domestic and intimate-partner violence, substance abuse, mental health, gerontology, hospice and palliative care, rehabilitation, disabilities, and recovery from trauma have become significant aspects of social work education, training, and practice. Now issues of workplace abuse, particularly the trauma of bullying, should be a primary concern of the social work profession. To date, this has not occurred.

Only a generation ago, the clinical community was beginning to understand the trauma associated with combat. As military personnel returned from Vietnam, treatment protocols and technologies were developed, and recovery and rehabilitation became possible. Until recently, victims of sexual assault and domestic violence have been unable to seek and receive redress for their victimization. Today both have protections provided by the law that were unheard of two decades ago. Social work has had a visible and viable role in participating in finding solutions for these and other vulnerable populations.

The profession and the community as a whole would be well served to identify workplace abuses as social and societal problems and to participate in dialogue and technology development for treatment and prevention. Social workers have had a historic role in assisting and advocating for many vulnerable and disenfranchised groups, such as new immigrants, victims of child abuse, abused spouses and elders, psychiatric patients, substance abusers, older adults, and hospice and palliative-care recipients. Finally, the profession needs to address its responsibility to act on public policy.

Social Work's Response to Bullying

While social work has said little about workplace bullying, it has addressed a variety of workplace issues. Social work theorists Germain and Bloom (1999) addressed how two factors must be considered in addressing the dimensions of the person–work environment. These broad factors are *productivity* and *worker satisfaction*. Organizational factors and small group factors can further influence satisfaction and productivity. Worker satisfaction is cast as a cluster of factors that address how workers feel about approaching and carrying out the jobs they are hired to perform, the contexts in which they carry out these jobs, and the compensation they receive for performing the work.

The *human relations model* (Germaine & Bloom, 1999) has evolved to address the importance of the informal relationships between workers and the impact on organizational life these informal relationships can have, even though such relationships do not appear on organizational charts. Nineteenth-century social work evolution culminated in various approaches to industrial or occupational social work. When one considers the systems-theory foundation of much of social work thinking, it follows that social workers should be very actively involved with interventions in the workplace. Occupational social work usually means providing direct services within the confines of the workplace, a naturally occurring setting for most adults.

As of 2015, little social work research or literature has directly addressed bullying at work. However, Elizabeth Pomeroy (2012) offered one of the most insightful articles about working with victims of abuse from a social work perspective. Pomeroy cautioned social workers about the fragility of clients once they reach a social worker's office. Clients who have been bullied will often display profound symptoms. Unless the social worker has a history with the client, he or she will know little about the client's psychosocial functioning prior to the bullying experience. Pomeroy also observed that social workers may be in a pivotal position to provide employee assistance, thus making a difference in the lives of many.

In addition to advocating for the injured worker, Pomeroy (2012) suggested the following:

- Social workers should develop a good working knowledge of workplace emotional abuse via professional development.
- When working with a new client who has been bullied, social workers should get as clear a picture of the client's work history, relationships, and experiences as possible.
- A worker may suggest that the client keep a journal, not just as a therapeutic intervention but also for purposes of documentation.
- The social worker can encourage an injured client to have a support system outside of work.
- The advocacy role is an important one for social workers. Specifically, a worker can help by dealing with those in authority on behalf of injured workers.
- Clients can be helped to feel supported if the social worker will get information about workplace emotional abuse.
- Finally, the social worker can assist the client in making decisions about the future, including job-related choices.

A social work study by Meyer (2004) examined organizational response to conflict and the relationship to future conflict and negative work outcomes. In a cross-sectional study of 3,374 government service workers at 387 worksites in the southeastern United States, managers' conflict-handling styles were examined in relation to productivity. Meyer categorized results as four styles of conflict management: adaptive, forcing, avoiding, and abusive. Interestingly, as managers used more forced conflict–handling styles, accidents, absenteeism, and overtime increased. The prevalence of more abusive styles of handling conflict—for example, yelling, threatening, and pushing—correlated with less favorable outcomes. In addition, when managers used a more adaptive style, accidents, absenteeism, and overtime all decreased. These results suggest that conflict-management skills training could be helpful in organizations (Meyer, 2004). To the degree that mobbing is a process that often begins with an unresolved conflict situation, analyses of conflict-handling styles and the conflict-resolution skills of managers and supervisors can be important determinants of containment or escalation of discord and could ultimately affect mobbing. One role for social workers in work environments could be to provide assessment and coaching to managers and supervisors about their conflict-management styles and train them in skills that are most correlated with good outcomes.

A multifaceted role for consulting psychologists in addressing workplace bullying was proposed by Ferris (2009). While few social workers conduct the personality testing recommended by Ferris, most are skilled at assessment processes, so most can effectively manage organizational assessment processes. In addition, social workers, like consulting psychologists, can and often do participate in multiple "human" factors in work environments, including coaching and performance management. These can include diagnosing organizational orientation toward bullying, identifying processes that create and sustain bullying behaviors, and basic interventions within organizations such as awareness building, policy development, training, and conflict resolution. Like consulting psychologists, social workers have competencies to help leaders examine their own behaviors. Social workers wanting to work with organizations can hone these skills.

How can social workers weigh in with their personal experiences while working in organizations? A quantitative study of 234 social workers from 26 hospitals in a large urban area setting with a total population of about 2.5 million was conducted by Gellis (2001). In this study, social workers clarified their perceptions of their own managers' leadership practices. Leadership behavior was measure by Multifactor Leadership Questionnaire, Form 5X (MLQ 5X). The MLQ 5X is a 45-item measurement using five subscales: idealized influence attributed, idealized behaviors, inspirational motivation, intellectual stimulation, and individualized consideration. Participants were asked how frequently their social work manager engaged in specific transformational MLQ behaviors, such as address job-related needs of social workers, represent needs of direct-service social workers to administrators, contribute to organizational effectiveness, and the leader's work group performance. Results suggested that transformational leadership had the significant perceived effects of social workers' satisfaction with their leaders. An add-on hypothesis was supported that transformational leadership increases levels of subordinates' effort and performance beyond what other processes accomplish. Outcomes also suggested that transformational factors may be effective in enhancing positive attitudes and behaviors among social workers on the job, but whether social work leaders have a positive or negative effect on organizational functioning may depend on selection and training (Gellis, 2001). Social work practitioners and social work administrators need training in leadership for both social work education and social work practice. The degree to which social work administrators have sufficient leadership training can affect the prevalence of emotional abuse in those administrators' organizations. Adequate administrative experience and management training, with constant attention to organizational practices and processes, could prevent workplace dysfunction.

Social work within the workplace has been part of the profession's applied domain for many years. However, little has appeared to date in social work literature to address the identification, prevention, treatment, and remediation of actual workplace bullying. Social work tradition would advocate for treatment of the work environment where problems occur, but most non-social-work-oriented organizations do not have the benefit of social workers' expertise to address problems in the work environment (Woods & Hollis, 2000). It may be that highly challenging work environments could minimize their risks of bullying by utilizing social workers and social work principles in organizational practices.

Direct Intervention with Workers Who Have Been Bullied

Many social workers today are clinicians, so the clinical guidelines in chapter 6 are relevant as social work issues. Social work theorists Woods and Hollis (2000) asserted that the tension created by crisis needs to be relieved. When people are in an unsteady state, egos are fluid, defenses are shaken, and emotions are high. Clinicians and therapeutic responders will need to determine the meaning of the crisis to the individual and assess the person's adaptive capacities. To understand the impact of the crisis and to set realistic treatment goals, knowledge of the person's precrisis level of functioning is important. To link the person in crisis to that person's own adaptive capabilities, identifying relevant earlier life experiences can be very helpful. Finally, when examining resources and strengths, assessing a person's family circumstances and attitudes while identifying support system needs can all help with stabilization.

As mentioned in chapter 6, Hollis (1972) suggested that all therapeutic relationships begin with the professional asking three questions: What is the problem? What contributes to the problem? What can be changed or modified?

Social workers engaged in treating injured workers need to grasp that the client is in distress not only because of the failure of unique coping strategies but also because the client has experienced a grave social injustice in a significant life institution.

Dewees (2005) identified the therapeutic relationship as the very heart of social work practice and advised clinicians to hear the client's whole story, even if it is long, and to notice the client's view of situations and their meanings. Social work educators and theorists Woods and Hollis (2000) cited clinicians' characteristics of nonpossessive warmth and concern, genuineness, and empathy, along with optimism and objectivity, as conditions necessary to the healing relationship. Northern (1995) reminded professionals that even voluntary clients may have ambivalent feelings when they begin treatment. They usually have anxiety about the new relationship and concerns about how they might be perceived. Even with those clients with a highly positive commitment to seek help for themselves and their problems, ambivalence is often present. Citing countless medical evidence of the positive influence hope has on outcomes, Northern also reminded clinicians of the powerful motivating force of hope for clients in crisis.

When social workers provide psychotherapy, they will undoubtedly come into contact with clients or patients who have been bullied. One view represented by the media and some in the general public holds that bullied targets are themselves responsible for their situations. Unless clinicians who treat victims of mobbing are specifically sensitized to the issues involved with mobbing, they may not believe that the severe symptoms observed in the victims are primarily a result of the victims' work context. Instead, they may assign diagnoses that focus on internal states, such as generalized anxiety disorder and major depressive disorder, and ignore the context from which the distress has emerged. They may also conclude that these disorders existed before the mobbing process began (Zapf, 1999). This logic would make psychiatric symptoms a cause rather than a result of the mobbing process. Social workers are somewhat unique in their ability to acknowledge the context in which people exist and the stressors present in the micro- and macrosystems of the client that may precipitate the onset of emotional and psychological distress.

Kilburg (2009) suggested some direct responses that clinicians, including social workers, may find helpful:

- Help clients to clarify what is happening to them if they are the targets of bullying.
- Remember that therapeutic work has, at its core, the need to help clients create the time and space for reflection.
- Help clients test reality.
- Be prepared to share the emotional journey of the bullied client.
- When invited to comment, be mindful of how easy it is to judge those in the situation. Many situations do not have clear beginnings, middles, or endings.

In a study from India (D'Cruz & Noronha, 2012), researchers examined the threat that bullying creates for the bullied target's sense of identity. Although, to obtain data, the study examined a small sample of only 10 participants who underwent intensive and thorough interviewing, the findings suggested core themes, including both a threatened sense of security and diminished sense of self in those who had been victims. After the bullying experiences were over (through the target's departure from the workplace or the cessation of the abuse), victims were tasked with a need to rebuild personal security, create insulation for themselves, regain equilibrium, regain their dignity, and reestablish meaning for themselves. Certainly, it would be within a social worker's purview to assist an injured worker in addressing these concerns.

Although the relationship between leadership and organizational functioning and the prevalence of bullying or mobbing at work have already been established, little attention has been given to concepts of leadership and organizational performance within many of the domains of social work theory and practice. Until very recently, theories or models of leadership had been rarely advanced in social work practice, especially in social welfare (Gellis, 2001). Nonetheless, examining management characteristics and behavior is a relevant and critical area for social work study. The practice of *transformational leadership* is a force that could be instructive within the field of social work. Transformational leadership includes such concepts as vision, strategy, and organizational culture.

IMPLICATIONS FOR SOCIAL WORK PRACTICE

As mentioned in chapter 1, social work within the workplace has been part of the profession's applied domain for many years. However, little has appeared to date in social work literature to address the identification, prevention, treatment, and remediation of the actual workplace emotional abuse that is created, and sustained, by bullying in the workplace. While social work tradition would tend to advocate for addressing the problem in the work environment itself, most non–social work oriented organizations do not have the benefit of social workers' expertise to do so

(Woods & Hollis, 2000). Many of social work's basic principles are highly relevant in addressing workplace bullying.

Relationship of Social Work's Model to Bullying: Person in Environment

Risk, protective, and *resilience factors* affect social and health problems (Fraser et al., 1999). Risk factors affect the likelihood of a future event, given a set of conditions. Risk is a central concept in the field of public health, where it is used along with the concept of covariation and prediction. Risk factors may be individualistic such as traits, they may be related to life events or experiences, or they may be related to context or environment. Risk factors are markers or correlates but are not necessarily causative. Nonspecific risk factors include combinations of individual, familial, and extrafamilial factors, including child abuse; chronic family conflict; unskilled parenting; academic failure; peer rejection; poverty; racism, sexism, and other types of discrimination; and environmental factors. The combination of these factors lead scholars to use the term *cumulative risk factors* when implying risk. With these cumulative risk factors, an implicit need exists for an integrative perspective in identifying vulnerable populations and high-risk environments (Fraser et al., 1999).

Protective factors are not just the opposite of risk factors. They may be individualistic factors, such as easygoing temperament; family factors, such as parental warmth and supervision; or conditions outside the family, such as neighborhoods, schools, churches, and communities (Fraser et al., 1999). Other protective factors may be compensatory—that is, they may directly reduce a person's individual risk.

Finally, resilience factors involve those accumulations of wisdom and experience that have allowed people to adapt to circumstances and to achieve positive and unexpected results, even in adversity. Individual adaptation results from individual exposure to risk, followed by experience in successful response to the risk (Fraser et al., 1999).

In examining workplace issues, a number of perspectives are needed, including occupational choice and character style, problems with career success encountered by workers, task analysis, boundary issues, lines of authority, management changes, and interorganizational changes (Czander, 1993).

Gellis (2001) acknowledged that models of transformational leadership have rarely been advanced in social welfare but that the most appropriate model emphasizes a pattern of interaction between the worker, supervisor, and environment. Social work literature emphasizes the importance of social contexts in human functioning. Approaches to understanding human functioning need to include systems theories and human-development theories, as well as an understanding of ego functioning, biophysical factors, values and cultural differences, communication styles, and the effects of stress on individual and collective behavior (Northern, 1995).

Theories about the causes and conditions of workplace bullying are many and varied. Researchers would be naive to point to one condition or variable and conclude that it is *the* cause of bullying. Rather, one can identify many conditions or factors that are correlated with bullying and perhaps concur that there are relationships between some of these variables and workplace emotional abuse. Just as there is no one cause, there is no one solution or intervention. The remaining sections will identify a variety of solutions to bullying problems at the micro, mezzo, and macro levels of human interaction.

Social Work Settings

Today's social work challenges include increased pressures to produce measurable outcomes, to provide supervisory and managerial training for direct-service providers prior to promotion, and to manage organizational politics by settling disputes, managing distrust, minimizing blame, and dispelling feelings of hopelessness in both clients and staff. All of these workplace pressures may increase the risk of mobbing if left untreated, even in human services organizations. Regarding social work organizations, Ginsberg and Keys (1995) conceptualized human services agencies as political arenas tied to public policy, serving as ends to means (getting services to target populations) while being sensitive to the needs of interest groups. While human services managers need to protect their organizations from risk of emotional abuse, they also need to understand the politics of social service administration by thinking politically. They should consider such acts as diagnosing interests, assessing power, controlling agendas, controlling decision alternatives, and controlling the promises that are made. Human services administrators must also behave politically by operating with self-awareness, displaying communication skills, creating networks, building alliances and consensus, playing by the rules, performing useful functions, and managing the impressions that outside interests have of them (Ginsberg & Keys, 1995).

Max Weber coined the term "bureaucracy" as a concept rather than an actual structure, and a number of concepts are inherent in his definition. Each position in the organization has identifiable but limited scopes of authority. Responsibility for the organization and control of its functions are mainly concentrated at the top of a well-defined hierarchy. Centralized units house records and data. Workers are hired based on education and training. Being a staff member of the organization is a full-time commitment, and employees regard their positions as careers. Rules clearly define the organization's activities. Most relationships between employees are characterized as impersonal. Recruitment and hiring practice base selection on knowledge, skills, and abilities. Private lives for all members of the workplace remain separate from work lives. Finally, promotions in the organization are usually based on seniority (Dewees, 2005).

Contrast this with today's organizations, in which many of these concepts are not inherent assumptions. Social work must also address the changing face of the workplace by integrating new groups of inexperienced workers, consulting with business about how to address diversity issues, and helping to strengthen the relationships between the world of work and the community. Social work has long since held a role in working both *in* and *with* organizations. Social work practice in social service agencies requires an understanding of the organization's culture, including mission, physical surroundings, self-identity, and procedures, along with the organization's understanding of social justice and diversity factors (Dewees, 2005). Attention to organizational culture, mission, vision, values, physical plant, professional identity, processes and procedures, and diversity are part of minimizing the risk of mobbing. Thus, an inherent role for social work may be key in the prevention of workplace emotional abuse.

As noted earlier, the NASW (2008) *Code of Ethics* tasks social workers to promote social justice and social change with and on behalf of clients. This is accomplished with

- direct practice,
- community organizing,
- supervision,
- consultation,
- administration,
- advocacy,
- social and political action,
- policy development and implementation,
- education,
- research, and
- evaluation.

These activities are the foundation of the profession's purpose and practice. Clearly, the issue of emotional abuse at work, the personal and organizational causes of emotional abuse at work, and efforts toward remediation fall within the definition of social work's mission and values.

Non–Social Work Settings: Social Workers as Organizational Consultants and Facilitators

When social workers themselves are placed in *host settings*—that is, those settings that are not social work organizations but rather that offer guest status to social workers as part of a multidisciplinary team—their responsibilities for organizational understanding are compounded. They may be responsible for, or participate in, organizational change and participate as partners in decision making and identifying innovative ways of doing business, and they may be critical in identifying the organizational values that will advance the goals of both the workplace and the community. These processes can all contribute to preventing and remediating workplace bullying.

THE NEED FOR MULTIDIMENSIONAL MODELS TO EXAMINE PERPETRATORS, VICTIMS, AND ENVIRONMENTS

The metaphor of a restaurant kitchen can serve as an example of how many factors combine to create bullying (Rayner et al., 2002). Visiting a commercial kitchen at peak business hours would reveal that during rush hours, the environment becomes tense. If no standards are set for appropriate behavior, circumstances can degenerate and conflict can ensue. The combination of time pressures, kitchens crammed with too many people and too much equipment, hot room temperatures, requirements for high quality, and little room for error all add up to an explosive environment where all staff work under stressful conditions. When chefs own their own restaurants, the pressures of profitability further compound matters. Connect this metaphor to more general bullying in the workplace. These are the types of workplace environments that can create workplace abuses.

To improve understanding of workplace bullying, Rayner et al. (1999) pointed to the need for methodologies that go beyond just interviews and questionnaires with people who admit to histories of being victimized by bullying. The quest for truth may be "out there," but researchers must examine different realities and multiple perceptions as part of the process of studying emotional abuse at work. This would require developing data-collection methods that are multidisciplinary and multidimensional, as well as coordinated. Collaboration between researchers is imperative. If too much fragmentation exists between disciplines, the patterns that lead to mobbing may be unclear, and solutions will not be identified (Rayner et al., 1999). Gellis (2001) acknowledged that models of transformational leadership have rarely been advanced in social welfare, but the most appropriate model emphasizes a pattern of interaction between the worker, supervisor, and environment. Social work literature emphasizes the importance of social contexts in human functioning. Approaches to understanding human functioning need to include systems theories and human-development theories, along with an understanding of ego functioning, biophysical factors, values and cultural differences, communication styles, and the effects of stress on individual and collective behavior (Northern, 1995).

EMERGING TRENDS AND LEGISLATION

Emerging trends and legislation have been discussed at length in previous chapters. David Yamada (2000) suggested that policy objectives toward developing a formal, legal response to workplace bullying need to reflect the following:

- Laws should encourage employers to use preventive measures to reduce bullying.
- When bullying does occur, the law should protect workers who use self-help measures to address problems and seek resolution.
- Relief, compensation, and restoration should be available if preventive measures and self-help measures are not sufficient. (The legal system should provide a means of relief, ensure compensation for injuries, and assist victims in returning to their jobs or securing other employment.)
- Finally, the law should ensure that bullies are punished. Bullies should have punitive measures as a consequence of their behaviors. And, according to Yamada, the punishment should be dire enough to discourage future bullying.

Trends in Litigation

Trends in litigation have been varied. As of 2000, case law has ruled in favor of plaintiffs on the basis of severe emotional distress, harassment, and hostile work environment. Arguments of emotional distress due to job termination have been rejected by most courts. Workers' compensation may provide limited benefits, depending on the employer and the circumstances. Courts have generally allowed employers to conduct their own internal investigations of allegations of emotional abuse. The Title VII hostile work environments doctrine is relevant to an analysis of emotional abuse at work. David Yamada (2000) argued that Title VII now encompasses a sexual harassment doctrine. It also could provide a useful framework for understanding a broader, status-blind, hostile work–environment standard that responds more effectively to the problem of emotional abuse at work. Yamada's contention is that the hostile-environment doctrine and statutes could achieve all four of the policy goals stated earlier—that is, the role of prevention, self-help, remediation/compensation, and punishment for addressing workplace bullying, including but not limited to sexual harassment.

The National Labor Relations Act

First enacted by Congress in 1935, the NLRA provides some rights and responsibilities that can help to put a check on workplace bullying in two ways, according to David Yamada (2000). First, the NLRA grants employees "the right to self-organization, to form, join, or assist labor organizations, to bargain collectively through representatives of their own choosing" (NRLA, 1935). If a union can discourage workplace bullying, then the right to form and join unions serves an important means toward the goal of stopping workplace bullying. Second, the NLRA gives workers the right to engage in activities for their "mutual aid or protection" whether they belong to a union or not.

However, according to David Yamada (2000), the NLRA in its current form is of very limited value in combating workplace bullying. There are number of reasons for this. First, the NLRA places severe limits on the types of employees who can organize and join unions and engage in union activities. Expressly excluded from the NLRA's protections are supervisors, independent contractors, domestic and agricultural workers, and family-member employees. Second, the NLRA offers protection of employees who undertake collective measures to oppose workplace bullying and states that employers may not interfere with, restrain, or coerce employees in executing their rights. The problem is that for nonunion employees, the "concerted activity" section of this provision is limited as a legal weapon (D. Yamada, 2000).

Occupational Safety and Health Act

A part of the U.S. Department of Labor, OSHA was established to protect all working men and women in the United States, to ensure safe and healthful workplaces, and to preserve human resources. Unfortunately, Congress has decided that when personal injuries and illnesses occur in the workplace, they place substantial burdens on the U.S. economy (D. Yamada, 2000). Although OSHA's main concern is ensuring that workplaces are free from hazards that caused or are likely to cause death or serious harm to workers, the definition of "serious harm" is not always interpreted the same in all jurisdictions (D. Yamada, 2000). Even if some types of bullying fall within the purview of OSHA, the statutes do not really address the goals of prevention, self-help, compensation, and punishment (D. Yamada, 2000). Those advocates of worker protections as a main goal of employment policy support regulatory policies such as those of OSHA. In addition, those who think policy should provide workers safeguards against employer negligence support such policies as the Employee Retirement Income Security Act and the FMLA. For others, if the goal of employment policies is to reduce poverty by getting more people to work, then such policies as minimum wages and earned income credit are generally supported (Midgley & Livermore, 2009).

If employers were required to have workplace bullying policies and practices in place in the same way they are required to have written policies to prevent discrimination, sexual harassment, and workplace injuries, they would be forced to work to prevent such abuses. If workers had training about the nature of workplace bullying, they would be both able to identify it when it occurs and take personal responsibility for avoiding engaging in such behavior. Workplaces could also provide for the advocacy of information about redress and information about tangible supports to self-help, such as groups, mental health referrals, and communication training. If injured workers had more opportunities for compensatory income during their recovery time, and if laws regarding compensation were in place for emotionally injured workers, workers could know that the legal system treated the injury as valid. Finally, if laws were in place to consistently provide negative consequences—that is, punishment—to perpetrators, potentially abusive bullies would at least be aware of the risks of their abusive behavior. Public employees' speech is protected only when it pertains to matters of public concern. According to David Yamada (2000), everyday bullying typically falls outside of that standard because private employees' speech is not included in the constitutional protection, so private employers are not necessarily bound by the free-speech provision of the Constitution.

Employers have offered a variety of defenses in response to charges of workplace emotional abuse, among them that the employer used reasonable care to prevent and promptly correct any inappropriate behavior and that the plaintiff (the injured worker) unreasonably failed to take advantage of any preventative or corrective opportunities provided by the employer (D. Yamada, 2000).

The preceding discussion of protections and case law application is by no means exhaustive. Limitations of the law and legal precedents help to clarify employer liabilities are daunting for victims seeking legal recourse for bullying or mobbing. Yamada (2009) has stated that consensus has not been reached on addressing and preventing workplace bullying. He has suggested that policies, programs, and procedures need to be in place in organizations. Some limitations are that research or precedent for developing guidelines and programs has not been developed. Yamada has advised that those who would engage in the challenge of developing guidelines should act inclusively, involving stakeholders. He has also proposed a multidisciplinary team approach to workplace bullying, with representation and expertise provided by mental health, public health, management and HR, law and dispute resolution, and education.

The Healthy Workplace Legislative Initiative: The HWB

In response to a general question about why there is a need for regulations to protect workers, a discussion at the HWB Web site (http://www.healthyworkplacebill .org) advises that employers tend to respond to laws with internal policies. The true value of workplace laws and the intent of the HWB is to motivate employers to prevent workplace bullying practices with universal policies and procedures relevant to all employees in their organizations. The HWB, crafted by David Yamada for the Healthy Workplace Campaign (a grassroots initiative), gives employers incentives to do the right thing by avoiding expensive litigation.

The opinion of many is that the HWB that has been introduced in state and territorial legislatures over the past 10 years could be crucial in changing norms, values, and practices around emotional abuse at work. As of 2015, 27 states and two territories (Puerto Rico and the Virgin Islands) have introduced the HWB in their legislature.

Key aspects of the HWB for employers include the following:

- Provides precise language about the definition of "abusive work environment" and provides for high standards for the definition.
- Requires proof of injury or harm by a qualified (licensed) health-care practitioner.
- Gives protection from vicarious liability for those employers who are already conscientious about workplace protections via prevention, policies, and practices.
- Requires that claimants use private attorneys (and therefore bear the financial burden of legal representation).
- Fills gaps in current state and federal laws protecting civil rights.

For workers, these are some key aspects of the HWB:

- Allows paths for legal response to workplace emotional abuses.
- Lets targets sue the individual perpetrator while holding employers accountable
- Provides an avenue for restoring lost wages.
- Puts a burden on employers for prevention and correction.

Contrary to popular myth, the HWB does not

- involve state-level departments to police or enforce any part of the law,
- involve any additional costs for states,

- require the plaintiffs be members of a protected status group (such as those protected by civil rights laws), or
- use the term *workplace bullying*.

Although the contents make such good sense, the bill has met with delays, opposition, and derailment, despite its virtues. While most U.S. states offer some types of protection, they are not uniformly in place, and as of 2015 bullying in general was *not* illegal in the United States unless it involved harassment based on one of the civil rights protections against discrimination. The 27 states and two territories where bills have been introduced as of April 2015 are indicated in Table 8.1.

As of July 2015, the HWB defeated earlier was refiled in Massachusetts. A total of 58 sponsors and cosponsors in the statehouse and senate supported the bill. This sponsorship is a substantial increase from prior sessions and is in response to growing support for HWB among constituents (D. Yamada, 2015).

Other legislative activity in states has included Georgia, where, in 2012, the Fulton County (Atlanta) commissioners voted unanimously to adopt a workplace antibullying policy that covers county employees. Under this policy, suspension and even termination may result for those who severely bully others in county work environments. Much of the language for this action came from the HWB drafted by Yamada and introduced across the United States. The Fulton County policy includes insults, threats, and sabotaging of another's work as offenses (D. Yamada, 2012).

New York's legislature actually passed a bill in 2008 that was vetoed by the governor. None of the bills has yet been enacted. How ironic that in a country so deeply committed to democracy and human rights, legislation preventing abuse at work has tended to be cast by critics as the government's attempts to regulate "civility." Unfortunately, even with the momentum created by the legislative success of such states as New York, no state has been successful in both legislative and administrative approval. The New York State Senate passed another bill in May 2010 that, again, was vetoed. In spite of the vetoes and the legislative failures, continued efforts have provided hope to those who have pioneered the initiatives around the country. In January 2015 Assembly Bill 3250 was reintroduced, and supporters are hopeful that it may both pass and be signed.

California governor Jerry Brown signed legislation (Assembly Bill No. 2053) in early September 2014, requiring employers of 50 or more workers to ensure that supervisors received training and education about workplace bullying. This legislation amended a previous California law requiring employers to engage in training and education for sexual harassment. Employers are now required to include "prevention of abusive conduct" in training and education programs for supervisors and managers. The definition of "abusive conduct" draws heavily from versions of the HWB, covering

> conduct of an employer or employee in the workplace, with malice, that a reasonable person would find hostile, offensive, and unrelated to an employer's legitimate business interests. Abusive conduct may include

Table 8.1. Healthy Workplace Bill (HWB) Activity

States and Territories That Have Introduced HWBs as of April 2015	First Introduced
States (*n* = 27)	
California	2003
Connecticut	2007
Florida	2013
Hawaii	2004
Illinois	2009
Kansas	2006
Maine	2013
Maryland	2011
Massachusetts	2009
Minnesota	2011
Missouri	2006
Montana	2006
Nevada	2009
New Hampshire	2010
New Jersey	2006
New Mexico	2013
New York	2006
Oklahoma	2004
Oregon	2005
Pennsylvania	2013
Tennessee	2014
Texas	2015
Utah	2009
Vermont	2007
Washington	2005
West Virginia	2011
Wisconsin	2010
Territories (*n* = 2)	
Puerto Rico	2014
U.S. Virgin Islands	2014

Reprinted by permission of Gary Namie, national director of the Healthy Workplace Campaign.

repeated infliction of verbal abuse, such as the use of derogatory remarks, insults, and epithets, verbal or physical conduct that a reasonable person would find threatening, intimidating, or humiliating, or the gratuitous sabotage or undermining of a person's work performance. A single act shall not constitute abusive conduct, unless especially severe and egregious. (Assembly Bill No. 2053)

Unfortunately, the new California law does not provide any basis for a legal claim for workplace bullying. While the governor's signing of the bill represents a modest step forward, it is still a step forward and perhaps will help to open the door for California's legal system to better address workplace bullying. The California law follows a related law in Tennessee enacted in early 2014 that requires a state commission to create a workplace antibullying policy for employees in Tennessee's public sector (D. Yamada, 2014a).

Avenues for redress for victims in the United States and internationally can vary significantly. No legislation currently exists to address workplace bullying at the national level, although Sen. Tom Harkin (D-IA) introduced an omnibus bill called the HELP America Act (S2558) in 2004 (Von Bergen et al., 2006). It did not specifically address workplace mobbing, and it did not pass. Although workplace bullying is not yet Title VII protected, there may be a trend toward awarding judgments in favor of plaintiffs if the workplace emotional distress meets four criteria: Was the distress inflicted intentionally, was the behavior extreme, did the defendant's actions cause the plaintiff emotional distress, and was the resulting emotional distress severe (Von Bergen et al., 2006)?

Unfortunately, these success stories are relatively few compared to the efforts over the past 10 years to ensure that workers in every state can have safety and protection from workplace bullying. Nonetheless, modest successes can contribute to larger momentum, offering continued hope for many. Fox and Stallworth (2009) reminded us that in the absence of legislative protections, strategies remain, including antibullying policies in organizations, training for all staff at all levels in the organization, and implementing conflict-resolution processes such as alternative dispute resolution.

Social Work, Advocacy, and Macro Policy Issues

Social workers have long enjoyed a reputation of being "change agents." Such activism requires passion for social justice, personal and professional commitment, and concrete skills. David Yamada (2013b) offered some suggestions for change agents:

- Be responsibly bold: Real change isn't reckless or timid.
- Take a next step: If you're stuck, take a next step. It may lead to something important.
- Put ideas on paper: Writing helps one to think logically about passionate issues. Let the creative and the logical sides of your brain inspire each other.
- Persevere: Stay with it long enough to have an impact.

- Learn: Change agents are lifelong learners. Continue to learn, read, write, etc.
- Affiliate and organize: While it's possible for individuals to make changes, it's easier when one works with others. Affiliate with those who share your passion and whose skills complement yours.
- Take a break: Avoid burnout.
- Plan, do, evaluate, repeat: Use this as your mantra.
- Celebrate victories, but get back to work: Don't celebrate too long, but celebrate to recharge your energy.
- When despairing, dig deep: Changing a small part of the bigger picture can be challenging and frustrating. When setbacks occur, dig deeper to renew faith, devotion, or connection with others.

SUMMARY

As highlighted in chapter 1, social conditions become social problems when interest groups raise public awareness about the existence of the conditions at question. The term *claims-making* describes the activities of interest groups (claims makers) whose grievances about a social condition are brought to public awareness (Hewitt, 2007). Claims-makers express concern about a condition they find unacceptable. When the claims-makers' cause becomes widely recognized by a society, the social condition becomes known as a *social problem*. The process from initial claims-making to widespread social recognition of the concern as a social problem takes time—often years or decades. The social problem of abusive work environments has undergone such a claims-making process. It began in continental Europe, migrated to the United Kingdom and Australia, and is finally gaining recognition in the United States. The United States has been very tardy in moving the issue of workplace emotional abuse to the level of social problem. The relatively slow claims-making process for identifying and defining social problems may account for the marked lag in data collection and analysis in the United States as compared to other developed nations in the West.

Through its long tradition of influencing public policy via advocacy, social work is well positioned to take up this cause. One obvious role for social workers would be to lobby for the passage of the HWB in their individual state legislatures. Social workers could also join the ranks of "coordinators" within states who gather to strategize for influence in state legislatures. Like any other citizen, social workers can become active by sharing information with friends; engaging in letter writing to news media and politicians; and becoming activists at local, state, and even national levels.

9

Additional and Alternative Explanations for Increased Bullying

Why is bullying so prevalent in the United States? Although this text has examined workplace bullying from a wide variety of perspectives, questions do remain about why it remains a problem in the 21st century, especially in the United States.

EFFORTS TO EXPLAIN BULLYING IN THE UNITED STATES

Swedish researcher Salin suggested that globalization and the liberalization of markets, the trend toward performance pressures, and emphasis on efficiency are correlates. McCarthy (1996, in Salin, 2003b) stated that these types of pressures "lower the threshold" at which managers might adopt bullying as a supervisory strategy, especially if they are not skilled at leading others. Sheehan (1999, in Salin, 2003b) proposed that with such pressure to produce outcomes, managers may resort to any behavior needed to accomplish tasks, including emotional abuse. Salin also noted that since the 1990s, the emphasis on efficiency for schools and health-care settings may negatively affect worker well-being and motivation. High-pressure organizations emphasizing bottom lines above all else can create environments in which managers ignore or even dismiss hard-working, loyal employees in favor of those aggressive individuals who contribute most to profits. While much of the data from the United Kingdom, the United States, and Australia has focused on superior-to-subordinate bullying, in Scandinavia bullying is often peer to peer. These more equal-power relationships can be affected by the same pressures of top-down bullying.

As mentioned earlier in this text, David Yamada (2000) asserted that the reasons for increased bullying include growth of the service industry, global profit squeeze, decline of unionization, diversification of the workforce, and increased reliance on contingent workers. Yamada linked workplace bullying to the historical relationship between employers and employees ("master and servant") as background for emotional abuse. Based in English laws from much earlier centuries, labor laws in the United States are among the most archaic. The basic structure of an employer's rights to choose, hire, exert power, and dismiss a worker creates a disparate balance of power that puts any employee at risk. Making this power imbalance even more significant is the increase in what is known as "at-will" employment as a possible correlate of bullying (D. Yamada, 2013a).

Modest cover-ups commonly protect bosses who harass and protect their organizations from accountability. Unless bullied workers elect to file lawsuits as a remedy, they are usually left to fend for themselves. An employer's response to complaints is an indication of the integrity of the organization (D. Yamada, 2010). Quite simply, bullying persists in the 21st century because it is allowed to go unchecked, and workers in general have no protections against it. In a November 2010 blog posting, David Yamada (2010) suggested that cultures of fear in organizations teach employees to ignore the plight of a bullied target because they are afraid to become one of the targeted. Yamada stated that not just in extreme cases does this phenomenon occur, but also in schools and workplaces where bullying goes unchecked (D. Yamada, 2010).

School-aged children learn early that the group ignores or casts out victims of bullying. Why? The personal risk to one's social standing or emotional security is often too great to help someone who is being targeted. Bad schools do not take preventative or remedial action to prevent or address bullying, especially if the perpetrators are students who tend to be popular or high functioning. In the adult world of work, cycles of abuse and abandonment repeat themselves when someone bullies another in the workplace. Then, like in childhood, the victim is typically abandoned by coworkers and by management (D. Yamada, 2010).

A similar type of abandonment and a relevant quote can be referenced in the writings of Martin Niemöller, a Protestant minister in Germany who opposed the activities of the Nazi regime. For the last seven years of Adolf Hitler's rule, he lived in a concentration camp under Nazi control. The following quotation is translated from the Martin Niemöller Foundation Web site (Niemöller, n.d.):

> When the Nazis came for the communists, I remained silent, I was not a communist. When they locked up the social democrats, I remained silent, I was not a social democrat. Then they came for the trade unionists, I remained silent, I was not a trade unionist. Then they came for me, there was no more, left to speak out.

Much controversy has surrounded the statement, and it has been printed in a variety of forms, with mention of diverse groups such as Jews, Jehovah's Witnesses, gay men, and Catholics, depending on which version one reads. Niemöller's point, whichever variation is used, was that leaders of the Protestant churches were complicit through their silence during the Nazi persecution of millions. Not until 1963 did Niemöller admit to his own anti-Semitism and offer his regrets (Gerlach, 2000). Still, Niemöller was one of the first Germans to talk openly about complicity in the Holocaust and a collective guilt for what had happened to the Jews. In his 1946 book *Über die deutsche Schuld, Not und Hoffnung* (published in English as *Of Guilt and Hope* [1947]), Niemöller said that his people (that is, Christians and Christian laity) had sinned against Jewish people and that he and his peers in faith bore guilt for the harm they had allowed to occur to Jews and to many others targeted by the Nazis. This passage is relevant in the discussion of workplace bullying and the abandonment of targets by peers, colleagues, coworkers, and bystanders. What is it about human nature that allows one to ignore the suffering of others? Why, in the face of cruelty and unfairness, do many remain silent?

The WBI, founded by Gary and Ruth Namie, suggests that policies and laws would not be required if bystanders, witnesses, and peers did not ignore their moral responsibility to help colleagues targeted by bullies. The answer to the question "Why doesn't anyone do anything?" can be answered simply by understanding that witnesses and colleagues fear for their own survival. Victims of bullying understand this when they are harmed by the inaction of their peers (Namie & Namie, 2011). The dilemma for bystanders is, however, that through their silence, as Niemöller points out, they may become the next target.

Globalization

Harvey et al. (2009) has cited the increase in globalization with reduced levels of management oversight as predictors of increasing workplace abuse. In addition to the increase in diversity and the decrease in management oversight inherent in a global economy, legal environments in which workers and managers operate can vary greatly. In most developed countries, workplace bullying has received much recent attention, but in emerging economies with a lack of supervision or legal protections, and with often desperately needy workers, organizations may be at risk for bullying. The authors suggested actions to address and monitor bullying in global organizations. Like organizational protection and remedies discussed in earlier chapters, these include assessing organizational culture, assessing the incidence of bullying, assessing management's philosophy and response to bullying, assessing policies, developing reporting procedures, and creating a due-diligence mechanism for investigating bullying, including an audit process.

Vandekerckhove and Commers (2003) have also suggested that globalization is an important feature of the current trends in workplace bullying. Asserting that downward mobbing is the most prevalent form, they posited that the increase in bullying matches organizational shifts that occur within the context of globalization. The authors argued that it is not the organizational shifts themselves but the failure of leadership to respond to these shifts by adjusting and transforming organizations and power structures within organizations that create bullying climates. The specific issue is that organizational changes involve new people and new sources of knowledge but that bullying involves the misuse of power outside the rules of the new rules of work. We need to understand how bullying in organizations is an escalating type of pathological response to organizational shifts due to globalization and new trends in workplaces. It can be viewed as an extreme reaction to these new types of pressures. As pressures toward decentralization and transition to more flexible and competitive organizations increase, leaders' stress levels increase as well. These changes are accompanied by fear responses manifested as bullying behaviors of managers toward subordinates.

Is This a Function of the Downturn in the U.S. Economy?

Logic would suggest that the answer is "yes"—things have become worse since the economic downturn. Data from the WBI, however, have suggested that bullying in the United States has become only slightly worse since the economic crisis of 2008. Most respondents in this study (data collected in 2008) indicated that bullying was already a serious problem before the recent economic downturn (Namie, 2009). A 2012 instant poll by the WBI suggested that the top reasons that bullying persists are the absence of consequences for the perpetrator, no laws to protect workers, no one in the organization having the strength or inclination to stop it, and passivity of onlookers/colleagues toward the bullied target (Namie, 2012). Systemic rewards for bullies were also mentioned by respondents as a key determinant.

Lack of Self-Awareness (but Not Pathology) of the Bully

Forbes Magazine staff writer Jacqueline Smith (2014) suggested that bullying is related to lack of self-awareness on the part of the bully, stating that the bully is not aware of how the bullying behavior is perceived and its effects on targets. She also suggests that bullying is related to silence about bullying behaviors and offers suggestions for giving clear but kind verbal feedback that the bully can understand.

Other explanations could explain or add to theories of bullying. These include the critical environmental issues facing nations of the world, which have led to extreme competition for ever-declining resources; a recent history of violence and combat; the very tight job market with the highest unemployment rates since the Great Depression; and the general attitudes of lack of respect for individuals and differences. How these factors may interact is an area of future study.

Attachment

The role of attachment style has not yet been addressed in this text, but it is relevant for brief discussion. British psychiatrist John Bowlby is credited with the formulation of attachment theory. Bowlby described attachment as a strong emotional bond that ties an individual to an intimate companion. Attachment serves an evolutionary survival function, helping our ancestors care for their young (and helping us to care for ours) and adapt to the environment. Unlike theories of imprinting (the term for an innate form of learning, coined by ethnologist Konrad Lorenz), attachment is a process that develops over months and years in a child's life and serves as an internal working model for later relationships. While imprinting is automatic and not learned, attachment is a process dependent on caregivers' responsiveness to a developing infant. Bowlby claimed that early parent–child attachment has significant and lasting effects on development.

Bowlby's colleague Mary Ainsworth, a developmental psychologist from the United States, elaborated on Bowlby's theory by conducting mother–child studies to assess the quality of infant attachment. Ainsworth's attachment theory can be summarized simply. First, the capacity of an organism for attachment is part of evolution. Second, attachments develop because of interaction between biological and environmental influences during sensitive periods in life. Third, the quality of this attachment between infant and caregiver(s) will shape the developing infant's later relationships, including those in adulthood. Finally, the quality of attachment will shape internal working models of self and others (Ainsworth, cited in Sigelman & Rider, 2014).

Secure attachment style is revealed when an infant protests separation from a familiar caregiver. An attached child has developed the capacity to use the caregiver as a secure base and haven to which he or she can return for comfort. Because attachment relationships develop so early and are so lasting, they influence relationships for the remainder of a person's life. Securely attached children grow into adults with secure attachment styles, predicting good abilities at romantic attachments and social relationships, including those in work settings. However, attachment studies suggest that only about two-thirds of infants are securely attached. For infants who are not securely attached, up to 10 percent display resistant attachment (also called anxious–ambivalent). They appear needy for security and comfort while outwardly displaying anger. Children with avoidant attachment (up to 15 percent) seem emotionally distant and appear to deny any need for affection. Children with disorganized–disoriented attachment (up to 15 percent) come from high-risk families and have a poor ability to regulate negative emotions, thus negatively affecting relationships for the remainder of their lives.

The three domains primarily affected by attachment styles are intellectual curiosity, social competence, and emotional regulation. A type of psychopathology, insecure attachment can take many forms. When severe abuse and or neglect has occurred in very early development, the results can be very serious, including an inability to experience remorse, a lack of empathy, and disregard for the well-being of others. Since these are often qualities found in those who bully others, the origins of these developmental shortcomings may link to early development and attachment.

PSYCHOPATHS

Boddy (2011) stated that narcissism, a lack of self-regulation skills, and an inability to experience remorse can be identified as characteristics of bullies. New studies in neurobiology have indicated that abnormal brain chemistry and wiring may account for the emotional coldness and lack of empathy of those with sociopathic or psychopathic features (Brinkley et al., 2004, in Boddy, 2011). Studies have suggested that people with high scores on a psychopathy-rating scale are more likely to engage in bullying, crime, and drug use than are other people, indicating that psychopaths are also usually bullies (Nathanson, William, & Paulhus, 2006, in Boddy, 2011).

Corporate Psychopaths

Boddy developed the concept of "corporate psychopaths" (2005, in Boddy, 2011). This combines the concepts of *corporate* from a business perspective with *psychopath* from a psychological one. The idea suggests that psychopaths can work, even thrive, in an organization. Other terms for people with these traits include "executive psychopaths," "industrial psychopaths," "organizational psychopaths," and "organizational sociopaths" (Pech & Slade, 2007, in Boddy, 2011). The Psychopathy Checklist–Revised (PCL-R) is an assessment instrument widely respected for its ability to identify those with psychopathic or sociopathic traits. Developed by Hare, it is very helpful in identifying corporate psychopaths who share the characteristics of glibness, superficial charm, grandiosity, manipulativeness, shallowness, lack of empathy or remorse, and cold response styles (Babiak & Hare, 2006; Deutchman, 2005, in Boddy, 2011).

Far too often, those with psychopathic traits are in supervisory or leadership positions in an organization and use intimidation to keep their employees submissive and fearful (Babiak & Hare, 2006, in Boddy, 2011). Supervisors play a significant role for employees in organizations by having the power to place both job demands and performance evaluations on their subordinates. Managers with psychopathic traits may harm their staff via public criticism, harsh and humiliating comments, sudden dismissal, and other types of intimidation. The presence of corporate psychopaths in a workplace has a strong influence on both bullying and unfair supervision. Unfortunately, organizations are often reluctant to acknowledge the presence of corporate bullies and discount reports by injured workers, thus leaving problem supervisors unchecked.

IS THE UNITED STATES A "BULLYING-TOLERANT SOCIETY"?

A major problem in preventing and remediating bullying in the United States is that America has values and beliefs that have created a "bullying-tolerant society." Namie et al. (Einarsen et al., 2011) asserted that U.S. labor laws have historically favored employers, tolerating a "master–servant" power imbalance. These laws have favored hierarchy and control of workers by employers. In the legislature, few lawmakers have been willing to expand worker rights. Namie and Namie (2011) also cited American beliefs about the free market as part of the wider backdrop where bullying has been tolerated. Worker treatment has generally not been as important as productivity where governance is concerned. In addition, the American myth of rugged individualism places blame on people, not conditions or culture, when things go wrong. As stated many times throughout this text, victims are often blamed when the world treats them unjustly!

An Uninformed General Public

Another possible correlate of bullying in the United States is the lack of awareness and understanding of bullying by the general public. Although workplace bullying is beginning to be understood as a type of trauma like long-recognized types of violence, the plight of the bullied worker has not yet lost its stigma (Namie et al., cited in Einarsen et al., 2011). One can hope that if more information is provided to the general public, more people may feel empowered to confront bullying when it occurs. Moreover, with more live media exposure and op-ed articles on the topic, bullying can be recognized for what it is: a type of workplace violence that can cause severe and lasting harm to victims, organizations, and the public at large.

SUMMARY

This text has provided a historical review of definitions and explanations for the phenomenon of workplace bullying. Theoretical explanations for mobbing have been explored in depth. Data from around the globe have been cited, along with the well-developed public policies of many Western, industrialized countries. Reactions and experiences of injured workers and costs to organizational functioning have been highlighted. Recommendations for mental health clinicians and other health-care providers have been identified. Organizational practices to prevent and remediate workplace emotional abuses via clear policies, consistent sanctions, and improved communications have been provided. Public policy issues and a clear role for the profession of social work have been emphasized. Finally, a few alternative explanations for the continuation of workplace bullying have been offered.

An unintended consequence of the development of laws that protect certain classes of people is that the bully may simply redirect his or her focus onto unprotected classes. Then, whether the total amount of workplace abuse has decreased or has just become redirected will be an open question. The corporate psychopath may be wise enough to avoid bullying those who can take action through laws and regulations and instead direct his or her energies toward those who do not have such protections. All of this points to the need for policies and laws that protect all workers. Social workers, as a profession, can have a hand in taking our workplace protection standards to a higher level.

It remains a mystery about why bullying is so prevalent in American work life. Whether the United States will begin to consider this workplace malady seriously remains to be seen. The decade-long efforts at enacting healthy workplace legislation have yet to produce conclusive action in any of the states or territories. Nonetheless, the moral imperative of social work and social workers in the promotion of human rights and social justice is very clear. As recommended by Tracy Whitaker (2012), social work can have a vital role in prevention and education via research, training in symptoms and solutions, social work education, and organizational advocacy. Social work needs to treat workplace emotional abuse of all types, against all people, as a problem as serious as mental illness, substance abuse, poverty, family violence, and access to health care.

References

Aiello, A., Deitinger, P., Nardella, C., & Bonafede, M. (2008). A tool for assessing the risk of mobbing in organizational environments: The "Val.Mob" scale. *Prevention Today, 4*(3), 9–24.

Aleassa, H. M., & Megdadi, O. D. (2014). Workplace bullying and unethical behavior: A mediating model. *International Journal of Business and Management, 9*(3), 157–169.

Ambrosino, R., Heffernan, J., Shuttlesworth, G., & Ambrosino, R. (2005). *Social work and social welfare*. Belmont, CA: Thomson Brooks/Cole.

American heritage dictionary (2nd college ed.). (1983). Boston: Houghton Mifflin.

American Psychiatric Association. (2013). *Diagnostic and statistical manual of mental disorders* (5th ed.). Arlington, VA: Author.

Applegate, J. S., & Shapiro, J. R. (2005). *Neurobiology for clinical social workers: Theory and practice*. New York: W. W. Norton.

Armstrong, K. R., Lund, P. E., McWright, L. T., & Tichenor, V. (1995). Multiple stressor debriefing and the American Red Cross: The East Bay Hills fire experience. *Social Work, 40*, 83–90.

Assembly Bill No. 2053, California Legislature 2013–14 Regular Session. Retrieved from http://www.leginfo.ca.gov/pub/13-14/bill/asm/ab_2051-2100/ab_2053_bill_20140220_introduced.htm

Ayoko, O. B. (2007). Communication openness, conflict events and reactions to conflict in culturally diverse groups. *Cross Cultural Management: An International Journal, 24*(2), 106–124.

Ayoko, O. B., Callan, V. J., & Hartell, C. E. J. (2003). Workplace conflict, bullying, and counterproductive behaviors. *International Journal of Organizational Analysis, 11*(4), 283–302.

Babiak, P., & Hare, R. (2006). *Snakes in suits*. New York: Harper Business.

Bairy, K., Thirumalaikolundusubramanian, P., Sivignanam, G., Saraswathi, S. Sachindananda, A., & Shalini, A. (2007). Bullying among trainee doctors in Southern India: A questionnaire study. *Journal of Postgraduate Medicine, 53*(2), 87–90.

Balducci, C., Alfano, V., & Fraccaroli, F. (2009). Relationship between mobbing at work and MMPI-2 personality profile, posttraumatic stress symptoms, and suicidal ideation and behavior. *Violence and Victims, 24*(1), 52–68.

Bamberger, P. A., & Bacharach, S. B. (2006). Abusive supervision and subordinate problem diagnosis: Taking resistance, stress, and subordinate personality into account. *Human Relations, 59*, 723–724.

Bandow, D., & Hunter, D. (2007). The rise of workplace incivilities: Has it happened to you? *Business Review,* pp. 212–217.

Barlow, D. H. (2002). *Anxiety and its disorders: The nature and treatment of anxiety and panic* (2nd ed.). New York: Guilford Press.

Baron, R. A., Byrne, D., & Branscombe, N. R. (2006). *Social psychology* (11th ed.). Boston: Pearson Education.

Barsky, A. E. (2007). *Conflict resolution for the helping professions* (2nd ed.). Belmont, CA: Thomson Brooks/Cole.

Beck, A. T. (1986). Hopelessness as a predictor of eventual suicide. *Annals of the New York Academy of Science, 487*, 90–96.

Beck, A. T., & Alford, B. A. (2009). *Depression: Causes and treatment.* Philadelphia: University of Pennsylvania Press.

Beck, A., & Emery, G. (1985). *Anxiety disorders and phobias: A cognitive perspective.* New York: Basic Books.

Beck, A. T., Emery, G. T., & Greenberg, R. L. (1990). *Anxiety disorders and phobias.* New York: Perseus Book Group.

Beck, A. T., Epstein, N., Brown, G., & Steer, R. A. (1988). An inventory for measuring clinical anxiety: Psychometric properties. *Journal of Consulting and Clinical Psychology, 56*, 893–897.

Beck, A., Steer, R., & Brown, G. (1996). *Beck Depression Inventory-II.* San Antonio, TX: Psychological Corporation.

Beck, A. T., Weissman, A., Lester, D., & Trexler, L. (1974). The measurement of pessimism: The Hopelessness Scale. *Journal of Consulting and Clinical Psychology, 42*, 861–865.

Beugre, C. D. (2005). Reacting aggressively to injustice at work: A cognitive model. *Journal of Business and Psychology, 20*(2), 291–302.

Bible, J. D. (2012). The jerk at work: Workplace bullying and the law's inability to combat it. *Employee Relations Law Journal, 38*(1), 32–51.

Bilgel, N., Aytac, S., & Bayram, N. (2006). Bullying in Turkish white collar workers. *Occupational Medicine, 56*(4), 226–231.

Blanchard, K. (1999). *The heart of a leader: Insights on the art of influence.* Tulsa, OK: Honor Books.

Blank, I. (2008). Selecting employees based on emotional intelligence competencies: Reap the rewards and minimize the risks. *Employee Relations Law Journal, 34*(3), 77–98.

Blase, J., & Blase, J. (2006). Teachers' perspective in principal mistreatment. *Teacher Education Quarterly, 33*(4), 123–142.

Blase, J., Blase, J., & Du, F. (2008). The mistreated teacher: A national study. *Journal of Educational Administration, 46*(3), 263–301.

Boddy, C. (2011). Corporate psychopaths, bullying, and unfair supervision in the workplace. *Journal of Business Ethics, 100,* 367–379.

Bond, S., Tuckey, M., & Dollard, S. (2010). Psychosocial safety climate and symptoms of posttraumatic stress disorder. *Organizational Development Journal, 28*(1), 37–56.

Boyett, J. H., & Boyett, J. T. (1998). *The guru guide: The best ideas of top management thinkers.* New York: John Wiley & Sons.

Branch, S., Ramsey, S., & Barker, M. (2007). Managers in the firing line: Contributing factors to workplace bullying by staff; an interview study. *Journal of Management and Organization, 13*(3), 264–282.

Breckler, S. J., Olson, J. O., & Wiggins, E. C. (2005). *Social psychology alive.* Belmont, CA: Thomson Higher Education.

Brennan, W. (2003). Sounding off about verbal abuse. *Occupational Health, 55*(11), 22–25.

Bridges, W. (1997). *Managing transitions: Making the most out of change.* Reading, MA: Perseus Books.

Bruch, H., & Ghoshal, S. (2002). Beware the busy manager. *Harvard Business Review* (February), pp. 5–11.

Bulutlar, F., & Öz, E. U. (2009). The effect of ethical climates on bullying behaviour in the workplace. *Journal of Business Ethics, 86,* 273–295.

Buttigieg, D., Bryant, M., Hanley, G., & Liu, J. (2011). The causes and consequences of workplace bullying and discrimination: Results from an exploratory study. *Labour and Industry, 22*(1), 117–142.

Cameron, K. S., & Quinn, R. E. (1999). *Diagnosing and changing organizational culture.* Upper Saddle River, NJ: Prentice Hall.

Carden, L., & Boyd, R. (2013). Workplace bullying: Utilizing a risk management framework to address bullying in the workplace. *Southern Journal of Business Ethics, 5.*

Chalosky, N., & Griffin, M. G. (2005). *Work-life programs and organizational culture: The essence of workplace community.* Retrieved from http://www.ERIC.ed.gov

Chapell, M. S., Hasselman, S. L., Kitchin, T., Loman, S., MacIver, K. W., & Sarulio, P. L. (2006). Bullying in elementary school, high school, and college. *Adolescence, 41*(164), 633–648.

Church, A. H., & Waclawski, J. (1998). The relationship between personality orientation and executive leadership behaviour. *Journal of Occupational and Organizational Psychology, 1*(Part 2), 99–125.

Clark, D., & Beck, A. (2012). *The anxiety and worry workbook: The cognitive behavioral solution.* New York: Guilford Press.

Clark, L. A., Watson, D., & Mineka, S. (1994). Temperament, personality, and mood and anxiety disorders. *Journal of Abnormal Psychology, 103,* 103–116.

Clarke, N. (2006). Emotional intelligence training: A case of caveat emptor. *Human Resources Development Review, 5,* 422–442.

Cooke, R. A., & Lafferty, J. C. (1987). *Organizational culture inventory: Strengthening organizations through individual effectiveness.* Plymouth, MI: Human Synergistics International.

Cooper, M. G., & Lesser, J. G. (2002). *Clinical social work practice: An integrated approach.* Needham Heights, MA: Allyn & Bacon.

Covey, S. R. (1991). *Principle-centered leadership.* New York: Fireside.

Cusack, S. (2000). Workplace bullying: Icebergs in sight, soundings needed. *The Lancet, 356*(99248), 2118–2119.

Czander, W. M. (1993). *The psychodynamics of work and organizations: Theory and application.* New York: Guilford Press.

Davenport, N., Schwartz, R. D., & Elliott, G. P. (2002). *Mobbing: Emotional abuse in the American workplace.* Ames, IA: Civil Societies.

D'Cruz, P., & Noronha, E. (2012). Clarifying my world: Identity work in the context of workplace bullying. *Qualitative Report, 17*(Article 16), 1–29.

Dehue, F., Bolman, C., & Pouweise, M. (2011). Coping with bullying at work and health related problems. *International Journal of Stress Management, 19*(3), 175–197.

DePree, M. (1989). *Leadership is an art.* New York: Random House.

Dewees, M. (2005). *Contemporary social work practice.* Boston: McGraw-Hill.

Djurkovic, N., & McCormack, D. (2006). Neuroticism and the psychosomatic model of workplace bullying. *Journal of Managerial Psychology, 21*(1), 73–88.

Djurkovic, N., McCormack, D., & Casimir, G. (2004). The physical and psychological effects of workplace bullying and their relationship to intention to leave: A test of the psychosomatic and disability hypothesis. *International Journal of Organization Theory and Behavior, 7,* 469–498.

Djurkovic, N., McCormack, D., & Casimir, G. (2005). The behavioral reactions of victims to different types of workplace bullying. *International Journal of Organization Theory and Behavior, 8,* 439–460.

Doka, K. J. (Ed.). (2002). *Disenfranchised grief: New directions, challenges, and strategies for practice.* Champaign, IL: Research Press.

Drucker, P. (2008). *The five most important questions you'll ever ask about your organization.* New York: Jossey-Bass.

Edwards, P., & Edwards, S. (2001). *Changing direction without losing your way.* New York: Penguin Putnam.

Einarsen, S. (1999). The nature and causes of bullying at work. *International Journal of Manpower, 20*(1–2), 16–27.

Einarsen, S., Hoel, H., & Cooper, C. L. (2002). *Bullying and emotional abuse in the workplace: International perspectives in research and practice.* New York: Taylor & Francis.

Einarsen, S., Hoel, H., Zapf, D., & Cooper, C. L. (2011). *Bullying and harassment in the workplace: Developments in research, theory, and practice* (2nd ed.). New York: Taylor & Francis.

Einarsen, S., & Raknes, B. I. (1997). Harassment in the workplace and the victimization of men. *Violence and Victims, 12,* 247–262.

Ewing, J. A. (1984). Detecting alcoholism: The CAGE questionnaire. *JAMA, 252,* 1403–1407.

Ferris, P. A. (2009). The role of the consulting psychologist in the prevention, detection, and correction of bullying and mobbing in the workplace. *Consulting Psychology Journal: Practice and Research, 61*(3), 169–189.

Fitness, J. (2000). Anger in the workplace: An emotional script approach to anger episodes between workers and their superiors, co-workers, and subordinates. *Journal of Organizational Behavior, 21,* 147–162.

Foa, E. B., Davidson, J.R.T., Frances, A., & Ross, R. (1999). Expert consensus treatment guidelines for posttraumatic stress disorder: A guide for patients and families. *Journal of Clinical Psychiatry, 60*(16), 69–76.

Fox, S., & Stallworth, L. (2009). Building a framework for two internal organizational approaches to resolving and preventing workplace bullying: Alternative dispute resolution and training. *Consulting Psychology Journal: Practice and Research, 61,* 220–241.

Fraser, M. W., Richmond, J. M., & Galinsky, M. (1999). Risk, protection, and resilience: Toward a conceptual framework for social work practice [Introduction]. *Social Work Research, 23,* 131–143.

Friesner, T. (2014). *History of SWOT analysis.* Retrieved from http://www.marketing teacher.com/history-of-swot-analysis/

Gardner, S., & Johnson, P. (2001). The leaner, meaner workplace: Strategies for handling bullies at work. *Employee Relations Today, 78*(2), 22–36.

Geffner, R., Braverman, M., Galasso, J., & Marsh, J. (Eds.). (2004). *Aggression in organizations: Violence, abuse, and harassment at work and in schools.* Binghamton, NY: Haworth Maltreatment and Trauma Press.

Gellis, Z. D. (2001). Social work perceptions of transformational and transactional leadership in health care. *Social Work Research, 25,* 17–25.

Gerlach, W. (2000). *And the witnesses were silent: The confessing church and the Jews.* Lincoln: University of Nebraska Press. Cited in the United States Holocaust Museum.

Germain, C. B., & Bloom, M. (1999). *Human behavior in the social environment.* New York: Columbia University Press.

Ginsberg, L., & Keys, P. R. (Eds.). (1995). *New management in human services* (2nd ed.). Washington, DC: NASW Press.

Giorgi, F. (2009). Workplace bullying risk assessment in 12 Italian organizations. *International Journal of Workplace Health Management, 2*(1), 34–47.

Girardi, P., Monaco, E., Prestigiacomo, C., & Talamo, A. (2007). Personality and psychopathological profiles in individuals exposed to mobbing. *Violence and Victims, 22*(2), 172–188.

Glasser, W. (1998). *Choice theory: A new psychology of personal freedom.* New York: HarperCollins.

Glendinning, P. M. (2001). Workplace bullying: Curing the cancer of the American workplace. *Public Personnel Management, 30*(3), 269–287.

Goodrich, B. (2013, October 9). SWOT analysis: Examples, templates, and definition. *Business News Daily.* Retrieved from http://www.businessnewsdaily.com/ 4245-swot-analysis.html

Gravois, J. (2006). Mob rule. *Chronicle of Higher Education, 52*(32), 10–16.

Gray, J. A. (2004). Is a constructive discharge resulting from a supervisor's environmental harassment a tangible employment action? *Labor Law Review, 55*(3), 179–196.

Gummer, B., & Edwards, R. (1995). The politics of human services administration. In L. Ginsberg & P. R. Keys (Eds.), *New management in human services* (2nd ed., pp. 51–72). Washington, DC: NASW Press.

Hartig, K., & Frosch, A. (2006). *Workplace mobbing syndrome: The silent and unseen occupational hazard*. Presented at the National Conference on Women and Industrial Relations, Queensland Working Women's Services and Griffith Business School, Griffith University, Brisbane, Australia.

Harvey, M. G., Buckley, M. R., Heames, J. T., Zinko, R., Brouer, R. L., & Ferris, G. R. (2007). A bully as an archetypal destructive leader. *Journal of Leadership & Organizational Studies, 14*(2), 117–123.

Harvey, M. G., Heames, J. T., Richey, R. G., & Leonard, N. (2006). Bullying: From the playground to the boardroom. *Journal of Leadership & Organizational Studies, 12*(4), 1–11.

Harvey, M. G., Treadway, D., Heames, J. T., & Duke, A. (2009). Bullying in the 21st century global organization: An ethical perspective. *Journal of Business Ethics, 85*, 27–40.

Hauge, L., Einarsen, S., Knardahl, S., Lau, B., Notelaers, G., & Skogstad, A. (2011). Leadership and role stressors as departmental level predictors or workplace bullying. *International Journal of Stress Management, 18*(4), 305–322.

Hazler, R. J., Carnay, J. V., & Granger, D. A. (2006). Integrating biological measures into the study of bullying. *Journal of Counseling and Development, 84*(3), 298–301.

Heames, J., & Harvey, M. (2006). Workforce bullying: A cross-level assessment. *Management Decision, 44*, 1214–1228.

Heine, H. (1995). An underestimated workplace terror: Mobbing. *Managing Office Technology, 40*(5), 41–43.

Hewitt, J. P. (2007). *Self and society: A symbolic interactionist social psychology* (10th ed.). Boston: Allyn Bacon.

Hoel, H., & Cooper, C. L. (2000). *Destructive conflict and bullying at work*. Manchester, UK: University of Manchester, Institute of Science and Technology.

Hoel, H., Cooper, C. L., & Faragher, B. (2001). The experience of bullying in Great Britain: The impact of organizational status. *European Journal of Work and Organizational Psychology, 10*, 443–465.

Hollis, F. (1972). *Casework: A psychosocial therapy* (2nd ed.). New York: Random House.

Home, A. M. (1997). Learning the hard way: Role strain, role demands and support in multiple-role women students. *Journal of Social Work Education, 33*(2), 335–347.

Hutchinson, M., Vickers, M. H., Jackson, D., & Wilkes, L. (2006). Like wolves in a pack: Predatory alliances of bullies in nursing. *Journal of Management and Organization, 12*(3), 235–250.

Hutchinson, M., Wilkes, L., Vickers, M., & Jackson, D. (2008). The development and validation of a bullying inventory for the nursing workplace. *Nurse Researcher, 15*(2), 19–30.

Hutton, S., & Gates, D. (2008). Workplace incivility and productivity losses among direct care staff. *AAOHN Journal, 56*(4), 168–176.

International Labour Organization. (2001). *Collective agreement on the prevention and resolution of harassment-related grievances*. Retrieved from http://www.ilo.org/public/english/staffun/docs/harassment.htm

James, R. K., & Gilliland, B. E. (2005). *Crisis intervention strategies* (5th ed.). Belmont, CA: Brooks/Cole.

Johnson, D. W., & Johnson, S. J. (2003). *Real world treatment planning.* Pacific Grove, CA: Thomson Brooks/Cole.

Johnson, P. R., & Indvik, J. (1994). The impact of unresolved trauma on career development. *Employee Counselling Today, 6*(4), 10–16.

Johnson, P. R., & Indvik, J. (2006). Sticks and stones: Verbal abuse in the workplace. *Journal of Organizational Culture, Communications, and Conflict, 10*(1), 121–127.

Johnson, S. (1998). *Who moved my cheese?* New York: Penguin Putnam.

Kanel, K. (2007). *A guide to crisis intervention.* Belmont, CA: Thomson Higher Education.

Kaplan, H. I., & Sadock, B. J. (1996). *Concise textbook of clinical psychiatry.* Baltimore: Williams & Wilkins.

Keashly, L. (2001). Interpersonal and systemic aspects of emotional abuse at work: The target's perspective. *Violence and Victims, 16*(3), 233–241.

Keashly, L., Trott, V., & MacLean, L. (1994). Abusive behavior in the workplace: A preliminary investigation. *Violence and Victims, 9,* 341–356.

Kelly, D. (2007). Workplace bullying, women and work choices. *Hecate, 33*(1), 112–127.

Kennedy, D. B., Homant, R. J., & Homant, M. R. (2004). Perception of injustice as a predictor of support for workplace aggression. *Journal of Business and Psychology, 18*(3), 323–336.

Kilburg, R. R. (2009). Sadomasochism, human aggression, and the problem of workplace mobbing and bullying: A commentary. *Consulting Psychology Journal: Practice and Research, 61*(3), 268–275.

Kivimäki, M., Virtanen, M., Vartia, M., Elovainio, M., Vahtera, J., & Keltikangas-Järvinen, L. (2003). Workplace bullying and the risk of cardiovascular disease and depression. *Occupational and Environmental Medication, 60,* 779–783.

Koonin, M., & Green, T. (2004). The emotionally abusive workplace. In R. Geffner, M. Braverman, J. Galasso, & J. March (Eds.), *Aggression in organizations: Violence, abuse, and harassment at work and in schools* (pp. 71–79). Binghamton, NY: Haworth Maltreatment and Trauma Press.

Kotter, J. (1996). *Leading change.* Boston: Harvard Business School Press.

Kouzes, J., M., & Posner, B. Z. (1995). *The leadership challenge.* San Francisco: Jossey-Bass.

Kouzes, J. M., & Posner, B. Z. (2001). *Leadership practices inventory* (2nd ed.). New York: Jossey-Bass.

Kowalski, R., Harmon, J., Yorks, L., & Kowalski, D. (1998). *Reducing workplace stress and aggression: An action research project of the United States Department of Veterans Affairs.* Washington, DC: U.S. Department of Veterans Affairs.

LaVan, H., & Martin, W. M. (2008). Bullying in the U.S. workplace: Normative and process-oriented ethical approaches. *Journal of Business Ethics, 83,* 147–165.

Lawrence, C. (2001). Social psychology of bullying in the workplace. In N. Tehrani (Ed.), *Building a culture of respect: Managing the bully at work* (pp. 61–75). London: Taylor & Francis.

Lee, S. J., & Tolman, R. M. (2006). Childhood sexual abuse and adult work outcomes. *Social Work Research, 30,* 83–92.

Lewis, J., Coursol, D., & Wahl, K. H. (2002). Addressing issues of workplace harassment: Counseling the targets. *Journal of Employment Counseling, 39*(3), 109–116.

Leymann, H. (1990). Mobbing and psychological terror at workplaces. *Violence and Victims, 5*(2), 119–126.

Liefooghe, P. D., & Davey, K. M. (2002). Explaining bullying at work: Why should we listen to employee accounts? In S. Einarsen, H. Hoel, D. Zapf, & C. Cooper (Eds.), *Bullying and emotional abuse in the workplace: International perspectives in research and practice* (pp. 219–230). New York: Taylor & Francis.

Lind, K., Glasø, L., Pallesen, S., & Einarsen, S. (2009). Personality profiles among targets and non-targets of workplace bullying. *European Psychologist, 14*(3), 231–237.

Lopez Cabarcos, M. A., & Vazquez Rodriguez, P. (2006). Psychological harassment in the Spanish public university system. *Academy of Health Management Journal, 2,* 21–39.

Lutgen-Sandvik, P. (2003). The communicative cycle of employee emotional abuse. *Management Communication Quarterly, 16,* 471–501.

Magnuson, S., & Norem, K. (2009). Bullies grow up and go to work. *Journal of Professional Counseling: Practice, Theory, and Research, 37*(2), 34–51.

Manning, C. (2001). Issues for general practitioners. In N. Tehrani (Ed.), *Building a culture of respect: Managing bullying at work* (pp. 185–201). London: Taylor & Francis.

Matthiesen, S. B., & Einarsen, S. (2007). Perpetrators and targets of bullying at work: Role stress and individual differences. *Violence and Victims, 22,* 735–752.

Martin, W. (2008). Is your hospital safe? Disruptive behavior and workplace bullying. *Hospital Topics: Research and Perspectives on Healthcare, 86*(3), 21–27.

Mayhew, C., McCarthy, P., Chappell, D., Quinlan, M., Barker, M., & Sheehan, M. (2004). Measuring the extent of impact from occupational violence and bullying on traumatized workers. *Employee Responsibility and Rights Journal, 16*(3), 117–134.

McCormack, D., Casimir, G., Djurkovic, N., & Yang, Y. (2006). The concurrent effects of workplace bullying, satisfaction with the supervisor, and satisfaction with co-workers on affective commitment among schoolteachers in China. *International Journal of Conflict Management, 17*(4), 316–332.

McDonald, J. J., Jr. (2006). Humpty Dumpty goes to court. *Employee Relations Journal, 32*(2), 61–71.

McKay, R., Arnold, D. H., Fratzl, J., & Thomas, R. (2008). Workplace bullying in academia: A Canadian study. *Employee Responsibilities and Rights Journal, 20,* 77–100.

Meseguer de Pedro, M., Soler Sanchez, M. I., Saez Navarro, M. C., & Garcia Izquierdo, M. (2008). Workplace mobbing and effects on workers' health. *Spanish Journal of Psychology, 11*(1), 219–227.

Meyer, S. (2004). Organizational response to conflict: Future conflict and work outcomes. *Social Work Research, 28,* 183–191.

Midgley, J., & Livermore, M. (2009). *The handbook of social policy.* Thousand Oaks, CA: Sage Publications.

Milgram, S. (1963). Behavioral study of obedience. *Journal of Abnormal and Social Psychology, 67,* 371–378.

Namie, G. (2000). *U.S. hostile workplace survey 2000.* Bellingham, WA: Workplace Bullying Institute. Retrieved from http://www.workplacebullying.org/multi/pdf/N-N-2000.pdf

Namie, G. (2003). *2003 report on abusive workplaces.* Bellingham, WA: Workplace Bullying Institute. Retrieved from http://www.workplacebullying.org/multi/pdf/N-N-2003C.pdf

Namie, G. (2007). *U.S. Workplace Bullying Survey.* Bellingham, WA: Workplace Bullying Institute. Retrieved from http://workplacebullying.org/multi/pdf/WBIsurvey2007.pdf

Namie, G. (2008). *U.S. Hostile Workplace Survey 2000.* Bellingham, WA: Workplace Bullying Institute. Retrieved from http://www.workplacebullyinginstitute.org

Namie, G. (2009). *The economic crisis and bullying.* Bellingham, WA: Workplace Bullying Institute. Retrieved from http://www.workplacebullyinginstitute.org

Namie, G. (2012). *2012 instant poll-C: Why bullying happens.* Bellingham, WA: Workplace Bullying Institute. Retrieved from http://www.workplacebullying institute.org

Namie, G. (2013). *2013 instant poll-E: Mental health professionals' grasp of workplace bullying.* Bellingham, WA: Workplace Bullying Institute. Retrieved from http://www.workplacebullyinginstitute.org

Namie, G., Christensen, D., & Phillips, D. (2014). *2014 Workplace Bullying Institute: U.S. workforce bullying survey.* Bellingham, WA: Workplace Bullying Institute. Retrieved from http://www.workplacebullyinginstitute.org

Namie, G., & Namie, R. (2003). *The bully at work: What you can do to stop the hurt and reclaim your dignity on the job.* Naperville, IL: Sourcebooks.

Namie, G., & Namie, R. (2009). U.S. workplace bullying: Some basic considerations and consultation interventions. *Consulting Psychology Journal: Practice and Research, 61*(3), 202–219.

Namie, G., & Namie, R. (2011). *The bully-free workplace: Stop jerks, weasels, and snakes from killing your organization.* Hoboken, NJ: John Wiley & Sons.

National Association of Social Workers. (2008). *Code of ethics of the National Association of Social Workers.* Washington, DC: Author.

National Institute for Occupational Safety and Health. (1996). *Actions to mitigate exposure to workplace homicides and assaults: NIOSH risk factors and prevention strategies.* Washington, DC: Author.

National Labor Relations Act, Title 29, 7 U.S.C. § 157 (1935). Retrieved from http://www.gpo.gov/fdsys/pkg/USCODE-2011-title29/pdf/USCODE-2011-title29-chap7-subchapII-sec157.pdf

Neuman, J. H., & Baron, P. A. (1998). Workplace violence and aggression: Evidence concerning specific forms, potential causes, and preferred targets. *Journal of Management, 24*, 391–419.

Neuman, J. H., & Baron, P. A. (2002). Social antecedents of bullying: A social interactionist perspective. In S. Einarsen, H. Hoel, D. Zapf, & C. Cooper (Eds.), *Bullying and emotional abuse in the workplace: International perspectives in research and practice* (pp. 185–202). New York: Taylor & Francis.

Niedhammer, I., Chastang, J., & David, S. (2008). Importance of psychosocial work factors on general health outcomes in the national French SUMER survey. *Organizational Medicine, 58*, 15–24.

Nielsen, M., Matthiesen, S., & Einarsen, S. (2008). Sense of coherence as a protective mechanism among targets of workplace bullying. *Journal of Occupational Health Psychology, 13*(2), 128–135.

Niemöller, M. (1947). *Of guilt and hope.* New York: Philosophical Library.

Niemöller, M. (n.d.). *Als die Nazis die Kommunisten holten* [When the Nazis came for the Communists . . .]. Retrieved from http://www.martin-niemoeller-stiftung.de/search/a31

Noring, S. (2000). Mobbing: Emotional abuse in the American workplace. *American Journal of Public Health, 90,* 636.

Northern, H. (1995). *Clinical social work: Knowledge and skills.* New York: Columbia University Press.

Ohlson, C., Soderfeldt, M., Soderfeldt, B., Jones, I., & Theorell, T. (2001). Stress markers in relation to job strain in human service organizations. *Psychotherapy and Psychosomatics, 70*(5), 268–276.

Olson, C., & Agina, I. O. (2009). Is higher education soft on workplace bullies? *AFT [American Federation of Teachers] on Campus: The National Publication of Higher Education Faculty and Staff, 28*(5), 5.

Olweus, D. (2002). Bully/victim problems in school: Basic facts and an effective intervention programme. In S. Einarsen, H. Hoel, D. Zapf, & C. Cooper (Eds.), *Bullying and emotional abuse in the workplace: International perspectives in research and practice* (pp. 62–78). New York: Taylor & Francis.

O'Moore, M., & Lynch, J. (2007). Leadership, working environment, and workplace bullying. *International Journal of Organizational Theory and Behavior, 10*(1), 95–117.

Ortega, A., Høgh, A., Pejtersen, J. H., Feveile, H., & Olsen, O. (2009). Prevalence of workplace bullying and risk groups: A representative population study. *International Archives of Occupational and Environmental Health, 82,* 417–426.

Oshry, B. (1996). *Seeing systems: Unlocking the mysteries of organizational life.* San Francisco: Berrett-Koehler.

Oxenstierna, G., Widmark, M., Finnholm, K., & Elofsson, S. (2008). A new questionnaire and model for research into the impact of work and the work environment on employee health. *Scandinavian Journal of Work, Environment and Health, 36*(2), 150–163.

Ozturk, H., Sokmen, S., Yilmaz, F., & Cilingir, D. (2008). Measuring mobbing experiences of academic nurses: Development of a mobbing scale. *American Academy of Nurse Practitioners, 20*(9), 435–443.

Pignotti, M., & Thyer, B. A. (2009). Use of novel unsupported and empirically supported therapies by licensed clinical social workers: An exploratory study. *Social Work Research, 33,* 5–18.

Pomeroy, E. C. (2012). The bully at work: What social workers can do. *Social Work, 58,* 5–8.

Poulin, J. (2005). *Strengths-based generalist practice.* Belmont, CA: Brooks/Cole, Thomson Learning.

Proctor, B., & Tehrani, N. (2001). Issues for counselors and supporters. In N. Tehrani (Ed.), *Building a culture of respect: Managing bullying at work* (pp. 165–183). London: Taylor & Francis.

Quine, L. (1999). Workplace bullying in National Health Service community trust staff. *British Medical Journal, 318*(7178), 228–233.

Ramage, R. (1996, October–November). Mobbing in the workplace. *New Law Journal.* Retrieved from http://www.law-office.demon.co.uk/art%20mobbing-1.htm

Randle, J., Stevenson, K., Grayling, I., & Walker, C. (2007). Reducing workplace bullying in healthcare organisations. *Nursing Standard, 21*(22), 49–58.

Rayner, C. (1999). From research to implementation: Finding leverage for prevention. *International Journal of Manpower, 20*(1–2), 128–135.

Rayner, C., & Cooper, C. (1997). Workplace bullying: Myth or reality—Can we afford to ignore it? *Leadership and Organizational Development Journal, 18*(4), 211–214.

Rayner, C., Hoel, H., & Cooper, C. L. (2002). *Workplace bullying: What we know, who is to blame, and what can we do?* London: Taylor & Francis.

Rayner, C., Sheehan, M., & Barker, M. (1999). Theoretical approaches to the study of bullying at work. *International Journal of Manpower, 20*(1–2), 11–15.

Roscigno, V. J., Lopez, S. H., & Hodson, R. (2009). Supervisory bullying, status inequalities, and organizational context. *Social Forces, 87*(3), 1561–1589.

Rospenda, K., & Richman, J. (2004). The factor structure of generalized workplace harassment. *Violence and Victims, 19*(2), 221–239.

Rospenda, K. M., Richman, J. A., Ehmke, J.L.Z., & Zlatoper, K. W. (2005). Is workplace harassment hazardous to your health? *Journal of Business and Psychology, 20*(1), 95–110.

Ryan, L. V. (2006). Current ethical issues in Polish human resources management. *Journal of Business Ethics, 66,* 276–290.

Salin, D. (2003a). Ways of explaining workplace bullying: A review of enabling, motivating, and precipitating structures and processes in the work environment. *Human Relations, 56,* 1213–1232.

Salin, D. (2003b). *Workplace bullying among business professionals: Prevalence, gender differences, and the role of organizational politics* (Unpublished doctoral dissertation). Swedish School of Economics and Business Administration, Helsinki, Finland.

Segal, D., & Hersen, M. (2010). *Diagnostic interviewing* (4th ed.). New York: Springer.

Seigne, E., Coyne, I., Randall, P., & Parker, J. (2007). Personality traits of bullies as a contributory factor in workplace bullying: An exploratory study. *International Journal of Organization Theory and Behavior, 10*(1), 118–132.

Senge, P. M. (1990a). *The fifth discipline.* New York: Doubleday.

Senge, P. M. (1990b). The leader's new work: Building learning organizations. *MIT Sloan Management Review, 10*(1), 7–39.

Senge, P. M. (1994). *The fifth discipline fieldbook.* New York: Doubleday.

Senge, P. M., Lichtenstein, B. B., Kaeufer, K., Bradbury, H., & Carroll, J. S. (2007). Collaborating for systemic change. *MIT Sloan Management Review, 48*(2), 44–53.

Shallcross, L., Sheehan, M., & Ramsay, S. (2008). Workplace mobbing: Experiences in the public sector. *International Journal of Organisational Behaviour, 13*(2), 56–70.

Sheehan, M., Barker, M., & Rayner, C. (1999). Applying strategies for dealing with workplace bullying. *International Journal of Manpower, 20*(1–2), 50–56.

Sigelman, C., & Rider, E. (2014). *Lifespan human development*. Belmont, CA: Cengage Learning.

Simms, C. (2000). Stop the word war. *Nursing Management, 31*(9), 65–71.

Skogstad, A., Matthiesen, S. B., & Einarson, S. (2007). Organizational changes: A precursor of bullying at work? *International Journal of Organizational Theory and Behavior, 10*(1), 58–94.

Smith, J. (2014, June 25). What workplace bullying looks like in 2014—and how to intervene. *Forbes.com*. Retrieved from http://www.forbes.com/sites/naomishavin/2014/06/25/what-work-place-bullying-looks-like-in-2014-and-how-to-intervene/

Sperry, L. (2009). Mobbing and bullying: The influence of individual, work group, and organizational dynamics on abuse workplace behavior. *Consulting Psychology Journal: Practice and Research, 61*(3), 190–201.

Sperry, L., & Duffy, M. (2009). Workplace mobbing: Family dynamics and therapeutic considerations. *American Journal of Family Therapy, 37*(5), 433–442.

Spratlen, L. P. (1995). Interpersonal conflict which includes mistreatment in a university workplace. *Violence and Victims, 10*(4), 285–298.

Steensma, H., & van Dijke, R. (2005–2006). Attributional styles, self-esteem, and just world belief of victims of bullying in Dutch organizations. *International Quarterly of Health Education, 25*(4), 381–392.

Stevenson, K., Randle, J., & Grayling, I. (2006). Inter-group conflict experiences of bullying and the need for organizational solutions. *Online Journal of Nursing, 11*(2).

Stewart, S. M. (2007). An integrative framework of workplace stress and aggression. *Business Review, 8*(1), 223–234.

Sue, D. W., & Sue, D. (1990). *Counseling the culturally different: Theory and practice* (2nd ed.). New York: John Wiley & Sons.

Support Center. (2002). *What are the steps of a strategic planning process?* Retrieved from http://www.unc.edu/~wfarrell/SOWO883/Readings/strategicsteps.htm

Tehrani, N. (Ed.). (2001). Victim to survivor. In *Building a culture of respect: Managing bullying at work* (pp. 43–58). London: Taylor & Francis.

Tepper, B. J., Duffy, M. K., Henle, C. A., & Schurer-Lambert, L. (2006). Procedural injustice, victim precipitation, and abusive supervision. *Personnel Psychology, 59*(1), 101–123.

Thomas, K. W., & Kilmann, R. H. (2007). *Conflict mode instrument*. Mountain View, CA: CPP.

Thomas, M. (2005). Bullying among support staff in a higher education institution. *Health Education, 105*(4), 273–288.

Townsend, A. (2008). How to tackle workplace bullies. *British Journal of Administrative Management* (Autumn), pp. 26–27.

Tracy, S. T., Lutgen-Sandvik, P., & Alberts, J. K. (2006). Nightmares, demons, and slaves: Exploring the painful metaphors of workplace bullying. *Communication Quarterly, 20*(2), 148–185.

Tuckey, M., Dollard, M., Hosking, P., & Winefield, A. (2009). Workplace bullying: The role of psychosocial work environment factors. *International Journal of Stress Management, 16*(3), 215–232.

Tuckey, M., & Neall, A. (2014). Workplace bullying erodes job and personal resources: Between- and within-person perspectives. *Journal of Occupational Health Psychology, 19*, 413–424.

Um, M.-Y., & Harrison, D. F. (1998). Role stressors, burnout, mediators, and job satisfaction: A stress-strain-outcome model and an empirical test. *Social Work Research, 22*, 100–115.

U.S. Department of Labor. (2002). *OSHA* [Fact sheet]. Washington, DC: Author.

U.S. Department of Labor. (2011). *Field manual: OSHA*. Washington, DC: Author.

U.S. Department of Labor. (2015). *OSHA guidelines for preventing workplace violence for health care and social service workers*. Washington, DC: Author.

Valle, M. (2005). A preliminary model of abusive behavior in organizations. *Southern Business Review, 30*(2), 27–35.

Vandekerckhove, W., & Commers, M.S.R. (2003). Downward workplace mobbing: A sign of the times? *Journal of Business Ethics, 45*(1), 41–50.

Vartia, M.L.A. (2001). Consequences of workplace bullying with respect to the well-being of its targets and the observers of bullying. *Scandinavian Journal of Work Environment and Health, 1*, 63–69.

Vega, G., & Comer, D. R. (2005). Sticks and stones may break your bones, but words can break your spirit: Bullying in the workplace. *Journal of Business Ethics, 58*, 101–109.

Vickers, M. (2001). Bullying as unacknowledged organizational evil: A researcher's story. *Employee Responsibilities and Rights Journal, 13*(4), 205–217.

Von Bergen, C. W., Zavaletta, J. A., Jr., & Sober, B. (2006). Legal remedies for workplace bullying: Grabbing the bully by the horns. *Employee Relations Law Journal, 32*(3), 27–41.

Voss, M., Floderus, B., & Diderichsen, F. (2001). Physical, psychosocial, and organizational factors relative to sickness absences: A study based on Sweden Post. *Occupational and Environmental Medicine, 58*(3), 178–185.

Westhues, K. (1998). *Eliminating professors: A guide to the dismissal process*. Lewiston, NY: Edwin Mellen Press.

Westhues, K. (2002). At the mercy of the mob. *OHS* [Occupational Health and Safety] *Canada, 18*(8), 30–36.

Westhues, K. (Ed.). (2005a). Checklist of mobbing indicators. In *Workplace mobbing in academe: Reports from twenty universities* (pp. 58–60). Lewiston, NY: Edwin Mellen Press.

Westhues, K. (2005b). *Winning, losing, moving on: How professionals deal with workplace harassment and mobbing*. Lewiston, NY: Edwin Mellen Press.

Whittaker, C. (2009). Head-on approaches to bullying. *Occupational Health, 61*(7), 16.

Whitaker, T. (2012). Social workers and workplace bullying: Perceptions, responses, and implications. *Work, 42*(1), 115–123.

Woods, M. R., & Hollis, F. (2000). *Casework: A psychosocial therapy* (5th ed.). Boston: McGraw-Hill.

Wornham, D. (2003). A descriptive investigation of morality and victimization at work. *Journal of Business Ethics, 45*(1), 29–34.

Yagil, D. (2005). Employees' attribution of abusive supervisory behaviors. *International Journal of Organizational Analysis, 13*(4), 307–327.

Yamada, D. (2000). The phenomenon of "workplace bullying" and the need for status-blind hostile work environment protection. *Georgetown Law Journal, 88*(3), 475–537.

Yamada, D. (2008, June). *Multidisciplinary responses to workplace bullying: Systems, synergy, and sweat.* Presented at the Sixth International Conference on Workplace Bullying, University of Quebec at Montreal.

Yamada, D. (2009). Understanding and responding to bullying and related behaviors in healthcare workplaces. *Frontiers of Health Services Management, 25*(4), 33–37.

Yamada, D. (2010, November). *Do organizations suppress our empathy?* Retrieved from Minding the Workplace: The New Workplace Institute Blog, http://newworkplace.wordpress.com

Yamada, D. (2012, November). *Georgia's Fulton County draws from Healthy Workplace Bill in adopting anti-bullying policy.* Retrieved from Minding the Workplace: The New Workplace Institute Blog, http://newworkplace.wordpress.com

Yamada, D. (2013a, September). *"Master and servant": The roots of American employment law.* Retrieved from Minding the Workplace: The New Workplace Institute Blog, http://newworkplace.wordpress.com

Yamada, D. (2013b, May). *10 ways to make a difference: Advice for change agents.* Retrieved from Minding the Workplace: The New Workplace Bullying Institute Blog, http://newworkplace.wordpress.com

Yamada, D. (2014a, June). *Tennessee directs commission to develop workplace anti-bullying policy for state's public employers.* Retrieved from Minding the Workplace: The New Workplace Institute Blog, http://newworkplace.wordpress.com

Yamada, D. (2014b, October). *Our economic system, psychopathology, and bullying at work.* Retrieved from Minding the Workplace: The New Workplace Institute Blog, http://newworkplace.wordpress.com

Yamada, D. (2015, February). *Massachusetts Healthy Workplace Bill draws 58 sponsors and co-sponsors for the 2015–16 session.* Retrieved from Minding the Workplace: The New Workplace Institute Blog, http://newworkplace.wordpress.com

Yamada, S., & Cappadocia, M. C. (2014). Workplace bullying in Canadian graduate psychology programs: Student perspectives of student–supervisor relationships. *Training and Education in Professional Psychology, 8*(1), 58–67.

Yildirim, D., Yildirim, A., & Timucin, A. (2007). Mobbing behaviors encountered by nurse teaching staff. *Nursing Ethics, 14*, 447–463.

Zapf, D. (1999). Organizational, work group related and personal causes of mobbing/bullying at work. *International Journal of Manpower, 20*(1–2), 70–85.

Zapf, D., & Einarsen, S. (2002). Individual antecedents of bullying: Victims and perpetrators. In S. Einarsen, H. Hoel, D. Zapf, & C. Cooper (Eds.), *Bullying and emotional abuse in the workplace: International perspectives in research and practice* (pp. 165–184). New York: Taylor & Francis.

Zapf, D., & Leymann, H. (1996). Mobbing and victimization at work. *European Journal of Work and Organizational Psychology, 5*(2), 161–307.

Zimbardo, P. (1973). On the ethics of intervention in human psychological research: With special reference to the Stanford prison experiment. *Cognition, 2*(2), 243–256.

Zunker, V. G., & Osborn, D. S. (2002). *Using assessment results for career development* (6th ed.). Pacific Grove, CA: Brooks/Cole.

Index

In this index, *t* denotes table.

A
absenteeism, 21–22, 90, 115, 125, 210
ABUSED questions, 144
accountability, 30–31, 112
acute stress disorder (ASD), 1, 156–157
    See also posttraumatic stress disorder (PTSD)
adaptations (systems theory), 61
administration. *See* organizations and organizational
    administration
AFT on Campus (American Federation of Teachers),
    105
age differences, 71–72, 73, 107
Age Discrimination in Employment Act, v, 8
aggression, 7, 12, 27–31, 42, 55–56, 143
    See also bullying
aggression assessments. *See* Conditioned Reasoning
    Test of Aggression (CRTA)
aggressive personality, 84, 87
Agina, I., 105
Ainsworth, M., 229
Alberts, J., 6
alcohol abuse, 144, 145
    See also problem drinking; substance abuse
Aleandri, E., 20
Alford, B., 150
alternative life centers, 190
American Red Cross study, 56, 141
Americans with Disabilities Act (1990), v, 8,
    173–174
Anderson, L., 95

angry scripts, 40
animal mobbing, 66
anomie, 37–38
anonymous reporting procedures, 133
antisocial personality disorder, 40–41
anxiety, 43, 151–154
    See also panic disorder; victimization predictors
The Anxiety and Worry Workbook (Clark and Beck),
    154
Applegate, J., 144
Armstrong, K., 141
ASD. *See* acute stress disorder (ASD)
Ashforth, B., 87, 117, 131
assertiveness, aggressiveness versus, 55–56
assessments. *See* diagnostic interviews; medical
    evaluations; risk assessments; *specific tools*
attachment styles, 228–229
attitude functions, 32–33
attorney selection, 171
attorneys. *See* Yamada, D.
attribution theory, 33–35
Australia, bullying in
    conditions for, 72
    consequences of, 22, 126–127, 128
    high-risk professions and, 97, 107–108
    legislation and, 10, 185
    litigation and, 184
    prevalence of, 17, 18
authoritarian personality styles, 41
Ayoko, O., 35, 36